CW00696713

Going for Goal

Going *for* GOAL

A Century of Ulster Hockey

1896 – 1996

By Alf McCreary

First published in the United Kingdom, 1996
by W. & G. Baird Ltd, at the Greystone Press
for the Ulster Branch of the Irish Hockey Union.

© Text: Alf McCreary

ISBN 1 870157 23 0

Cover: Olympic Gold Medallist Jimmy Kirkwood playing for his home club
Lisnagarvey. Picture courtesy of the News Letter.
Frontispiece: Stephen Martin (left) and Jimmy Kirkwood, two outstanding
Ulster hockey players with their Olympic Gold medals which they won as
members of the Great Britain team in the 1988 Seoul Olympics.

Designed by: Rodney Miller Associates, Belfast
Printed in Northern Ireland by W. & G. Baird Ltd., Antrim.

CONTENTS

Foreword

At long last the Centenary of Ulster hockey has arrived and the celebratory events to commemorate this historic milestone are in place. It does not seem like ten years ago, when the imminence of this meritorious achievement was first mentioned at a Branch Council meeting (with desultory references in subsequent years) until in due course the Council appointed a Centenary Committee to put flesh on the bones! Indeed in these early references to the Centenary no-one then was sure when the Ulster Branch officially came into existence, despite references to it in Dagg's Hockey in Ireland and Ninety Years of Irish Hockey. Certainly Antrim, Cliftonville and North Down were thought to be the Founding Clubs and there was a reference to an Ulster Hockey Union in 1896.

Dixon Rose

It is not for this Foreword to provide the answer to such an intriguing mystery. This and much more about the history of hockey in Ulster will all be revealed later in this book so elegantly and skilfully put together by Alf McCreary. His feel for the ethos of the game which he graced as a player as well as a reporter gives this Centenary Book a unique flavour which humanises and enhances what otherwise would be just the bare statistics of our history.

Much research has been involved in providing the material facts, and if nothing else is achieved, the book has been responsible for a number of Clubs having to research their own records to find out or confirm how and when they began, and to trace their changing fortunes as depicted in the Section on Club Histories.

Obviously more Club Centenaries will be celebrated as time passes, and those whose birth took place in more recent years perhaps already have cut their teeth on twenty-five, fifty or even seventy-five years of existence, or indeed some other variation on the longevity theme. We congratulate them all on their present achievements and wish them well in their continuing endeavours to both improve and prosper. In fact it would seem not unreasonable to conclude that in celebrating the events of the past, it can in turn generate a desire to preserve and build on the rich legacy left by our predecessors whose basic love of hockey must surely have been their underlying motivation.

Referring again to the research for the Book it is only right to pay tribute to the painstaking work by Drew Francey a stalwart of the Antrim Club and the Branch Council. The offices of the Linenhall Library, the Belfast Telegraph and the News Letter must by now notice the absence of this intrepid researcher. It was largely the information gleaned from these sources together with Drew's in-depth research and synopses of all the available Branch Minute Books that proved so helpful to Alf McCreary in his role as Author and Editor. We are pleased to have the opportunity to record our appreciation and thanks to Drew for his labours of love.

Naturally, to publish a book of this nature there is a cost factor, and in this respect the Ulster Branch is deeply grateful for the special financial contribution by our sponsors Harp Lager towards the production expenses. Harp Lager, as part of the Guinness Group, have been generous sponsors of Ulster hockey for many years and it is a partnership which we value very highly. It has enabled many of our plans for the development of the game to be implemented and sustained. We thank very sincerely Harp Lager, and their Marketing Manager Ken Morrison, for their continuing interest and in particular their involvement with the Centenary celebrations.

The point has now been reached when the journey through the pages of Ulster hockey can commence, with no doubt a touch of nostalgia thrown in for good measure when fond and happy memories of hockey friends, places and incidents are recalled. Hopefully when the journey is finished, the memories and the recorded achievements will leave a feeling that even if hockey is only a game, life has been and is the better for it.

It is our sincere wish and intention that the Centenary year celebrations will be shared and enjoyed at some stage by everyone involved in Ulster hockey, including our many friends in the other Provinces. May this Book bring much pleasure, and may it also act as the catalyst for another one hundred years of progress and achievement.

Dixon Rose
Chairman
Ulster Branch Centenary Committee

Introduction

"It was the best of times. It was the worst of times" - the best of times being the first hundred years of hockey in Ulster and the worst of times the conflict off the pitch caused by two World Wars and our own tragic problems in Northern Ireland. The libraries of Ulster are groaning under the weight of volumes recording this worst of times and it is therefore a singular delight to peruse Alf McCreary's History of Ulster Hockey in the past 100 years.

History is perhaps an unfitting description as the word does not do justice to a warm lively stroll through a century of hockey pausing occasionally to explore and absorb the atmosphere of a particular time and event.

Michael Graham

There have been changes over a hundred Seasons, but the reader may well contend that little has really changed. The debates that ensure Club Committee Meetings extend after closing time in this decade differ little from those which enlivened many a winter's evening in the preceding one hundred years. Umpires, pitches, fund-raising, training, discipline, Branch fees, and Branch decisions - it was ever thus.

You will read that the Branch was formed 'to further the interests of hockey', an admirable objective which has challenged Branch Councils throughout the years and should remain our maxim as we plan into our second century. The Branch was formed by the Clubs, and ownership abides with the Clubs. The Branch can only be as strong and successful as its constituent bodies. Election to the Governing Council continues under the control of the Clubs and the future is in their charge.

The Clubs are, of course, the past, the present and the future of our great game. Whether one played in the First XI in the Senior League or the Sixth XI in the Junior League the satisfaction of a game well played, the laughter, enjoyment and comradeship were and continue to be of the same high level. Memories of a goal scored, a shot saved, a Cup win or a League victory are all precious and important to each one of us irrespective of the status of the match. We have all recounted numerous humorous incidents from Club Tours which improve and develop as the years pass. We rarely remember Tour matches but have total recall of the social events. We all have opinions which we will express ad nauseum on any hockey-related subject. This history "Going for Goal" will no doubt introduce new topics for discussion and debate. The history of our Clubs will make fascinating and, at times, surprising reading and it is pleasing that the contribution of every Club is recorded in this book.

Monsieur Etienne Glichitch, President of the Federation International Hockey, often refers to "the family of hockey". This is particularly appropriate in Ulster where it is always a joy to renew old friendships and develop new ones, both on and off the pitch. Regrettably, I understand that it is not possible to play for ever. There is, however, a life after the final stick has been confined to the attic.

Coaching, managing and administration play an important part in our sport and provide the opportunity for us all to continue our love affair with hockey, in which there are many challenging, rewarding and enjoyable posts. Those who have had the privilege to be Council Members will look back with considerable satisfaction on their contribution to furthering the interests of Ulster Hockey. The Council is an excellent debating forum, with a rich vein of humour never far from the surface.

My own special memories include the eloquence of Gordon McIlroy; the passion and experience of Dixon Rose and Francis Baird; the erudite majestic style of Ronnie McNamee supporting the unsupportable; that great gentleman Walter Dowdall upholding the standards of sportsmanship and tradition; Drew Francey and 'any other business'; and Brian Hanna producing a solution to every problem and a problem for every solution. I could mention with great fondness many more members but hockey owes a special debt of gratitude to all of those who have served on Council during our hundred years. The growth and development of our sport is a tribute to their character and ability and is a justification for all their efforts.

I wonder what our founding members would make of it all now? They would certainly enjoy this book and derive considerable pride from the manner in which we have grown from the solid base which they laid on our behalf.

This living book gives an insight into our heritage and soul and embodies both our tribute to the past and our legacy to the future.

Michael Graham
President
Ulster Branch, Irish Hockey Union

Author's Preface

It has been a pleasure to write this Centenary history of the Ulster Branch of the Irish Hockey Union, partly because hockey holds for me many pleasant memories of my boyhood and later development, and partly because hockey in my lifetime has witnessed so many important and far-reaching changes.

When I began playing at Newry Grammar School in 1951 it was a matter of 'Hobson's Choice' - there was no alternative! Newry Grammar did not play Rugby, and my progression - or regression - from a centre-forward to become a hockey goalkeeper was a matter of pure chance. As a youngster I had played soccer in goal, and shortly after going to Newry Grammar, I sustained a broken wrist when an over-enthusiastic soccer centre-forward followed through during a Saturday morning kick-about in my native Bessbrook, and implanted his massive boot on my right arm.

Sadly my future 'Olympic' career as an International hockey centre-forward was abruptly terminated, but the then hockey master at Newry - Eddie Agnew who went on to Campbell College - drafted me as a makeshift goalie during a Wednesday afternoon practice. Gradually my broken wrist healed, my positional sense as a soccer goalie stayed with me, and within a few years I was a member of the Ulster Schools team with such luminaries as Derek Shaw of Friends School, Lisburn and Roy 'Charlie' Forsythe of Banbridge Academy. For a couple of Seasons I was an Irish Schools trialist but, greatly to my disappointment, I could not dislodge Wesley Griffiths of King's Hospital, Dublin, who was the 'sitting' goalie. (I suppose that today I would have been included as the reserve goalie in an Irish Schools Squad!)

Alf McCreary

Hockey at Newry taught me three things - one, that hockey goalies must never be caught in the indecision of no-man's land; two, that enterprising wingers could (and often did) utilise the wall at the famous 'Hen-run' in Newry for the old 'one-two' to pass the full-back when the umpire wasn't looking; and three, that continued membership of the First XI meant adventures to Belfast, with a game at Inst or Campbell, followed by a furtive attendance at a cinema in Great Victoria Street to watch a 'French Film', and then fish and chips near Great Victoria Street Station before returning by train to Newry - heady days indeed!

My other random memories include arriving at the Station, as Captain, to welcome the Inst team to darkest Newry, with Ralph 'Wrigley' Spearman, as ever shepherding his city charges to that border town. Another memory is that of the ageless Wally Mercer arriving to play at Newry and looking as mature and worldy-wise then as he does today. I also recall watching David Kernohan, the then Irish Schools and Campbell College goalie, playing in an all-white strip that took my breath away - country boys like me did not rise to such style. Only a couple of years later, to my surprise, I replaced 'Kernie' as the Queen's University regular goalie - a development which did not affect our friendship and my relationship with a sportsman and a professional whom I regard highly.

My years at Queen's University were a wonderful and broadening experience. My first game, straight out of school, was against Banbridge, and I still recall the force of the shots from the Irish winger Aubrey Allister and the skill of centre-half George McElroy. Later that Season I recall fierce games against YMCA, with George Glasgow sporting as ever, but as hard as nails; our do-or-die struggles against Parkview in the mud at Doagh; and frightening encounters against Antrim at Castle Park, with Sammy Wallace and the late Francis Baird chattering continually at the umpires and anyone else within earshot; and with the ever-youthful Paddy Marks running like a gazelle. I recall, too, one full-toss clearance by Antrim full-back Tom Allen which whizzed past the ear of Geoffrey Martin and landed in my own circle. If it had hit Martin he would not now be the Head of the EU Office in London! I also remember being kicked in the teeth by 'Garvey's John Kennedy during a goal-mouth melee, but the thump - I hasten to stress - was purely accidental!

My days at Queen's involved foreign travel, which in 1960 was still a remarkable privilege. Our first trip was to Hamburg in 1960 (with the Ladies First XI) and later to Essen and Cologne. One of our major achievements was to beat the outstanding 'Berliner' team, from West Berlin, in a game which, I recall, was broadcast. Perhaps the highlight of my career was playing for the British Universities against the German Universities in Munich in 1964 - a game which we won. Again two memories stand out - the night before the big game, the British Ambassador had to be called out of the local Opera House to bail out half of our team who had been arrested following a fracas with several members of the German public on a Munich tram! I also recall that we won the match fairly easily and that I kept a clean sheet in goal until the dying minutes when, in my then bachelor days, I spotted a group of gorgeous Frauleins on the line and took my eye off the ball - which is a cardinal sin for any goalkeeper!

My other memories of Ulster hockey during the Sixties include being chosen on the Possibles side for an Ulster Senior Trial - the other goal-keeping 'trialist' was Harry Cahill, then of YMCA and one of the greatest goalkeepers in Ireland and Great Britain. Incidentally, when I turned up late in the changing-room, I was given a lecture by Andy Hayes who told me that I ought to have 'checked the time in the newspapers'. (I don't believe I was even notified by post!)

I also remember playing in goal for the Queen's team which lost 0-2 to Portrush in the 1962 Anderson Cup Final, and also winning the Mauritius Cup (the Irish Universities Championship) several times, and most notably by beating Trinity College Dublin in the elegant atmosphere of the College Grounds in the heart of Dublin.

My mind goes back to some outstanding Queen's colleagues, including Bob Poots, and Ken Shooter who tragically died in his early Twenties. I recall, too, the flawless radio reports of Jack Carroll from Cherryvale and elsewhere; the kindness of Jack 'Sweetie' Hagan who as umpire used to share sweets with the players on both sides; and Hugh Patton, the redoubtable goalie from Portrush who used to unbuckle his pads and walk the length of the field to take the penalty 'bully' against the opposite goalie, and many other characters.

After Queen's, I joined the Belfast Telegraph and as a member of Malcolm Brodie's Ireland's Saturday Night sports staff my playing days were effectively finished. However, having swopped the goalie's pads for the reporter's pen, I stayed in touch with the game for almost the next 30 years and joined the Press Corps with Carl Anderson, Graham Hamilton, Sammy Jones, John Flack, Gary McDonald, and other colleagues.

During this time I was welcomed wherever I went, and I renewed friendships with those hockey-playing and umpiring stalwarts of my youth who mellowed (not in every case) to become administrators, umpires and the backbone of the game at Club and Branch level - people like Alex Glasby, Des Simon, Dixon Rose, Ronnie McNamee, Bobby Howard, Brian Hanna, the late Francis Baird, and many others, including my old friend Wally Mercer. The Annual Kirk Cup Final on Boxing Day is a Mecca for all golden oldies, and those not-so-old!

Despite a heavy professional commitment over the years, involving the Belfast Telegraph, Queen's University and freelance writing and broadcasting, I have kept a friendly eye on Ulster hockey - not only as a Saturday reporter but also as a person who appreciates and enjoys sport in general. I am delighted by the progress made by Ulster and Irish hockey on the field, in terms of skill and commitment, and also off the field where the work of a dedicated band of administrators has provided the organisation and the financial and other resources to underpin the successes on the pitch.

This personal recollection also mirrors the development of hockey in general in the past half-century or so, from an essentially amateur sport in every sense to a game that is now much more professional and International without losing the best spirit of 'amateurism'. It is a record of which we can all be proud. This book gives a snapshot picture rather than a graphically detailed account of the past 100 years of Ulster Hockey which could become bogged down by details and statistics. Instead I have chosen to write, with most helpful research by many others, a broad-brush account of hockey in all its aspects, and also with an eye for the humour, the personalities, the characters and the human fraility of a sport which we all love. If, in the following pages, the reader can spot a glimpse of himself or herself or friends, and most importantly a picture of Ulster hockey as we know and have known it, I will regard my enforced choice in swopping the goalie's pads for the writer's pen to have been well worthwhile.

Alf McCreary
Belfast, 26 September 1996

Acknowledgements

The use of material from many sources is gratefully acknowledged - including the Clubs themselves; the Branch Minutes; the Local and Regional Press, including particularly the News Letter, the Belfast Telegraph, and the Ireland's Saturday Night; the publication Hockey in Ireland by TSC Dagg and 90 Years of the Irish Hockey Union, edited by Chris Glennon; and other source material.

I would like to thank many people for their help including all those from the Clubs who took the trouble to carry out research and to provide relevant information and photographs; also those individuals who supplied important information and who made particular contributions to the first Eight Chapters, including Carl Anderson, John Smyth, George Glasgow, George Compston, Brian Hanna, Carson Clarke, and others.

I pay special tribute to the Editorial Board which included Ronnie McNamee with his Schoolmaster's eagle-eye for proof-reading; Dixon Rose, whose organisational and entrepreneurial abilities proved invaluable; and Drew Francey, whose generous assistance and wealth of research on the Minutes and Appendices, and other matters, are deeply appreciated.

I also thank Rodney Miller Associates, the Designers, and Bryan McCabe, the Managing Director of W & G Baird Ltd, the Printers, for their skill in the design and production of this Book.

My particular thanks are expressed to Pauline Allen for her great skill in preparing the Manuscript for the Printers; to Ivan Ewart for photographic help; and to my wife Hilary for her cheerful acceptance of the domestic and personal sacrifices required while yet another book project developed from an idea to become a reality.

Finally, I would like to thank all those not mentioned by name, or inadvertently omitted, for their help in what has been a considerable team effort. No doubt, as with all complex operations of this nature, a number of inaccuracies and omissions may well become apparent with time, but as a former goalkeeper who knows all about the responsibility of the last line of defence, I trust that those destined to write the 150th History of the Ulster Branch and beyond will build on the material already assembled between these covers.

Alf McCreary
Belfast, 26 September 1996

In the Beginning

The origin of the Ulster Branch of the Irish Hockey Union is stated clearly in the Minute Book. It reads:

> A meeting was held in the Royal Avenue Hotel Belfast on Friday, 11 December 1896 for the purpose of forming an Ulster Hockey Union to further the interests of hockey in Ulster.
>
> The following delegates attended. Messrs O Andrews and Dickson (North Down), Oldham and Reilly (Cliftonville).
>
> The Convenor of the meeting Mr J Moore (Cliftonville) was also in attendance. Mr Andrews proposed and Mr Dickson seconded that Mr Reilly take the Chair. The Convenor read the copy of the circular convening the meeting. Mr Oldham proposed and Mr Dickson seconded and passed unanimously that an Ulster Hockey Union be formed, and the matter of adopting rules, electing office bearers etc be held over till the next meeting. Mr J Moore, in the mean time, to write to the Honorary Secretary of the Irish Hockey Union, Dublin re affiliation with the 'Irish Hockey Union', Inter-provincial matches etc.

Signed	J Moore	Signed	E Blow
	Honorary Secretary		*Chairman*
	(Pro-Tem)		

Prior to this meeting, there were reports in the local Belfast newspapers of hockey matches taking place on an 'ad hoc' basis, which suggests a need for a more systematic approach to this growing sport. Indeed the Northern Hockey Union was founded in Londonderry on 10 October 1896, by representatives from The Route, Coleraine, Lacrosse (Derry), Ballymoney and Londonderry. The splendidly-named paper The Ireland's Saturday Night, which is still going strong, reported on page 2 of its edition of 9 February 1895:

> The first hockey match played in Belfast for many years took place on Tuesday 4 inst, between teams representing officers of the King's Own Yorkshire Light Infantry and the Dorset Regiment when the 'York's' won by 6 goals to 3 goals. Now that the game has been started here under auspices so favourable, perhaps the local gentlemen in civilian circles may be induced to give it their countenance. We want a few more winter games in Ulster than we have at present. Reports of hockey matches played in and around Belfast will always find a place in the columns of the Ulster Saturday Night.

The same newspaper reported on 4 February 1896:

> Hockey in Ulster - Several hockey Clubs have been organised in Belfast. The second public match in Belfast was played on Tuesday, 31 January 1896, between

two teams of schoolgirls and the impression on our representative was that it is well worthy of cultivation by both sexes. It is inexpensive and yields as much, or perhaps more fun than lacrosse or association football, with both of which games it may claim kinship. We hope that the hockey promoters will let the 'Saturday Night' know of their doings from time to time as we will always be glad to help the game along.

Around the same period, there were advertisements in the Belfast Newsletter and the now-extinct Northern Whig from the North Staffordshire Regiment requesting fixtures. Incidentally this confirmed one theory that the rise of hockey here was partly due to the influence of the English Regiments who were based in Ireland - which at that time was one country.

Although the origin of hockey in Ulster is reasonably well-documented, the emergence of hockey itself is more problematic. The link between hockey and hurling was investigated exhaustively by TSC Dagg in his book Hockey in Ireland (published by The Kerryman in 1944). A later book 90 Years of the Irish Hockey Union edited by Chris Glennon and published by the Leinster Leader Ltd, Co Kildare covers much of the same ground originally combed by Dagg who concluded on Page 49 of his wordy but nevertheless invaluable source book:

> There is little doubt that hurling as played at present, and hurley as played in the latter half of the last century had their origin in the ancient Irish game of camán, and that shinty and hockey, the Scottish and English variants, came from the same source. If this be true, then modern hockey is almost certainly a scientific development of the ancient Irish pastime, and to call it a foreign game in Ireland is as little reasonable as to say that our ancient Irish melodies cease to be Irish when presented in a modern setting.

Allowing for Dagg's burst of nationalistic fervour, it is probably true that hockey, or a form of the game, was played in many other parts of the world from earlier times. Dagg himself claims that a game akin to hockey was included in the early Olympics of the ancient Greeks and that a kind of hockey was played for hundreds of years by the Indians of North and South America, including a primitive stick and ball game played by the Araucanian Indians of Chile. (Some Ulster hockey observers would contend that a 'primitive stick and ball game' is still played in parts of this Province, though there is no truth in the rumour that some of the older Ulster Branch officials and players were present at the early Greek Olympic Games!)

The game in England is said to have originated in the seventeenth century, and the love of hockey was one of John Bunyan's "darling sins he could not let go". Indeed the historian Lord Macaulay in his essay on Bunyan states "bell-ringing and playing at hockey on Sundays seem to have been the worst vices of this depraved tinker." Hockey later began to take root in England - a Blackheath Hockey Club was formed around 1840 - and with the formation of the Hockey Association in 1886 (following an abortive attempt to establish a similar body 10 years earlier) a set of rules was drawn up. Within a short time these were accepted across the country.

Thus, although there is no definitive reason for the emergence of hockey in Ulster, it is likely that a combination of factors brought this about - the influence of English Regiments in Ireland, the establishment of a number of Clubs down South, and the growing reputation of the sport itself which was bound to have spread by word of mouth. Those men who came forward to establish an Ulster Hockey Union in 1896 were reflecting and giving form to

North Down First XI 1897-98
This picture of North Down, who with Cliftonville were the Founding Members of the Ulster Branch, is thought to be one of the earliest available in Ulster hockey. In their first-ever encounter (in 1896) North Down beat Cliftonville 8-0! Cliftonville had only 13 Members, including 11 players, one umpire and one linesman.

a growing trend that was inevitable. Hockey in Ulster was going to be developed, sooner or later.

The First President of the Ulster Branch was the Marquess of Dufferin and Ava who accepted the position after the Lord Mayor of Belfast the Right Honorable WJ Pirrie and Major General Geary CB had declined to serve. For two years the Branch Meetings were 'Chaired' by persons elected from the meeting until Herbert Andrews (North Down) became the first active President, elected on 19 September 1899.

The histories of each Club show the steady development of Ulster hockey at the turn of the century, and most were founded by a small group of young men who decided that they would like to play the game. In 1894 Antrim was established by a group of professional men, including linen barons, managers, solicitors and others. The first Annual General Meeting of Cliftonville was held on 12 October 1896. The Banbridge Club was formed in 1897 by a group of young men who used to 'knock a ball about on a Saturday afternoon'. Hockey came to Downpatrick in 1900, when it was played at the Saul military camp. In September 1901 a Meeting was held in Lisburn, with the idea of forming a Club, which later became Lisnagarvey.

There is something almost innocent about the way in which each group decided to form a Club. It was almost as if a few young fellows acquired a few sticks and a ball and played their first games in a local field, with their coats as goalposts. Self-help was paramount, and the early 'Garvey officials built their own pavilion, complete with toilet facilities. They could not afford to paint the building, but coated it with distemper - the cost not to exceed five shillings! The picture of these late Victorian and Edwardian days belongs to a different world, before the holocaust of the First World War which set the tone for one of the bloodiest and most vicious centuries in the history of mankind.

In the book "Degrees of Excellence - the Story of Queen's 1845-1995"[1] there is a most evocative picture showing a carefree day of tennis on the front lawns of the University - just three months before the outbreak of the First World War. This was one of the sunniest summers on record, and some of the light from this lost age still shines through. It was in this atmosphere of comparative innocence that hockey began to take root in Ulster, though then - as now - all of the Province's political life was under the shadow of violence as the Home Rule crisis steadily worsened. Happily, however, sport usually finds a way around even the greatest of political crises and learns how to survive for another day.

Following the initial moves of 11 December 1896, another meeting was held in the Royal Avenue Hotel on 5 March 1897. It was attended not only by representatives from Cliftonville and North Down, the original Clubs, but also by members from North of Ireland, Ards and Royal Hospital. The Honorary Secretary stated that the Irish Hockey Union, which was formed in 1893, intended to introduce special rules for the affiliation of Provincial Associations. He also said that an Inter-provincial game between Leinster and Ulster could not be "managed this season", but it is clear that the officials in both parts of Ireland were looking beyond their own territory.

The Irish Hockey Union by the end of November 1897 still had no rules for the affiliation of branches, and therefore representatives from Antrim, Cliftonville and North Down joined in order to organise Inter-provincial games. The first-ever Inter-provincials to be played in Dublin took place on 11 February 1898 against Munster, and against Leinster the next day. TL McElderry of Antrim and WT Graham of North Down were elected on 17 December 1897 as the first IHU delegates from Ulster. In fact Tommy Graham was the first Ulsterman to become President of the IHU. He succeeded the founder-President the Reverend TB Gibson in 1905, and held office for some

Antrim First XI 1898-99
The Antrim Club, which was founded in 1894, was one of the strongest in the early years of the Senior League. The above team won the Senior League and the Senior Cup in the 1898-99 Season.

[1] Written by Dr Brian Walker and Alf McCreary, and published by the Institute of Irish Studies at Queen's.

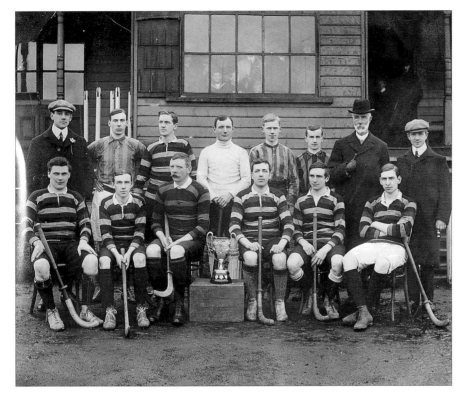

Banbridge First XI 1905-06 Winners of the Ulster Senior Cup The next Season the Club won the Irish Senior Cup, bringing the Trophy to the North for the first time. This is one of the earliest photographs of the Banbridge team, with the familiar 'hooped' jerseys.

16 years - the longest ever tenure. Mr Graham was also the Treasurer of the Ulster Branch from its inception for 24 years, and he was also an International Umpire. As such he was the prototype Branch official, many of whom have devoted long and enthusiastic service to the game.

Further meetings of the Ulster Hockey Union were arranged, and on 15 October 1897, it was decided to form a League, and to affiliate with the Irish Hockey Union. According to the ever-faithful Ireland's Saturday Night, Cliftonville was the first Northern Club to play in Dublin, and in December 1897 they lost 0-3 to Dublin Corinthians. Three months later, the newspaper reported that S McBratney (Ulster Club)[2] and O Andrews (North Down) were the first Ulstermen to play for Ireland.

Towards the end of the 1897-98 Season, the Irish Hockey Union altered their Rules to enable Provincial Branches to be formed, and at the AGM of 19 September 1898, the 'Ulster Hockey Union' changed its name to the Ulster Branch of the Irish Hockey Union.

Unfortunately, the Ulster Branch minute books between 1903 and 1928 are missing, but records of the progress of the Branch are fairly well covered by the local newspapers. The early pre-occupations of the Branch officials included finance, poor pitches, postponements and 'scratched' games, unruly crowds, umpiring problems and endless disputes about the interpretation of the rules of hockey. For example the AGM of 19 September 1899 noted that "'the Senior League' was again worked last year, but as a number of fixtures was still left unplayed at the end of the Season, it is questionable whether it will be advisable to continue the League competition during the coming Season." In 1908 the Branch held no fewer than 26 meetings to hear complaints from Clubs, some most trivial and mainly due to the ignorance of the laws of the game and the Rules of the Branch.

---

[2] S McBratney is listed in '90 Years of the Irish Hockey Union' as playing for Cliftonville.

Captain George Anderson, a Banbridge man who died on active service in France during the First World War. The Anderson Cup was presented by TN Anderson in memory of his brother. A large number of Ulster hockey players joined the Services and took part in the First World War. The Anderson Cup was first played for in 1920, and won, appropriately, by Banbridge.

The number of teams allowed to play in the League varied slightly over the years, and the Secretary's report to the AGM of 20 September 1901 gave a comprehensive list of Senior League placings. Antrim were top with 12 games won out of 14. During that 1900-01 Season, Antrim won the Ulster Challenge Cup Final, beating Banbridge 3-1, while Antrim Second XI won the Ulster Junior Shield Final, beating Portadown 5-0.

There is also an interesting snippet from the 1900-01 Minute Book - all matches were postponed on 12 February 1901 "in respect of Queen Victoria's funeral." In the early days many different Clubs became affiliated to the Branch, including Monaghan, Bessbrook, Enniskillen, Carrickfergus, Gilford, Ballyclare, Ballymoney, Malone, Windsor, Sydenham and others. But throughout the past century the familiar names of Antrim, Banbridge, Cliftonville, North Down, Lisnagarvey, Newry, Queen's, Down, East Antrim, Parkview, South Antrim and several others keep coming through.

The Belfast News Letter on 20 September 1899 reported a recurring worry at the Branch meetings of those, and later days. "The matter of appointing competent umpires for the different matches is becoming more and more necessary, but the difficulty is in finding umpires willing to act. The Council would urge upon all the Clubs the necessity of training one of their non-playing members to make himself up in the rules, so that if neutral umpires cannot be managed, at least one who understands the rules of the game may be depended upon." (The French have a philosophy for this which is, roughly translated, "the more things change the more they seem the same!")

The state of many grounds remained a major concern. Part of the AGM of 1905 was recorded thus by the Belfast Newsletter:

At the present time there is not a single ground in the city fit for a representative match unless favoured with the best weather, and as the playing of representative fixtures and cup ties outside the city means a heavy falling off in 'gates', the fact is in itself deplorable; but above and beyond the question of finance, the bare fact remains that good hockey cannot be played upon a bad ground. Until we can give the public better hockey the game will not be popular with the public. You must have better grounds before you can hope to improve your play sufficiently to warrant a claim to larger International representation. You must have better grounds before you can effectively banish foul and dangerous play. Compared with the result the individual expense is trifling, and for these reasons alone there should be no effort spared to make your city and your country grounds equally as good as those in Comber and Antrim - remembering at the same time (which with so many competitions we are liable to forget) that above all - 'the game is the thing'.

It wasn't until the 1911-12 Season, when the members of the Malone Club amalgamated with NICC, to become the North of Ireland Hockey Club, that the Branch thought that they had at last found a suitable enclosed ground in Belfast where all the important games could be played. Unfortunately, the Great War intervened, the North of Ireland Hockey Club did not reform itself again, and therefore the use of the Ormeau ground, as a 'Headquarters' was denied. Although the NICC ground was the venue for the Ireland v Wales match in 1920, the long search for a suitable enclosed ground in Belfast was to continue until the YMCA ground at Bladon Drive (1922) and Dunmore Park (1933) became available.

The 10th Annual Report of the Branch submitted at the AGM of 24 September 1907 offered congratulations to the Banbridge side which won the Irish Senior Cup in 1907 - the first time that it had been brought North. The

Branch noted "for the first time in the history of the game, this much-coveted Trophy has been brought north of the Boyne, and the Committee hope that the Cup may remain somewhere, if not on the banks of the Bann, within the confines of the Red Hand Province for many seasons to come."

Despite the happy moments, the war-clouds were gathering over Europe, and on the outbreak of war in 1914, all hockey was suspended. A Special Meeting of the Branch on 3 September 1914 was reported in the Belfast News Letter a few days later:

> The President, Mr W Heney, in addressing the members, pointed out that owing to the present crisis he had thought it advisable to summon a Special Meeting of the Branch to consider the question as to whether hockey should be played during the coming Season. Personally, he thought that in many ways it would be very inadvisable to arrange League fixtures; in fact, his opinion was that no hockey should be played at all for the present under the jurisdiction of the Branch. In the unfortunate crisis that had arisen it behoved every man to put aside the question of games and submit himself to training at least for the benefit of his country.
>
> Mr RW Glass in concurring with the President's remarks, said he would urge on all hockey players that were able to support the Empire by joining either one of the forces. Already many players, of the game they were so interested in, had joined and he sincerely hoped that there would be more.
>
> After other speakers had addressed the meeting it was unanimously resolved "the Ulster Branch of the Irish Hockey Union resolve that for the time being all Competitions with the Branch be postponed, and intimation to that effect be sent to the Irish Hockey Union and the Press."

Significantly, a large number of Ulster players joined the services and took part in the First World War. They included 43 from Lisnagarvey, of whom four were killed and four wounded, and four others were awarded the Military Cross for bravery; 36 from South Antrim; 31 from Cliftonville, of whom 6 died and 8 were wounded; and 27 from Banbridge, of whom eight were killed in action. Four of these men were Internationals, including Captain George Anderson who played for Scotland in 1910 as a student at Edinburgh University and who died on active service during the First World War. (The Anderson Cup was presented by TN Anderson in memory of his brother and it remains in competition to this day.) After the War ended, with its horrendous casualties - not least to the 36th (Ulster) Division - life gradually returned to normal, or to as much normality as was possible after such carnage.

The Ulster Branch AGM of 23 September 1919, the first since 1913, dealt with the events of the 1913-14 Season, but the details were unimportant compared to what had gone before. The President William Heney set the tone with a sombre and dignified statement, as reported by the Belfast News Letter:

> The Chairman said he was sure he was voicing the sentiments of all present when he said how pleased they were to renew active legislation in regard to the game of hockey. As they were all aware hockey had ceased during the four years of war. That war had its sadness and had also its pleasant memories. It was a great satisfaction to him and, he was sure, to all lovers of the game that the response made to the call of country by the players of that game of which they were the government was so voluntary and so extensive. He had taken the trouble to study the statistics of the different sporting organisations, and while not in any degree disparaging the efforts that other sport promoting organisations made in regard to the war, he thought, considering the number of men they had playing, that no organisation had made so large a response as the playing members of the Hockey

Union. In that response there were some very noticeable examples and those would remain a lasting credit to the game and an incentive to them all to see that its traditions were worthily upheld. In conclusion, Mr Heney moved a resolution placing on record their sense of the great loss sustained through the untimely deaths of so many of their members, and tendering to the bereaved relatives their heartfelt sympathy.

The resolution was passed in silence, all standing.

The old order had changed for ever. An age of comparative innocence had gone.

Between the Wars - and Beyond

The upheaval of the First World War and the contrasting details of life in Ulster were summarised in superb prose by the late Sir Winston Churchill. He wrote:

> Then came the Great War. Every institution in the world was strained. Great empires have been overturned. The whole map of Europe has been changed. The positions of countries have been violently altered. The modes of thought of men, the whole outlook on affairs, the grouping of parties all have encountered violent and tremendous change in the deluge that has swept the world. But as the deluge subsides and the waters fall short, we see the dreary steeples of Fermanagh and Tyrone emerging once again. The integrity of their quarrel is one of the few institutions that has been unaltered in the cataclysm that has swept the world.

It would be unfair to say that the administration of Ulster hockey was dreary - it was anything but - yet reading between the lines of the edited Minutes between 1919 and 1950 there were many very routine details of ordinary Branch business, and not a few quarrels both on and off the pitch which had their own unchanging and undiminished integrity.

In the Report for the 1919-20 Season there is a curious paragraph which states:

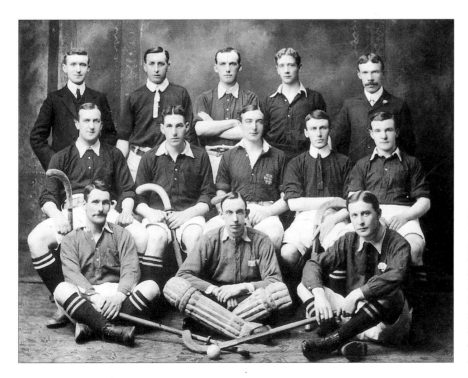

East Antrim 1906-07
The East Antrim Club dates from 1902, and one of its Founder Members was Andrew Burney, in this picture seated third from the left in the middle row. 'Andy' Burney who later became Ulster Branch President, presented the Burney Cup for Schools competition in 1920. In the first Final RBAI beat BRA 4-0.

South Antrim 1920-21
Winners of the Northern
Junior League.
The Club, which was formed in
1912, had a very successful
1921-22 Season and won the
Kirk and McMeekin Cups.

There is obviously something wrong with the official side of Ulster hockey. Complaints of various kinds are heard on all sides, and something will have to be done if the sporting traditions of the game are to be maintained. First of all we have North Down deciding to scratch all their home matches, and accordingly forfeit the points, and the latest is that the Honorary Secretary of the Ulster Branch (Mr WT Coates) has tendered his resignation. I understand that he did not resign for business reasons, but because of not seeing eye to eye with some of the decisions arrived at by the Council of the Ulster Branch.

Mr JH Church was appointed the new Branch Honorary Secretary. After discussions with the Branch, and the allegations of crowd misbehaviour were withdrawn, North Down agreed to restart playing home matches.

On a happier note, the Branch reported that there were no fewer than 37 competing Clubs at the end of the Season (some five more than in the Centenary Year) and the Senior League Championship was decided for the first time by a test match, with Antrim beating Banbridge 3-1. In hockey terms, Antrim were clearly a power in the land in those days.

There were changes at the top in Branch administration. William Heney of Antrim who had been President since the 1911-12 Season, and of course during the war years, stood down, as did the Treasurer Tommy Graham, who had served 24 years in office. The incoming President AG 'Andy' Burney presented the famous Burney Schools Cup, and the first Final in 1920 was won by the Royal Belfast Academical Institution who beat Belfast Royal Academy 4-0. This begs the question as to why such a large school as BRA has been conspicuously absent from the top ranks of Ulster School competitions for so many years.

Another important trophy - the Anderson Cup - was donated that Season, and the Branch also began to give regular donations from the gate receipts of the Anderson and other 'Charity Cups' to endow a bed in the Royal Victoria Hospital.

The Minutes for 1921-22 record that some 50 teams were by then playing under the jurisdiction of the Branch, and there is a somewhat testy note which states "an effort is being made to get the Antrim and North West League to affiliate. It is strange how the officials in the North West cannot see their way to become affiliated. There are some good players in that League, and it is a pity that they should be deprived of the chance of Inter-provincial and International honours."

The highlights of the Minutes for the following year included an important reference to a suitable war memorial to members who had served in the armed forces during the First World War. This was not necessarily a 'war memorial' in the accepted sense, ie a statue of a soldier on a granite plinth. Some members believed that this memorial should take the form of endowing a bed in a local hospital, like the Royal Victoria, but others felt in the words of the Honorary Secretary that "there appears to be a widespread desire to secure and equip a ground which will serve as a constant reminder to hockey players in the days to come of the sacrifices made by their predecessors in the Great War." Thus began a long search for suitable premises, which was not without its financial and other difficulties.

The other matter of note in the Minutes was the refusal of the Hockey Association to accept a proposal from the Leinster Regiment. To mark its disbandment, the Officers put forward £100 to provide a Trophy for annual competition between England and Ireland. The English rather stuffily declined the offer, much to the justified annoyance of the Irish, so the Leinster Regiment Cup was instituted and awarded each year to the champion Province in Ireland. Some £50 was spent on the Trophy, and the remainder invested in a War Bond to provide replicas for the winning team each year. It was only recently that this War Bond was cashed in. (Details of the Inter-provincial results are carried in the Appendices).

The Leinster Regiment Cup is awarded each year to the winning side in the Inter-provincial Championship. Money for the Trophy was given by the Leinster Regiment in the early Twenties to mark its disbandment. The original £100 was donated with the intention of providing a Trophy for the annual Ireland v England game, but the Hockey Association rather stuffily declined the proposal. Ulster Branch Centenary President Michael Graham, who managed Ulster sides for seven successive wins in eight Championships, is pictured holding the Cup.

During the 1925-26 Season, the Minutes recorded the early days of a long-running saga about promotion and relegation. A Wednesday League was started for those with a mid-week break, including military teams, and "the competition proved the least troublesome of all the Leagues." During that year the Branch recorded that charity not only began at home, with another £50 donated to the Royal Victoria Hospital from the 'Anderson Charity Cup', but also abroad, with the Branch giving five guineas to the Irish Women's Hockey Union for their forthcoming tour to America.

The relationship with the north-west was clarified in 1927 when the North West Union amalgamated with the Ulster Branch to become the North West District Committee. The Branch Minutes stated:

> Probably the most important happening of a busy Season was the satisfactory agreement reached with the North West Union, whereby all the Clubs in that district would play under the jurisdiction of the Irish Hockey Union. This was an important step forward, and the agreement had given much satisfaction to the officials of the Irish Hockey Union. Now the officials of the Ulster Branch were turning their attention towards South-East Ulster, where the game was played, but unofficially. It was hoped that in this district a similar agreement would be reached before the end of the coming Season.

The 1929-30 Minutes had little to report beyond the routine affairs of the

An action picture of an Antrim game in 1926. Note the huge curved hockey stick, which is a far cry from the sleeker version today.

Branch but there are fascinating references to the position of Branch Secretary. It is recorded that "Mr JH Church resigned as Branch Secretary. He could not accept the terms offered as the paid Branch Secretary. TH MacDonald accepted the position of Branch Secretary at a fee of £45 per year." Later on, however, there is a totally unexplained paragraph stating that "the Branch Secretary was given permission to destroy all papers etc prior to the 1928-29 Season, at his discretion." Such a Minute today would have investigative reporters knocking on the door. It may well be that the disappearance of a large number of the earlier Minute Books arose from that remarkable decision to allow the Branch Secretary to destroy "all papers etc" prior to 1928-29 "at his discretion".

The apparent harmony between the Ulster Branch and the North West was less than it seemed, and the 1930-31 Minutes record the following stinging resolution:

> That the Council of the Ulster Branch of the Irish Hockey Union greatly regrets the unfriendly criticism offered by the Committee of the North West District which has been published in the Press from time to time. That we would point out to the North West Committee that should they feel they have a cause of grievance and wish the matter investigated, the proper course is to lay it before the Council, either through their representatives on the Council or by an official letter to the Secretary. The Council are of the opinion, that to publish an alleged grievance in the Press before it has been submitted to the Council displays a desire to ventilate it rather than to have it adjusted.
>
> The Council also regrets that the North West Committee should view with suspicion any action of a Council of which two of its own members form a part, and of a Council which has always striven to do its utmost for the promotion and improvement of hockey in the North West District. The Council hopes that in future any matters which a District Committee wish brought to the notice of Council will be submitted in a proper manner.

So there! The Minutes for the next Season 1931-32 were less acrimonious, and they noted among other things, that 10 teams were 'elected' to the Senior League. Their names have a familiar ring - Antrim, Banbridge, Cliftonville,

Lisnagarvey, Holywood, South Antrim, East Antrim, North Down, YMCA and Queen's. By 1933-34, no fewer than 56 Clubs had affiliated to the Branch, and 34 had entered for the Irish Cups. A Mr FJ Bennett from Munster asked the Branch to buy 100 copies of his proposed Irish Hockey Annual at 1/6 each, for sale to the Clubs. The offer was declined. (One hopes that this is not a portent of things to come!)

Disillusion and discipline also featured in the Minutes. It was stated that "Killyleagh Club was unable to finish off the Season's fixtures due to lack of interest", and on discipline it was noted that the Parkview ground was closed for six weeks "following incidents which led to a game with Mossley being abandoned on 9 December, 1933." The Christmas spirit was no doubt conspicuously absent on that Saturday afternoon in darkest Doagh. There was no Christmas spirit in Ballynahinch either, with the local Club being suspended and its ground closed following incidents after a match with Bangor on the same day. However, Ballynahinch was judged not to have sinned as greatly as Parkview, and the former was reinstated by the Council on 9 January, 1934 - no doubt giving Ballynahinch cause to toast a 'Happy New Year'.

By the end of the 1936-37 Season the Branch had still failed to settle the complex issue of promotion and relegation, and a Notice of Motion to introduce the new proposals was defeated, a two-thirds majority vote in favour not having been obtained. The composition of the Leagues was finally agreed as follows:-Senior - 8 teams; Qualifying - 9 teams; Intermediate - two divisions of 8 teams; and Minor - 10 teams. There were 49 Clubs affiliated,

Ulster v Leinster 1927
The Ulster team won the Championship in 1923, '24, '26, '27, '28 and '29. Throughout the years the Competition has been dominated by Ulster and Leinster. The current holders are Ulster.

Replica of the Irish Senior Cup Presented by the Lisnagarvey Captain, JL Alderdice to each team member in recognition of the Club's first Senior Cup success in 1925. 'Garvey have won the Cup many times, including in recent years a remarkable seven consecutive Senior Cup victories, and four consecutive Senior League Championships, plus many other trophies and honours.

including 9 from the North West. The Anderson Cup was won by Cliftonville; North Down won the Kirk Cup and the Senior League; Parkview won the Qualifying League and the Intermediate Cup; and Banbridge Second XI won the Intermediate League.

There was still trouble with grounds and discipline. The Ballynahinch ground was closed for four weeks following incidents in a match with Cullybackey on 14 November 1936 "when their Captain was sent off and the team left the field." The Grounds Committee reported that the Ballynahinch ground was unfit for hockey and a new ground would have to be 'secured' for the next Season. The grounds problem seemed endemic, and the next year's Minutes record that Newry Olympic's pitch was 15 yards short, and that the Club then acquired a new ground which conformed to the rules. The Cullybackey pitch was found to be unfit for hockey and it was unanimously agreed by the Branch that unless another ground was found by the end of 1937, all their matches would have to be played away.

Such Minutes provide conclusive evidence that Branch officials were taking their duties seriously and were attempting to apply the rules rigorously during a period when Ulster hockey, though progressively better organised, had still many rough edges. Discipline remained a recurrent problem, and the Branch took a firm line not only with Clubs and players, but with spectators as well. It was reported in the 1937-38 Minutes that "the Mossley ground would be closed for four weeks from 19 November 1937 following incidents in a match where the Umpire (Mr Morrow) was intimidated and unnerved by abusive and threatening language both on and off the field."

"After another incident at the Mossley v Crossgar Minor League game, the Mossley Club was warned that if it did not give an assurance to the Council that such conduct would not happen again, it would be excluded from Ulster hockey." There was yet more trouble, this time at the Parkview v Saintfield Intermediate Cup Semi-Final. According to the Minutes "The game had to be stopped five minutes from time because several Saintfield players had joined in a fight that had started on the touchline. Umpire Johnston also reported that he had to leave the pavilion partly dressed after the game had been stopped."

The mind boggles at the state of poor Umpire Johnston leaving the pavilion 'partly dressed'. Had someone taken his shoes, hidden his trousers, stolen his shirt, or all three? Seriously, however, the somewhat stilted wording of the Minutes refers to what must have been a nasty situation, and the Council closed the Parkview ground and suspended Saintfield for the rest of the season. Parkview were later given permission to play the remainder of their home games at Dunmore Park. In all there were 23 Umpires' reports about Clubs and players and four about spectators that Season and "these were all dealt with in a very determined manner with the view to stamping out all unsporting actions by those involved."

The outbreak of the Second World War led to the suspension of official hockey, and the Council at a meeting on 12 September 1939 decided:

THE ADMINISTRATION OF ULSTER HOCKEY BE SUSPENDED, THAT THE COUNCIL STAND ADJOURNED SINE DIE, BUT THAT IN THE INTERESTS OF THE GAME AND AS A CONTRIBUTION TO NATIONAL FITNESS, PARTICULARLY OF THE MANY BOYS PARTICIPATING, CLUBS ARE RECOMMENDED TO ARRANGE AS MANY FIXTURES AS POSSIBLE ON A FRIENDLY SYSTEM.

Many Clubs responded enthusiastically. During the 1940-41 Season 416 games were arranged, and the next year 32 Clubs took part in friendly and Cup fixtures, to the extent that 400 games had been played between October and March. Banbridge were beaten by Dublin University and Mossley by Pembroke Wanderers in the all-Ireland Cups, the games being played in Belfast. In the 'unofficial' Inter-provincial series, Ulster beat Leinster and Connaught, but lost to Munster.

On 13 May 1943, the Branch decided to rescind its earlier decision, and proceeded to elect Officers and to carry out its 'ordinary duties'. RK Megran, who had been acting President since 26 September 1940, became President in his own right.

The Minutes during the rest of the War period were very matter-of-fact, with the only hostilities reported being those between Down and Mossley during the Second round Intermediate Cup tie on 28 October 1944. "The game had to be abandoned in extra-time after fighting had broken out between spectators and players. The Council decided, after three meetings, that both teams be dismissed from the competition and the Down ground be closed until 1 February 1945."

(It is interesting to note that the Ulster Branch was by no means the only institution to refer only obliquely to the War years in its Minutes. In my experience as the author of the history of other institutions in Ulster, the same attitude was apparent. It was as if the relevant Boards and Committees and Minute-writers believed that the whole world knew about the war and its ghastliness, and that there was no need to make reference to this in what were the everyday records of normally peace-time institutions.

Nevertheless, the person reading such Minutes would have a little clue about the colossal scale of both World Wars and about the way in which they affected the economic and social fabric of society for generations to come. On the other hand, the Minutes of the Ulster Branch - and of other institutions - during these years provide the reassurance that a kind of abnormal 'normality'

Banbridge First XI 1934-35 Winners of the Kirk Cup Banbridge is one of the most successful sides in Irish hockey, winning the Senior League 18 times, the Irish Senior Cup 9 times, the Kirk Cup 17 times, and the Anderson Cup 13 times.

The Lisnagarvey team in 1945-46, which won the Anderson Cup, the Irish Senior Cup, and the Senior League. Second from the left (front row) is Jimmy Corken, who died tragically in a drowning accident at San Remo in Italy. The Corken Cup was instituted in his memory in 1958. In the first three years it was won by 'Garvey who have held it 19 times, to date. Also in this picture is the famous Jack Bowden (second from right, front row), and a youthful Howdy Clarke, the current long-serving Honorary Secretary of the Club (extreme right, back row).

was operating in the Province at a time when much of the world was in a state of mayhem.)

By 1950, the Branch and Ulster hockey had weathered two World Wars, many internal upheavals, financial challenges, and discipline problems. The following decades would witness many changes in all aspects of the game, both on and off the field. But still only a few years past their half-century, the Branch could do little to alter one fundamental reality about sport - that was human nature. At the end of the Minutes for the 1949-50 Season there is one short sentence which tells a very long tale about discipline and human reactions to authority - "as the Secretary had been unable to get the suspended Crossgar Club to return the Minor League Cup, after many requests, it was agreed to place the matter in the hands of the Branch solicitor." The Crossgar Club had been suspended during the 1946-47 Season following an earlier assault on an Umpire during a game against Saintfield. Despite an appearance before Council of the Crossgar Captain, the suspension was not lifted, and in fact it stayed in operation for 20 years, being lifted only on 28 February 1967! The Ulster Branch took discipline extremely seriously, and in doing so its officials ensured that the highest standards had to be maintained in a sport which, if ever out of control, could prove to be extremely dangerous indeed.

The Fifties and Sixties

From the early Fifties, the game of hockey progressed steadily both on and off the field. The Ulster Branch officials provided important continuity, and many of them gave a lifetime's service. In doing so they helped to develop the administrative talents of younger men who eventually took over. In the Minutes for the 1950-51 Season, the President RS Craig conveyed the thanks of the Ulster Branch to Bob Coulter after his 30 years service as Honorary Treasurer, while a vote of sympathy was passed on the death of Sam Bulloch, a Past President and Secretary. Around the same time the Branch sent a letter of good wishes and thanks to George Bannister a Council Member, an Umpire and a member of the Rules Committee who expressed a desire to withdraw from the Council due to illness. Significantly, however, the Minutes of these years also record the names of those who had been or would be making an important contribution - including Andy Hayes, Alex Glasby, Des Simon and Dixon Rose.

At the AGM of 31 May 1951 - the Festival of Britain year - the outgoing President presented to the Branch a Chairman's Baton in the form of a miniature hockey stick, and expressed the hope that those people destined to preside in the years to come would only use it on the table for keeping members in order! It is difficult, however, to ignore the fact that each year's Minutes contain significant references to the vexed question of discipline, not only on the field but also among spectators.

It was decided unanimously at the AGM of 1951 to "send a circular to all Clubs directing them to take disciplinary action against players or spectators for abusing umpires, and that where possible all grounds should be roped off." It was also agreed that "a directive should be sent to the new Council and the Umpires Association from this AGM that severe disciplinary action should be taken in all cases reported, and that no case should go unpunished."

At the same meeting an application from Lissara for affiliation was accepted "under the guidance of the Reverend Sam Finlay" on condition that a member who was helping to form the Club and who was still under suspension with the previous Crossgar Club, should apply personally for reinstatement. This he did, and he was accepted.

The Minutes of the early Fifties contain routine details of matches played, further suspensions, and financial considerations. A Festival of Britain match between Ireland and the RAF was held at Bladon Drive at a loss of £25, and there was criticism at Council of the loss, venue, team selection and the date of the game! There was also criticism of the 'heavy expenditure' incurred at the dinner following the English international in Dublin. "It was felt that the Hockey Association had no business bringing so many guests to the dinner without paying for them."

On a slightly different note, the President reported that ties were now available (from him) for ex-International players at a cost of 12/6. It was also agreed to pay the fares "of any boys from Strabane and Lifford who were selected for the Schools Trial in Belfast on 1 March 1952." Clearly the Council kept a close eye on all financial transactions, whether they included the cost of free-loading dinners at a Hockey International, or the train fares of boys coming from the North-West to Belfast. Such details gave a homely touch to Branch deliberations, compared to some of the mega-spending of sport in general today.

The question of good behaviour still weighed heavily on the minds of Council members, and to prove that it was not only Mossley, Parkview and other familiar names which featured in disciplinary reports, there is a caustic note about Lisnagarvey in the Minutes for the 1951-52 Season:

> The President complained of the conduct of the Lisnagarvey players and supporters on the occasion of their Irish Cup Final against Pembroke Wanderers in Dublin. He said that every time Lisnagarvey scored a goal, the pitch was invaded by dozens of spectators, who hugged, slapped and carried the scorers shoulder high from one end of the pitch to the other. Many of the IHU and Branch Officials who witnessed these events were disgusted with this behaviour. The Council unanimously condemned the conduct of the players and spectators, and agreed that the Lisnagarvey Club should be written to accordingly.

One wonders what these august Council members would make of today's soccer stars who make hugging an art form, after scoring a goal!

Despite the best intentions of the Branch to control conduct on and off the field, it was not possible to legislate for human emotions and strong partisanship during the heat of play, or 'on the line', as this extract shows:

> Following an incident in the Senior League Test Final in 1951 between Mossley and Lisnagarvey played at Randalstown it was brought before the Emergency Committee on 28 May 1951. Mr S Preston (Mossley) denied using abusive language but admitted in being persistent in claiming for a goal which had been disallowed by the Umpire.
>
> Robert Burns (Mossley) who was a spectator at the game, said that he had not used abusive language and was merely supporting his team and criticised the Umpire on some of his decisions. He maintained that he had a just right in doing so as that was what the War was fought for so as people could have free speech. When asked about the Rules he said that he had not seen a Rule Book.
>
> It was unanimously agreed to suspend S Preston until 1 October 1952 and R Burns from participating in the game or any executive capacity for the same period, both to be cautioned as to their future conduct and the Mossley Club to be censured for forwarding the drastic letter relating to the appointment of umpires and it was hoped that they would make a point of controlling their spectators at visiting grounds in the future.

One of the issues which dominated the Minutes during these years was the purchase of a War Memorial Ground at Cliftonville. The purchase of such a ground had been on the agenda for many years. At the AGM held on 18 May 1944, the Honorary Treasurer, Mr RH Coulter proposed that £80 be lodged in the Belfast Savings Bank as a start for a Memorial Fund, in memory of those who had fallen in the last War and also in the present conflict, to secure a ground for the Ulster Branch.

At the first Council meeting of that Season it was agreed to impose a levy on each Club of 10/- per registered player per year as a minimum contribution to the provision of an Ulster Hockey Ground as a War Memorial. A Memorial Ground Fund Committee was elected and over the next two Seasons a sum of £792/12s/9d was raised.

At the Council meeting on 14 October 1948 it was agreed to write to all the donors of the Charity Cups noting now that the hospitals in Northern Ireland, and the welfare thereto, were under Government supervision, it was no longer necessary to forward money collected in connection with the four Charity Cups belonging to the Branch, and asking if "they would be agreeable for this Season's money to be handed over to the Memorial Ground Fund."

On 9 October, 1951 a Special Emergency Meeting was held to arrange a deputation of members who would meet representatives of Cliftonville Cricket Club, which had been offered the ground at £7,000 and wanted the Branch to raise half the cost. Some four months later, on 13 February 1952, the Branch accepted the deal in principle, and it was agreed that £1,500 should be transferred from the Memorial Fund towards the cost, along with £250 from the IHU. A year later the agreement was legally sealed with Cliftonville Cricket Club, and the Branch decided that this would be the 'Headquarters Ground' and would be called 'The Cliftonville War Memorial Sports Ground Ltd'.

From that time there were many references during Branch meetings to devising ways and means of paying off the debt, and at yet another Special Meeting on 4 September 1953 it was decided to place a levy of £15 on Senior Clubs and £7/10s on Junior Clubs to be paid not later than 31 January 1954. Some nine months later there were two more Special Meetings and the levy was increased to £25 and £12/10s respectively, to be paid before 1 January 1955.

A number of Clubs were unable or unwilling to pay these levies, and at a Special Meeting on 30 September 1955, it was agreed that the levy for the new Season would be £15 for Senior Clubs and £7/10s for Junior Clubs. Penalties of £2 and £1 were imposed on Senior and Junior Clubs for non-payment of the levies, and persistent offenders were liable to be suspended.

The Antrim Club, in typical fashion, expressed the frustration felt by others and the 1956-57 Minutes record a motion stating:

> That in view of the very poor condition of the Ulster Branch Hockey Ground at Cliftonville which has been, for the past two Seasons, in no condition for representative or international matches, and in view of the fact that an immense amount of money will be required, above the abilities of the Clubs to pay, to put the ground in order, IT IS RESOLVED that the interest of the Ulster Branch in the ground be sold and the proceeds be either retained on a Suspense Account for the purchase of a new ground or returned to the clubs in the proportion paid up by them.

Sammy Wallace of Antrim was a prime mover of the motion but as there was no seconder, it was lost. The Minute, however, gives a good indication of the feelings of some Clubs and players at that time. The Branch carried on with raising the necessary funds, and on 20 September the levy was fixed at £15 and £7/10s. It was agreed to organise a Carnival at the ground over the Christmas holidays to help clear off the debt, but the Carnival had to close a week earlier than planned, due to bad weather. The Council was asked, however, to obtain expert opinion on the cost of having the ground 'put into first-class order'. Perhaps Sammy Wallace's observations had not been entirely in vain!

Subsequently, there were more references to the levy, and to non-payers, but by 3 November 1958 a new note was creeping in, with the Branch endorsing a proposal to sell off a portion of the ground to the highest bidder.

Sammy Wallace, the popular Antrim former hockey player, and noted golfer. Pictured here with the Wallace Golf Trophy, he was President of his home Club Massereene in 1995, its Centenary year.

Irish Cup Medals, both Senior and Junior, are highly-prized. This picture features an Irish Junior Cup Medal presented in 1955 to John Hadden, the Captain of Lisnagarvey Second XI who won the Cup that year, for the first time. To date, 'Garvey have won this Trophy 15 times, which is more than any other Club.

One corner of the ground was sold for £3,500 and the debt was cleared. By May 1963, delegates at the AGM were questioning the future of the ground, and the cost of the upkeep "for the few games that were played on it each Season." Nevertheless at the end of 1964 plans were in hand to enlarge the pavilion at the finish of the 1965-66 hockey Season, and it was indicated that "all the overhead expenses would be paid by the Cricket Club." This offer was accepted by the Directors of Cliftonville Sports Ground Ltd. However by 12 October 1966, Dixon Rose was complaining about "the whole set up at the Cliftonville ground, the state of the pitch and the vandalism of the original pavilion."

In 1968, Cliftonville Cricket and Hockey Clubs amalgamated and produced a plan for ground improvements that would require a considerable amount of finance for the next few years.

A Branch Sub-Committee did not think that the Club should be hampered in their wish to make improvements by any disinclination of the Branch to become involved, for financial reasons. The Committee therefore unanimously recommended that the Branch's Directors give notice to the Board of their intention to withdraw from the Company at a convenient date and enter into negotiations with representatives of the Cliftonville Club for a formal ending of the partnership as set out in the Memorandum and Articles of Association of Cliftonville Sports Ground Ltd. In 1972 the Cliftonville Ground and Clubhouse were destroyed by vandals. It took five more years of protracted negotiations before the sale of the ground was approved and it was not until the 1982-83 Season that the Cliftonville Sports Ground Ltd was liquidated and £24,540 was received by the Branch.

This ended a long-running saga during which the Branch, for the best of reasons, wished to maintain a Headquarters Ground to commemorate in a fitting way the sacrifice of hockey players in two World Wars. It was extremely sad that this noble venture failed, and that the Ground itself was virtually destroyed by an ancient and bitter war at home.

Mossley Second XI Winners of the Irish Junior Cup in 1966. The Club, which was Founded in 1929, also won the Irish Junior Cup in 1944.

The question of relegation and promotion, and the composition of the various Leagues generated lively discussion. In 1957 it was decided to hold a ballot for places in Senior Leagues A and B. Despite strong objections, the ballot went ahead and was made "by a representative of the Press". At a Special Meeting of 13 September, George Blower supported a YMCA motion which asked that this be rescinded, and he said that drawing lots was not a suitable method of running a League Competition. Then "after a frank and free discussion" (the mind boggles!) it was decided to drop the ballot and to divide the League into two sections of 8. Parkview who had earlier made a plea for inclusion in Section A, after winning Section B six years out of seven, were granted their wish and were included in A, but not Portrush who had to play in Section B with such teams as Newry, East Antrim, South Antrim, Albert Foundry, Holywood, Mossley and Down!

On 30 September 1957, a Special Meeting was held to consider a motion from Portrush "that the resolution forming the present Senior League be rescinded and the action of the Council in relegating Portrush to the B Section without warning was unorthodox and callous." Council agreed to listen to representations from the Captain K Rodgers and N Cameron, a Committee member, but after discussion the Resolution was lost by 24-4 votes. The wisdom of Solomon himself could not have satisfied all concerned.

By the end of the Fifties promotion and relegation was established on a trial basis. (This writer remembers clearly, however, the angst of having to play in this rigorous system during his first year at Queen's and escaping with his life, after stern tussles with Antrim and Parkview! There was nothing like a points system to sharpen the already keen edge of competition.) Despite the initial reservations about relegation and promotion, the system gradually became established, but over the years there were few surprises. Teams which managed to win promotion to a more senior League often found it difficult to live in such company and returned to the lower level, while Clubs like Lisnagarvey, Banbridge, Instonians and others tended to become permanent fixtures in the Senior section.

Finance was always an issue, and the Branch had the uncanny knack of zoning in on pounds and pence, as well as somewhat larger aspects of funding. In the 1960-61 Season, the Secretary reported to Council that the players in the recent Home Scots v Ulster game had refused to pay their fares, with one exception. The relevant minute makes interesting reading:

> He had heard the news from Jack Carroll on the steamer going to Glasgow. He had subsequently returned the fare to the player who had paid and had written to Harold Cahill the Ulster Captain for an explanation. He had replied stating that as the Cliftonville Sports Grounds Fund debt was now cleared through the sale of part of the ground, the players felt that their expenses should now be paid. After voting down an amendment to ask the players to pay the full fare the proposal to ask the players to pay 50% of the fare was carried by 11 votes to 2. Mr Peacock was asked to write and tell the players that the Council regretted the way the case was handled and they had fourteen days to pay.

The matter still surfaced in the Minutes of 28 March 1963, where it was noted that three Ulster players had still not paid their fares for the game against the Home Scots in Glasgow. It was agreed that if payment was not made by 30 April, the players would be suspended, but no further reports appear in the Minutes, and the issue seems to have died a natural death. The payment of fares had been a vexed issue, with many players believing that

The social side of Club life has been an important part of Ulster hockey, both in fund-raising and in 'friend-raising'. These photographs represent two of the well-known Clubs in Ulster - the Annual Antrim Supper and Social Evening in 1955, and a Lisnagarvey 'Pirate Dance' on 9 December 1960. It is worth noting that admission to the Dance was 5/-, and that the music was provided by Derry's Gay McIntyre who still plays a good saxophone and clarinet!

representative hockey was an honour which ought not to be financed out of their own pockets, while the Branch equally had to keep a sensitive eye on expenditure. It was also to do with the concept of amateur 'purity' and the intrusion of money into sport which, some would argue, has been to the detriment of the original and noble instinct that the game itself is more important than winning.

Meanwhile, the North West District Committee of the Ulster Branch, which had been formed in 1927, stayed in business until the late Sixties, despite problems of postponed fixtures and periodic lack of players. The history of the North West was chronicled colourfully by its long-serving Secretary Arthur W Fielding. In the 1951-52 Annual Report, he noted that: "this Committee has now completed 25 years, having been Founded in the year 1927, and it is most gratifying to see that at this stage, hockey is very much alive in this area."

A couple of years later, however, life was not so sweet. Mr Fielding stated in his 1953-54 Annual Report:

> My Report so far has been encouraging but I must state that there have also been dark clouds on the horizon. There is that certain section in North West hockey who never attend meetings, never can support any venture, want everything for nothing, never attempt to keep to the rules, and are forever criticising. During my period of office, I have endeavoured to clean up the game in Derry and District, to play it on strict amateur and sportsmanlike lines. To a great extent I feel I have succeeded but if there are those people who believe they can do a better job than the present officers I say they are very welcome to the positions. We all live in a small city each man knows his neighbour but the considerable enjoyment I have got out of hockey administration I am not going to have it dulled by a few incompetents and troublemakers.
>
> The Protests and Appeals Committee had few meetings in the Season for which we are very thankful. At the same time I hate backbiting but deplore the attitude of a representative of one Club on the erring side, who had the audacity to infer that, I, personally upheld an Umpire in a certain case which to his way of thinking

The Dolphins Touring Team, a well-known 'temperance' side, circa 1965.

Antrim First XI 1966
Winners of the Kirk Cup
The Cup was first presented on 29
October 1897 by Mr John Kirk JP,
an Antrim man.

is still wrong. The influential and patient bearing Protest and Appeals Committee will bear me out in the action taken by me. Namely - nil. Perhaps the member concerned should consult a dictionary as to the duties of a Secretary at any meeting.

A number of Reports from the Sixties are not available, but towards the end of the decade it was clear that the problems were becoming insurmountable. In the Report for the 1966-67 Season, JHY Ferguson, who succeeded the redoubtable Arthur Fielding, stated:

At the last AGM I mentioned the conduct and attitude of certain players on and off the field. I am extremely glad to be able to state that there was not one meeting of the Protests and Appeals Committee. However, I received a few verbal complaints about players questioning umpire's decisions. As I have criticised a similar type of conduct before, I do not intend to repeat myself except to say that as soon as all the players are conversant with the rules, perhaps more people will volunteer to blow the whistle on Saturday afternoons. Have you noticed that the players who have not a good word to say about umpires very seldom offer their services when they hang up their sticks. At the present time, the umpire's panel is very small and it is up to the Clubs to increase it. It is a well known fact that every Club should have two umpires, but, unfortunately, that is not the case in this area. I hope that the Clubs will be able to produce two umpires during the 1967-68 Season.

What does the future hold for hockey in this area, gentlemen? Will the state of the game improve or will it go the other way? Will we get very far by keeping on ourselves or would it be better to ask the Ulster Branch to permit our Clubs to join their ranks? I would be very sorry to see the disappearance of the North West Branch but we must forget about sentiment, and think of the game and of our players. If our Clubs were in a section of one of the Ulster Branch's Leagues, the

Cliftonville Hockey Club 1966-67 Winners of the Senior League, the Corken Cup (awarded to the Winners of the Ulster Section of the Irish Senior Cup), and the Pembroke Wanderers Festival Trophy
Seated in the front row is Andrew Rose, the Club President, and his son Dixon, both of whom held the Office of President of the Irish Hockey Union. This 1966-67 team began a run of seven Senior League titles and two consecutive Irish Senior Cup victories, truly a golden era in the Club's history.

players would get more games and they would not see the same faces week after week. What do you think of this idea? I should like to hear your opinions before you leave here tonight.

By 1968, however, it was clear that the answers were negative, and in his Report, for 1967-68, Mr Ferguson sounded the final note.

For the last time, I am having the privilege and pleasure of reporting to you on the activities of the North West District Hockey Committee.

As most of you know, the North West, as the Committee has been commonly known since its inception, ceases to exist next September. I have no intention of stating all the reasons for this drastic action as you have been told them quite a few times during the last Season. However, I feel that I should repeat part of what I stated in my application to have the existing North West Clubs taken over by your Branch.

At the beginning of the 1967-68 Season, five Clubs entered for the League, 4th/7th Royal Dragoon Guards, Convoy, Raphoe, Magee University College and Strabane. Before the competition started, Raphoe withdrew and Magee vanished at Christmas. I have used the word 'vanished', because I still have to receive their official notice of withdrawal. Raphoe played in one round of the Irish Junior Cup and then withdrew from all Cup competitions ...

Unfortunately, gentlemen, I have nothing more to report and it only remains for me to convey my sincere thanks to the Ulster Branch for all its assistance to the North West District Hockey Committee.

On a personal note, I must offer my most grateful thanks to all officials and members of Council who have helped me in numerous ways, during my term of office as Honorary Secretary of the North West.

Thus ended the history of hockey in the North West District which had started with such brave hopes in 1896. It had given much to hockey, and not least the Festival Cup, from 1951, but in the end, the lack of support in depth was decisive.

Despite the demise of the North West Branch, the Minutes of these decades portray Ulster hockey as a sport firmly established and attempting, not without success, to inject discipline and more professionalism into the game, both on and off the field. It was a period, still, of relatively basic amenities, endless disputes about disciplinary matters, and relative insularity concerning International hockey compared to today. But it also had the basic honesty of individuals enjoying their amateur sport on a Saturday afternoon and being helped to do so by a dedicated, and sometimes misunderstood, minority of administrators and umpires. The game would change radically in the next decades but the solid foundations laid since the end of World War Two would pay great dividends in the years to come.

Troubles

The decades from the Seventies onwards witnessed some of the worst political deadlock and violence on the island of Ireland this century, yet the world of hockey went about its business relatively undisturbed. There was damage to property, including the headquarters pavilion and ground at Cliftonville which was situated in one of the heartlands of the Troubles. There was also reluctance on the part of some teams from outside to visit Northern Ireland, and in the Minutes of 1970-71 the Branch Secretary Des Simon reported that he had written to Cheshire and Lancashire endeavouring to arrange an alternative fixture to replace the cancelled Home Scots game, but neither was interested.

On occasions, the Minutes made a brief reference to one or other aspect of the Northern Ireland Troubles, and the very brevity of those references spoke volumes about the horrendous violence that was continuing all around, while people tried to continue with their business, social and sporting lives as best they could. For example, on 23 September 1976, the President Alex Glasby stated that the Belfast Telegraph was "to be congratulated on getting back to business after the recent no-warning bomb attack." In the "business as usual" spirit of Ulster in those days, it was further reported that team lists and results

Victims of the Troubles - a Newspaper cutting from the Belfast Telegraph of 6 February 1974. It shows Dixon Rose, the Cliftonville Secretary, and hockey writer Carl Anderson amid the rubble of Cliftonville Pavilion some 18 months after it was destroyed by vandals. The Club was never able to return to what had been the Headquarters ground of Ulster Hockey.

*Celebrating in Style -
Dixon Rose (left) pours
champagne into the Senior League
Trophy, while Des Simon holds
the Corken Cup and Alex Glasby
the Irish Senior Cup. This picture,
dating from the mid-Seventies,
was taken at a time when
Cliftonville had a great run of
League and Cup victories. All
three men are not only
outstanding Cliftonville Club
members but also former
Presidents of the Ulster Branch
and of the Irish Hockey Union.*

were to be phoned in to Carl Anderson as usual, and that a full reports and results service would be resumed as soon as possible."

The bomb in the Belfast Telegraph was one of the incidents that remains fresh in my mind, as I was on duty that day and managed to escape from the leader-writers' room and move swiftly down the back stairs before the bomb went off. One man died, and several people were injured.

Another incident remains fresh, concerning hockey in the Troubles. On Saturdays I exchanged my feature writer's hat for that of a sports reporter, and covered a Senior League or Cup game each week. On one particular Saturday I set out from my home in North Belfast to drive to Annadale in good time for the start of their home game. In the event, the city of Belfast was ringed with security forces' road-blocks, and I eventually arrived at Annadale School to hear the final whistle being blown. Happily, however, the players and umpires sportingly offered to give me a broad (if not ball-by-ball) account of the game, and a highly-readable account of the afternoon's proceedings appeared in the Ireland's Saturday Night. The Editor, Mr Malcolm Brodie MBE, would not have known that his reporter had not seen one second of the game which he had described so vividly, but in the circumstances the editor would have understood. No doubt many players, umpires and spectators had their own anecdotes about trying to maintain the normality of hockey in troubled times.

Over the years the friendly rivalry between the four Provinces of the island of Ireland did not spill over into political issues, which has been one of the strengths of sport in general. However, in the early Seventies a controversy arose which tested the goodwill on all sides and which underlined the feelings that lay beneath the surface. The issue was covered broadly by Chris Glennon in 90 Years of the Irish Hockey Union.

First signs of problems about the Munich Olympics came during the summer of 1971. It became apparent that the Ulster Branch Council would find difficulty in supporting the Ireland team entering for the Games. Concern was expressed about the financial burden the event would bring, the 'flag' issue would be a hindrance and political issues might arise leading to dissension. On the other hand, the Union had already accepted grants from the Olympic Council of Ireland on the basis that it was preparing for the Games, and the Executive Committee had indicated that it would favour applying for entry. While it remained uncertain whether an Ireland team's entry would be accepted, nevertheless the matter needed to be resolved.

At the Council meeting on 30 October 1971, Dr Bertie Blake took office for his second term, and the correspondence included a letter from the FIH indicating that entry to the Munich Games should be made through the Olympic Council of Ireland before 31 December 1971. A very full and reasoned discussion followed and a number of relevant issues were aired: the obvious desire to maintain a united Hockey Union; the political aspects of the matter whereby the 'Four Provinces Flag' or 'Danny Boy' could not be used; no player could be compelled to walk behind the tricolour; there was the commitment to the Olympic Council of Ireland and the possibility of having to refund the grants; the overall financial cost of attending the Games; there were the political implications and personal feelings, as well as the position of the Ulster Branch.

In the final analysis, the unity of Irish hockey was probably the dominant factor. The vote on a secret ballot resulted in a defeat by 27 votes to 25 for the motion that an application should be made for entry to the Munich Olympics. An immediate sequel was that Con Lynch stated that he could not then accept office. He drew attention to the following points (a) the considerable preparations made by the players, and the breach of faith with those players who were being denied their most cherished ambition; (b) the degree of public support for participation which had been sought through press and other publicity; (c) the decision implied a certain lack of integrity on the part of the IHU following the extent to which preparations had already progressed.

However, the Munich Olympics question, which simmered under the surface was re-opened at a Special General Meeting on 4 December 1971. The meeting was convened at the request of the Leinster Branch to reconsider and, if it thought fit, to rescind the motion passed at the October meeting.

The many sides of the debate were again presented in a realistic way and it was acknowledged that it was a most difficult question. Everyone in Ireland would be awaiting the outcome and the delegates were advised to vote with wisdom and according to their conscience. The outcome of the ballot was 27 in favour of the motion to rescind, with 21 against. As there was not a two-thirds majority, required to reverse a previous decision, the motion was lost. Ireland would not be entering for the Munich Olympics after all.

There still remained the question of the Irish players who were eligible for the Great Britain squad, and the GB Coach, Dr Bill Vans Agnew, asked for the Ulster players to be made available for Santander. This was an unexpected development. The Union had not anticipated such a request. The reply, predictably, was that Ireland would retain first claim on the players. When GB asked for this decision to be reconsidered the Union replied that the first allegiance of the players must be to Ireland. They expressed the hope that it would not prejudice the prospect of those concerned being chosen for the GB Olympic Squad. The position established at that time helped to consolidate the Union into a cohesive, forward-looking body ready to face all the challenges of the future.

By the time the Executive Committee met later in December 1971, the Union was back on course. The Ulster Branch re-affirmed its support for the principle that the IHU was responsible for governing all aspects of the game in Ireland.

The Union turned its mind to International matches again. The next major expedition was to participate in an 8-Nation Tournament in Santander, Spain, during May 1972. The success of the Irish team in Santander, allied to the way in which the officials dealt with some very difficult decisions, built respect and determination which was to carry Irish hockey into the forefront of hockey-playing nations. Some incidents at Santander relating to the use of flags and anthems led to a full and understanding discussion which produced a formula which was to stand the test of time. It meant that the acceptance of matches outside Ireland would be conditional on the use of the 'Four Provinces Flag' and the music of 'Danny Boy'. The Santander Trophy is one of the Union's proudest possessions gained on the hockey field.

Administrators All - This picture taken at the Cliftonville Annual Dinner in 1958 shows generations of Ulster Branch Officials. Back row, left to right, Ken Armour, Percy Taylor, Des Simon, Alex Glasby and Jack Ewing. Front row, left to right, Billy Jordan, Billy Cross, Andrew Rose, Billy Shooter and Andy Hayes. The silver-ware, and the wine-bottles, show the serious and the social sides of Ulster Hockey!

The Ulster Branch Minutes for the period mirror the above and this account of the debate, to a marked degree. However there is scant reference in the Minutes to reports from the Ulster representatives on the Executive Committee being presented to the Council of the Ulster Branch. There is a mention of a Special general Meeting of the IHU on 4 December 1971, and after a long discussion it was agreed to mandate the delegates to again vote against an Olympic entry. The main issue was not finance, but the choice of the Flag and Anthem to accompany a team representing the two political entities on the island of Ireland. The issue dragged on, and was exacerbated in Ulster eyes by the use of the flag and anthem of the Irish Republic during the international tournament at Santander in Spain.

The Ulster Branch minutes of 20 June 1972 recorded an acceptance of an IHU apology "for the unfortunate flag and anthem incidents in Santander" and accepted the arrangements for future matches, namely that the music of 'Danny Boy' and the 'Four Provinces Flag' would be used. Given that these incidents occurred during a time of widespread IRA terrorist violence in the North, and in an atmosphere of heightened tension and fear in the island as a whole, this compromise was no mean achievement. The issue would be raised in later years, but the people who achieved that compromise in 1972 displayed commendable common-sense all round.

The Minutes of Branch meetings during the Seventies were filled with the reassuringly normal business of the administration of hockey in Ulster, with notes about the winners of competitions, successful Branch dinners, promotion and relegation which seemed to be a tiresome yet tireless subject for discussion, and also the dire warnings about suspensions - as on 15 December 1977 when the Branch itself suspended any "compliments of the Season" and warned Queen's, Civil Service and Down that they would stand suspended if they did not make their returns, before 7 January, for the International match played the previous April! Obviously no prisoners were taken in the unceasing war against inefficiency.

Cecil Pearson was a highly-regarded and greatly-liked Official who made a significant contribution to Hockey. He was Branch Secretary for 30 years, Convenor of the Schools Committee for 20 years, Assistant Secretary of the Umpires Association for 13 years, and Ulster Branch President for 1958-59. His Reports as Branch Secretary had a style of their own - he once told the AGM "I have not a clue as to who won our Section of the Intermediate Cup!"

Unfortunately, the Minutes from January 1978 to March 1986 are missing, but the Annual Reports of the Honorary Secretary Des Simon provide valuable information for these years. His first Report recorded a significant piece of Branch history when he noted the retirement of his predecessor Cecil Pearson "after over thirty years wonderful work for hockey in Ulster and indeed Ireland." Cecil typified the unstinting service of Branch officials who devoted virtually a lifetime to the sport. He was a most popular man, invariably polite, and a familiar figure with his broad, smiling face and his dark hair slicked to one side in the style reminiscent of his generation who believed that every sportsman should follow the example of Denis Compton in making a fortune for Brylcreem.

His inimitable style is well-illustrated by the following excerpts from his Secretary's Report to the Branch for 1966-67:

Now I will make some attempt to let you know what happened in Junior circles as I expect that most of you, like myself, hardly knew all Season what was happening ... I have not a clue as to who won our Section of the Intermediate Cup. Our thanks are due to the two hard-working Secretaries of the Umpires Association for their work throughout the Season and to the umpires for turning out in all weathers, although I am quite aware (you have told me so!) that many of them do not know the Rules.

Cecil was honoured with a Queen's Silver Jubilee Medal, and later with a

Goal-keeping Styles

The styles and equipment of goal-keepers changed greatly over the years. In the top picture, dating from 1965, Cliftonville goalie Archie Wallace moves into a crunch tackle with only his pads and old fashioned kickers for protection. Billy Curran on the left is in close attendance, while the burly Eric Priestley of Lisnagarvey waits to snap up a rebound. Archie Wallace, incidentally, was widely-regarded as the best 'uncapped' goalie in Ulster.

A youthful Brian Hanna of Instonians, and later a President of the Ulster Branch and of the Irish Hockey Union contemplates the scene, a little grimly, from between the goalposts. He is wearing the regulation white pads and gloves. It is interesting to note the state of the grass and pitch in the goal-mouth.

Modern Style -
In this picture of action in a Cookstown v Raphoe game, the Raphoe goalie has all the necessary equipment for today - the pads, large gloves and elaborate head-gear. Former goalies looked more vulnerable, but they also seemed more uncluttered, and they were recognisable!

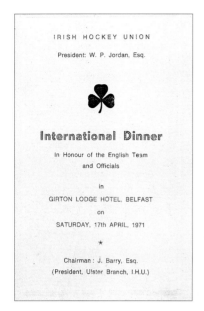

*International Duty -
These Dinner memorabilia
underline the social side of Irish
hockey. The 1966 Dinner for the
Scottish team and Officials shows
that the meal cost a princely 25/-.
The 1971 Menu for the Dinner in
honour of the English team and
Officials is interesting in that the
English party was still prepared to
visit Belfast at a time of a steadily-
worsening security situation. In
the Seventies, the Eighties, and the
Nineties the IHU and the Ulster
Branch had to face up to the
extremely difficult issue
concerning the entry of an Irish
team at the Olympics.*

British Airways Award for services to hockey. During the same year, 1978-79, the game suffered a loss in the death of Gerry Edwards, another amiable and dedicated official, who had first served on the Council in 1934. The Minutes, as usual, record details of Cup winners, and it was noted in 1980-81 that "for the second year running, both finalists in the Irish Senior and Junior Cups were from Ulster, thus illustrating the strength of club hockey in the Province." In 1981, the Senior Cup was won by Queen's who beat Lisnagarvey in the Final, while the Irish Junior Cup was won by Belfast YMCA Second XI who defeated Instonians Second XI, the Cup-holders. (Incidentally, Cecil Pearson played for YMCA Second XI in their previous Final 31 years previously, when they lost to Naas.)

During this period, the Olympic issue again emerged, and the topic was raised during the 1980-81 Season by the Leinster Branch. The Ulster Clubs opposed a resolution that Ireland should compete in the Los Angeles Olympics in 1984, and a similar resolution was heavily defeated at a Special General Meeting of the Irish Hockey Union. The Ulster Branch Secretary noted in his annual Report, somewhat optimistically "it is hoped that the Olympic question has been buried for ever, as the continued unity of the Irish Hockey Union, if at all possible, must be maintained."

The issue returned again in the early Nineties when the IHU put forward a proposal that an Ireland team be entered for a qualifying tournament for the 1992 Olympics. All the old questions were raised again - not about hockey on the field, but essentially about the identity of the team. An Ireland team would logically be regarded internationally as 'Irish', with the Irish national anthem and Irish flag. But a team which would include on merit the Northern players domiciled in the United Kingdom of Great Britain and Northern Ireland would not be 'Irish' in that sense.

The matter was debated at an Ulster Branch meeting on 30 October 1990, and the Minutes state clearly that "for most members the issue was a political one", and "that it would be difficult to reconcile what is in the best interests of Ulster and Irish hockey with our political views." The issue was faced head-on, and with honesty. The Minutes state:

> It became clear that members were faced with a hard decision. Whilst all were in favour of advancing the cause of Irish hockey, it was also a very political and emotive issue, involving the use of passports, flags and blazers. Many members asked that the overall view of Irish hockey be taken into account, and that to enter was the best way forward, despite divisions, in this one instance. Members felt that there would be problems for Ulster hockey whichever way the decision went.

The IHU's recommendation to participate in a qualifying Tournament for the Olympics was rejected by 22 votes to 19, thus indicating a fundamental division of opinion in the Ulster Branch. The issue rumbled on, and the Ulster Branch sent a large delegation to a special meeting of the IHU in Dublin on 19 January 1991. The debate raged intensely, to the point where friendships in some cases were strained. The outcome was recorded in a two-line note in the Minutes of the Ulster Branch meeting on 5 February 1991. The President, Carson Clarke, "referred to the IHU Council Meeting on the Olympic issue in Dublin on 19 January, where the motion to enter the Olympics was passed by 40 votes to 28."

In later discussion of the matter, the President stated that "while Ulster had lost the vote, he felt that the Branch had followed through the democratic process." The Minutes further recorded that "letters were read from Francis Baird, resigning from the International Senior Selection Committee, and from John Kennedy, resigning as Vice-President of the Irish Hockey Union."

Thus ended an episode that had created strong feelings but which had not led to permanent damage to relationships between the Branch and the Irish Hockey Union. At this remove it is not difficult to appreciate the arguments on both sides, but it was probably inevitable that an Irish team, and players from all parts of the island would be entered for the Olympics. The controversy also regularised a situation where Northern players could choose whether to play for Ireland or Great Britain but not for both. Most Ulster players keen to develop an International career opted for Ireland. What was remarkable, at this remove, was the way in which the issue was handled, given the current (and indeed prevailing) political atmosphere where fundamental Anglo-Irish issues and their local manifestations seemed almost irreconcilable.

The Professionals

The increasing professionalism in the administration of the game was apparent as time went on. Ulster Branch officials became more and more aware of the need for the systematic development of hockey and for proper funding. The financial developments alone were indicative not only of the progress that had been made since the early days but also of the increased responsibilities.

The Branch balance sheet in 1898 disclosed a surplus balance of £5-12-3 which had grown by 1899 to £18-1-8. Including under expenditure was the item "Athletic Stores hire of hockey balls £1" and "wages gatemen 3/6". Almost 100 years later, the Branch spends around £500 per annum on the purchase of balls but saves money by not paying the gatemen!

Whilst costs have naturally grown, the last ten years have seen a substantial increase in the financial requirements to run the Branch and Clubs. Branch annual expenditure is now circa £55,000 which is funded from Club affiliation fees, Sports Council Grants, Interest income, gate receipts and sponsorship from Harp Lager, which at the time of writing has been extended for another three years.

The advent of artificial surfaces has increased Branch expenditure for the hire of pitches for training and finals from virtually nil to £2,000 per annum. However, for Clubs this cost is often greater due to weekly training and matches. In 1970, one of the Belfast Clubs paid £25 per year for the use of two ash pitches and changing facilities. In 1995, the same Club paid £3,500 which included the hire of artificial pitches. A Club with six teams will pay affiliation fees of £2,000 per annum to the Ulster Branch and the Irish Hockey Union. Add these sums to the normal running expenses and the cost for the Season can be in the region of £9,000. The expenditure for a Club which has purchased an artificial pitch will be considerably higher, with additional costs for bank interest, loan repayments, rates, electricity and other outgoings. Inevitably, Clubs are now a business with annual accounts, budgets and cash flow forecasts. It is imperative that income must at least match expenditure. A professional approach has to be taken to maximising fund raising, sponsorship and pitch letting. As well as normal running costs, the price of success can be daunting. For example, a Club qualifying for a European competition can anticipate a cost of circa £8,000 for the tournament.

A number of Clubs have purchased artificial pitches. The current cost of a pitch and floodlights is £400,000 - £500,000 and this can grow to £1 million-plus if land has to be purchased and a clubhouse built. Joint schemes with schools or local Councils can ease the financial burden and grant aid from the Lottery Fund can be of further assistance. The sale of existing land for development purposes is also a method of raising a substantial portion of the

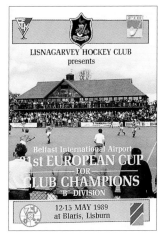

Showpiece - on and off the pitch This Programme for the 1989 European B Division Championships is also a striking illustration of the first-class facilities which Lisnagarvey have developed on their new site at Blaris, following the sale of their former premises to Marks & Spencer plc. This is perhaps the most impressive illustration of the progress of Ulster Hockey since its humble beginnings a Century ago.

Lisnagarvey set high standards in the evolution of their new pitch at Blaris, and many other Clubs have worked hard to develop their own, or gain access to, synthetic pitches. One of the most progressive Clubs is Newry Olympic who officially opened their new facilities in May 1993 with a number of social events and a sparkling 5-5 draw between a strengthened home team and the full Irish squad.

required expenditure. All of this is a long way from the hockey of a Century ago when a profit of less than £6 over the Season was considered 'satisfactory'.

The establishment of a Development Committee by the Ulster Branch in the mid-Seventies was a decisive step forward. Its main purpose was to provide guidance and direction in the administration and playing of hockey, and its very existence was evidence that the old 'ad hoc' system could no longer apply. The Committee also recognised the need for imaginative measures to underpin its work, but it was not until 1985 that money became available from the Sports Council in Northern Ireland to assist with the appointment of Stephen Martin, the Olympic player, as a part-time Development Officer. Two years later, due to further Sports Council funding, this key appointment became full-time. In 1992 a part-time Administrative Assistant was appointed, with grant aid from the Sports Council to provide a portion of the costs. A hockey office, complete with computer and modern equipment, was opened in the House of Sport, on the Malone Road in Belfast, to further underpin the important administrative changes taking place.

The Ulster Branch also systematically set about obtaining sponsorship, notably from such names as Harp, Guinness and Gilbey's and with the advent of International Tournaments, such as the 1990 Ulster Gilbey's Games, the sport began to attract substantial television coverage. Hockey is fast-moving, highly-skilled and exciting as a television sport, and it has a 'clean' image. It was little wonder that, for example, Dixon Rose was able to report that the Gilbey's Four Nations Tournament between Ireland, Australia, France and Russia at Blaris in 1990 had been a success "with good weather, excellent hockey (particularly from Australia), first-class television coverage, and a most satisfactory response from the hockey public." Hockey was indeed coming of age. On the debit side the Gilbey's Games lost £7,000, despite sponsorship and gate receipts of £14,000 but the venture had proved worthwhile in hockey terms alone.

It was re-assuring to know, however, that the Branch kept a tight control on all finance - at a meeting on 3 April 1990, shortly before the Gilbey's Games, the Council heard an appeal from Newry against the two-match suspension of a player. The suspension was maintained, but "a proposal from Mr McNamee that the appeal fee of £20 be forfeited was also carried." It was equally re-assuring that the best interests of young players were assured at all times - Mr Brian Hanna noted at a Branch meeting that young representative players had been seen in party mood at a Belfast Hotel on a Saturday evening near midnight, and wondered if this was proper behaviour. (Former hockey goal-keepers, myself included, occasionally become a little more responsible in middle-age!)

One particularly important development in Ulster hockey was the enlightened policy of creating good relationships with the media and of gaining maximum publicity for the sport. Carl Anderson, who would be described as 'the doyen' of hockey correspondents by his old boss Malcolm Brodie, reflects on some four decades of reporting on the sport he loves. Writing for the Belfast Telegraph and the Ireland's Saturday Night, and now the Newsletter, as well as broadcasting for BBC Radio Ulster, Carl has covered hockey everywhere from Portadown to Paris and from Banbridge to Buenos Aires. At my request, he reflected on a lifetime of reporting hockey and in so doing he provided a fascinating insight on the game and its characters.

Hockey in Ulster has chalked up a great many achievements during the past 100 years, but one of the sport's major gains has been the media attention it has

attracted during that period. It still owes a lot to the foresight of the Ulster Branch
Council who, 30 years ago, decided it was up to themselves to help hockey attract
the right degree of publicity. The then Council set up a media sub-committee
consisting of Percy Taylor, Des Simon, Alex Glasby and Billy Jordan.

I certainly remember the zest with which they tackled the job, writing to every
Sports Editor, setting up a face-to-face meeting with each, making the points they
felt necessary ... and offering ANY assistance hockey could offer the media.
Hockey is still reaping the rewards for that clever approach, and I'd encourage
current Branch and Club officials to give that matter a little thought.

If they can help a journalist to do his job, either by going out of their way to
provide information, or clearing the use of the Club telephone so an important
deadline can be met ... the profit, in the long-term, is likely to be theirs.

I'd also like to put on record in this important publication my appreciation, on
behalf of the media in general, of the assistance we received down the years from
the late George Blower, for 25 years the Ulster Branch Fixtures Secretary.

He never missed an opportunity to obtain publicity for the sport he loved, and
in doing so, helped make it a very successful organisation which can go into a new
century with considerable confidence.

From the reporter's point of view the passing years also have brought changes.
I've never sent a report by pigeon post, but modern technology in the shape of
mobile telephones and laptop computers has helped the journalists do the job
with less trouble.

When I began reporting hockey 40 years ago, only the privileged few had
telephones in their home and, from memory, only Cliftonville had one, in the
kitchen of their homely headquarters ground, from which they sadly were driven
in August 1972 by 'The Troubles'.

In those days I reported for the Ireland's Saturday Night and because
technology in the newspaper business also was less well developed, it was
necessary to telephone a report to a copy-taker at half-time ... and again on the
final whistle.

Certain venues, however, presented particular difficulties.

If, for example, Instonians were playing at Bladon Park, I had to leave the shale
pitch at the far end of the complex at half-time, climb that awful grass bank, plod
across three muddy rugby pitches to the car, drive down the Malone Road to a
public telephone box at Sans Souci Park to do my 'first take'. It then was a case
of dashing back to the pitch, picking up what I had missed from a colleague, or a
spectator, and repeating the leg-work at the final whistle.

At Lisnagarvey's old grounds, on the site now occupied by Marks & Spencer
at Sprucefield, the reporter at half-time dashed down the long lane to the
Hillsborough Road, across to Johnny Palmer's filling-station, and asked for the
use of the telephone, which was located in a store room at the back of the
premises.

On one occasion when the light had fused, I stumbled in the darkness, tripping
over cases of baked beans, found the instrument, dialled by using a cigarette
lighted for illumination, and then ad-libbed my copy, because I couldn't see the
notebook.

That day, Lisnagarvey were playing in a Cup match. The teams still were level
at the end of normal time, so I had to make the repeat journey at the end of 70
minutes to telephone a further piece, dashed back to the ground for the second
time, to be greeted by the players coming off the pitch with their job completed.
But my job wasn't finished. I had to get the facts, rush back to Johnny Palmer's
and phone the copy to my paper. And you think the reporter's job is a lot of fun!

There were also hazards presented by so-called colleagues.

When Ulster played the Home Scots on an annual home-and-away basis, it was
Ulster's turn to visit Paisley, in 1963. The game started late because the pitch had
been flooded, and my deadline was running out, so I dashed into the Anchor Club
when the final whistle sounded on a 2-2 draw (Angus Hamilton was the Ulster

*Carl Anderson, who has reported
for 40 years on Ulster and Irish
hockey. Formerly the Hockey
Correspondent with the Belfast
Telegraph and Ireland's Saturday
Night, he is currently the Hockey
Correspondent with the News
Letter, and he also reports on
hockey for BBC Radio Ulster. His
memories include reporting from
places as far apart as Lahore and
Johnny Palmer's filling station
near Blaris!*

All the Presidents' Men
This historic picture was taken
during the 1993 Celebrations to
mark the Centenary of the Irish
Hockey Union. This group
consists of seven former Presidents
of the Ulster Branch and also the
IHU, together with the 1993
President Crawford Tipping
from Leinster.
The Ulster group is (top left)
George Blower, Bobby Howard,
Walter Dowdall, Dixon Rose and
Des Simon; (front row) Billy
Jordan and Alex Glasby.

umpire that day), found the public telephone, shut the door, and started ad-libbing furiously.

After a few paragraphs, the door was jerked open by a Scottish reporter with the same problem ... time was running out on his deadline with the Sunday Telegraph ... and I was told in no uncertain terms that locals deserved first use of the facilities.

The argument became heated, the Scot was ejected, and I completed my report with back against the wall, one foot keeping the door firmly closed, and an irate home reporter screaming the house down in the corridor outside.

I've often joked that hockey reporting might drive a man to insanity, but I wasn't so relaxed when I reported Ulster's 6-0 Inter-pro victory against Connacht from the St Dympna's Mental Hospital grounds in Carlow in 1964.

(The number of the public telephone was Carlow 6!) The instrument was in the front hallway of the hospital, dusk was falling, and as I entered the premises from the rear door and walked to the front entrance, I was surprised not to meet a single member of staff.

Contact with Belfast was established, I began dictating, and two patients, obviously curious, joined me. Before long, there were 20 closely clustered, some sitting on the ground, one between my feet, and all listening intently to the story about Davy McManus's hat-trick.

With the light fading, I completed the job, dashed to the front door, found it locked, traced my way through gloomy corridors to the back of the hospital, found my way into the grounds, and then discovered that the entrance gates had also been secured.

I climbed the wall, returned to the Central Hotel, where Ulster were staying overnight (that's another story which I'll leave to Wally Mercer and Dixon Rose) and ordered a stiff drink. Easy job this hockey reporting!

Among other amusing incidents was the reaction of the waiter at breakfast in Faletti's Hotel in Lahore when I admitted my concern about the food quality in the Third World.

"The Game's The Thing!"

- Action Down the Ages

An action shot from an Antrim game in the 1920's with outside right Harold McKay in the foreground..

A tense moment in an Intermediate Cup Final in 1945 between Mossley and Downpatrick at Cliftonville. Mossley won 4-1. The hockey sticks, and the pitch, look distinctly agricultural!

Modern Style - Antrim's Leslie Allen in full stride during a game against Ballynahinch.

"You no worry, Sahib," he replied. "Pakistan much cleaner country than India, and Lahore cleanest city in Pakistan. I recommend the Corn Flakes and warm buffalo milk."

I tried it. The Corn Flakes and warm buffalo milk were delicious. I had them every morning ... but decided against the Brain Messalla!

Everything considered, I'll always be grateful for the day in 1966 when I turned down the offer from Sports Editor Malcolm Brodie to quit hockey and become Rugby Correspondent of the Belfast Telegraph.

I've nothing against rugby, even played the sport, but hockey has been my business for 40 years, and I've enjoyed every minute.

That characteristic report by Carl Anderson strikes a chord with me, not only as a former hockey reporter, but as someone who has known the game and its officials and players for virtually a lifetime. Hockey retains a sense of enthusiasm and an absence of hardened cynicism which seems to disfigure so many other sports. In the long haul of reading through the Minutes and Honorary Secretary's Reports since 1896, there is a discernible progress from humble beginnings to a modern approach. This is much more complex and professional, but it still retains an amateur dimension (in the best use of the word 'amateur') in its respect for the game, and for the best interests of all its participants.

The Minutes, right up to the present, record the essential business of the Branch which is and always has been about the standards of play, about discipline and good umpiring, and about respect for all those people, including Branch officials, who wish to continue contributing to hockey - in many cases when their playing days are over.

The Honorary Secretary's Report of 23 May 1996 is essentially the same as those of his predecessors of a century ago. It records the highlights of the year, the progress of the game, the winners of Leagues, important Cups and Tournaments, finance, umpiring, the state of grounds, and other matters. And, even 100 years or so later, there is still a strong line on misbehaviour. The 1996 Report states: "there was some concern towards the end of the Season that there had been a few incidents in which umpires had been physically abused - obviously this cannot be tolerated, and we would expect the Disciplinary Committee to take strong action if such incidents are deemed proven."

Some things never change, but most changes in Ulster hockey have been for the better. Its standards both on and off the field, and its contribution to Irish and indeed International hockey, have been exemplary. And the Ulster Branch has provided a firm base to carry hockey in this Province and on this island confidently into the next millennium. The handful of men who met in the Royal Avenue Hotel in Belfast on 11 December 1896 did so to form an 'Ulster Hockey Union' in order "to further the interests of hockey in Ulster." A century later it is abundantly clear that the vision and the initiative of these men, and of countless people who followed them down all the decades, have been honoured in full.

Blowing the Whistle
(The Ulster Hockey Umpires Association 1897-1996)

CHAPTER 6

Since the beginning, the need for Umpires to ensure fair play and the observance of the spirit of the Laws has been recognised. Umpires are all too prone to attack and criticism, but they have made an honourable and vital contribution to hockey in Ulster and far beyond.

At the first General Meeting of Clubs held on the 15 October 1897 it was decided to form an Ulster Hockey League. 'Rule 11' passed at that meeting stated "that two Umpires be appointed for League matches, one from each Club." In fact each team supplied its own Umpire, but following reports of rough play, that Rule was altered at a later Committee meeting on 26 November 1897 to read, "two Umpires shall be appointed for League matches, one from each Club, and one Referee (to be mutually agreed by the two Captains)." The role of the neutral Referee was to report back to Council, who would "disqualify any player found guilty of rough play from competing in further League matches."

At a Council Meeting on 2 October 1900 it was agreed that reference to Umpires and Referees be omitted from the League Rules and at the same time it was a recommendation from the Council to the League Committee to do their utmost to have neutral Umpires for the various League matches.

Over-robust play was a problem from the beginning, and at a meeting on 19 March 1901 a letter was read from Mr Roffey, the Referee in the Banbridge v North Down match reporting 'rough play'. There was also a report that a Cup game between Monaghan and Portadown was played as a friendly because the Official Referee had not turned up.

From the available early records (1897-1902), minuted appointments for Referees and Umpires continued to appear for both Senior and Junior Cup matches. There is an interesting reference from the AGM of 1902 - "they were all deeply obliged for the manner in which Mr Clayton had assisted the Council by refereeing important matches in almost every district of the province of Ulster. He had also refereed International contests to the entire satisfaction of everyone concerned."

Back in 1899, concern was being expressed on the appointment of competent Umpires, as the game in Ulster expanded, and annual appeals were made for neutral Umpires. However, it was not until the 1906-07 Season that a Referee's Association was formed, under the Secretaryship of Mr Ernest TS Wilson, of Lisburn, a position he held until hockey was suspended in 1914 due to the outbreak of World War One.

The 1907 AGM records the following. "To the members of

Andy Hayes, was elected Secretary of the Ulster Branch Umpires Association, and held the position for 35 years until illness forced him to retire. He was also President of the Ulster Branch, and of the Irish Hockey Union. A forceful, popular figure, he made an important contribution to hockey at Club, Inter-provincial and National level. During the Second World War he helped his home Club East Antrim to fulfill their fixtures by obtaining supplies of petrol during a time of strict rationing!
In this photograph he is pictured handing over the Richardson Cup to the youthful John Kennedy of Friends School U-15 team in 1950.

George Blower was one of the best-loved figures in Irish Hockey. He gave sterling service to YMCA, then Holywood 87, and to Ulster and Ireland at all levels. He was particularly interested in Schools hockey. George was a member of the Schools Committee for 37 years, Branch Fixtures Secretary for 25 years (and what a job that used to be!), a member of the Indoors Committee for 15 years and Chairman of the National Indoors Committee, Assistant Secretary of the IHU for 5 years and a member of the Umpires Association Committee for 19 years. He was Branch President in 1969-70 and President of the Irish Hockey Union in 1978-79. George, pictured extreme right, is characteristically umpiring a match between Instonians and Mossley in which goalie Brian Hanna is keeping his eye on the ball.

the Referee's Association also much credit is due. Under the direction of Mr ETS Wilson, the very courteous and hard working Honorary Secretary, the Association has supplied a long-felt want, and to a large extent has been responsible for the elimination from the Ulster game of much that was rough and unscientific, and which was allowed to run unchecked under the old order of club umpiring. Your committee takes this opportunity of offering their congratulations to Mr WT Graham and Mr ETS Wilson, both of whom were appointed by the IHU in several International and many other important engagements last Season." (Allowing for the sincerity of the above tribute, "much that was rough and unscientific" was still evident for many years to come!)

When hockey resumed in 1919, TH Tuke, of Bangor held the position for one Season. RC Bannister (Lisnagarvey) took over in 1920 and he was followed by his brother George W Bannister (Lisnagarvey) in 1928. At a meeting of Umpires held on 21 April 1931 it was decided to formalise the Association and a Committee was appointed to draft new Rules.

Des Simon, pictured here in celebratory mood, played occasionally for Cliftonville First XI at both cricket and hockey, but for many years he was the backbone of the Hockey Club. A former President of the Ulster Branch and the Irish Hockey Union, and an International Umpire, he succeeded Cecil Pearson as Honorary Secretary and retired in 1989 as a most effective, friendly and respected figure.

The Ulster Branch Referees' Association was reconstituted as follows; (a) "the Association shall be known as the Ulster Branch Referees' Association and shall be under the control of the Ulster Branch Council"; (b) "the Association shall have power to make by-laws governing its administration, such by-laws to be subject to the approval of the Ulster Branch Council"; and (c) "the Association shall be governed by a Council consisting of a President, Honorary Secretary and five others, who shall be elected annually from the members of the Association at a general meeting."

The First Office Bearers of the new Referees' Association were: President - RC Bannister; Honorary Secretary - GW Bannister; Council - Messrs JR Guiler, RH

Keers, W McCleneghan, A Rose and HD Montgomery; Representatives to Branch - GW Bannister and HD Montgomery. At the Annual General Meeting of the Ulster Branch held on 6 September 1932 "rules governing The Ulster Hockey Referees Association were submitted and passed, subject to the amendment in the title to the 'Ulster Hockey Umpires Association'."

The Association continued to progress, with occasional Council meetings and an Annual meeting each year. Presidents and Council members changed from time to time, but George W Bannister continued as Honorary Secretary up until 1935.

He was succeeded by RK (Dick) Megran who along with his Assistant Secretary, Mr Albert Hunter, held office until they retired in 1950. During Mr Megran's term, the Second World War intervened and only a handful of Umpires faithfully continued to officiate at the few matches which were played. The Association was revived in 1943 and Mr Megran reported that the Umpires Association had a membership of 22 compared to 48 in 1938-39. They officiated at 318 games out of the 450 played.

In 1950, Andy Hayes was elected Secretary, the position he was to dominate for 35 years, until illness forced him to retire. The Assistant Secretaries who worked with him were J Harwood (1950-58); W Tyrrell and C Wilkinson (1958-59); WP Jordan (1959-69); CC Pearson (1969-83) and E Coulter (1979-85).

At the Branch AGM on 28 May 1959 Andy Hayes, on behalf of the Umpires Association, presented a President's Chain of Office to the Ulster Branch. The Chain bore the names of all the Presidents of the Branch since its foundation. Amidst applause, he hung it round the shoulder of the outgoing President, Mr G Edwards who thanked the Association for their magnificent gift. Mr Edwards was also a stalwart of the Umpires Association, and served as President, Council Member, Selector and Grader and was Treasurer from 1952-76.

At the Branch AGM on 27 May 1965 Des Simon presented WA Cross, the outgoing President, with a Presidential Ulster Branch Plaque (the first one to be presented), as a gift from the Ulster Umpires Association. This presentation has continued every year since. At the 1960 AGM it was agreed that a grading system be introduced but when nothing happened, the matter was raised at the 1961 AGM. After a long debate it was decided by 19 votes to 10 to rescind the decision on grading.

This contentious issue was raised annually but it was 1966 before the AGM agreed to form a Pool of 20 Umpires for Senior and Qualifying A matches. The Senior Clubs were also asked to list their top 20 choice to further assist the Umpires Association in their selection of the new panel.

At a Special Meeting called by the Secretary in November 1966 it was agreed that it was essential to have grading, but the means of achieving this was in question. After a very animated discussion it was decided that the Umpires on the selected list of 20 be used singly as far as possible with other members for all matches in Senior and Qualifying A each week on a rota system.

However, the Secretary was opposed to the selection of an 'elite' squad of Umpires who would mainly officiate at the top games. His strategy was to keep as many Umpires as he could in the system by appointing everyone to an occasional Senior game. (One humorous quote from the 1967 Secretary's Report stated that "Mr Hayes expressed his sincere thanks to Billy Jordan who, as usual, did the lion's share of the work and never looked forward to Friday evenings or Saturday mornings.")

Billy Jordan, who has given outstanding service to Ulster and Irish Hockey. He was first elected to the Umpires Council in 1958, and for almost the next 40 years served in various capacities as Assistant Secretary, International Umpires Selector, President and later Vice-President. He was also President of the Ulster Branch, and also of the Irish Hockey Union. He is here pictured in his playing days, (bottom picture, right) with Jimmy Horner, and also in his Official capacity (top).

Alvin Carson won 90 Caps in a career which began in 1970 against West Germany in Dublin. For many years he was a patient understudy to the great Harry Cahill, before his opportunity came to take the leading role. The Irish goalkeeping position seems to have been occupied for many years by a combination of master and apprentice, and Alvin filled both roles excellently. Quiet and gentle off the field, he always seems content with his pipe and relaxed conversation. On the field he has played many brilliant matches for Ireland, relying on his positional sense, keen anticipation and great bravery.

Alvin is the most-capped Irish goalkeeper ever. He has also made 10 appearances for Great Britain.

His greatest Tournament was probably the first Intercontinental Cup in Rome in 1977, where he was an inspiration to the Irish team. His greatest disappointment was in 1976 when as a member of the Great Britain Team he waited in vain at London airport for the call to take the place of Kenya in the Montreal Olympic Games. On his retirement from playing in 1985, Alvin took up and quickly excelled at umpiring. Awarded his FIH Badge in 1990, he has umpired 19 International matches, and he is highly regarded and respected as one of the best umpires in Ireland.

Further unsuccessful attempts were made in 1968 and 1970 to implement proper grading structures. However, at the 1976 AGM concern was expressed as to whether the Association was keeping pace with modern developments in respect of the recruitment, coaching, grading, selection and appointment of Umpires. The consensus of opinion was to maximise resources and examine future policies. At a subsequent meeting of the Umpires Council a Working Party was formed with the brief to examine in detail all operations of the Umpires Association and to present proposals for future development.

The Working Party consisted of R Campbell (Umpires Association President); WRC Clarke; RW Jess; HD Simon; WA Williamson and LG Glasgow (Director of the Northern Ireland Sports Council). After seven months hard work their recommendations were accepted. The main points included; (a) a written Constitution containing the Association's Aims and Objectives and setting out its administrative structure; and (b) a system of induction, training, assessment and grading of Umpires.

In 1977 Alex Glasby was elected as the first Chairman under the new Constitution, and he held that Office for all but two years until 1989. He was elected President of the Irish Hockey Union in 1980 and during this time Angus Hamilton held the position. Alex returned as Chairman in 1983, and in 1989 was elected President of the Association, retiring in 1993. He was first

This is an early picture of Alex Glasby (centre) playing for Cliftonville in the mud and twilight of an Ulster Winter afternoon. Alex is another distinguished servant of Ulster hockey. He was elected as the first Chairman of the Umpires Association in 1977, and held that position for all but two years, until 1989. He was President of the Ulster Branch, and also of the Irish Hockey Union.

Richard Kendrick, a former Cliftonville player who stopped playing early to take up umpiring. He was the first Irish Umpire to be selected for the Olympic Games and World Cup panels. He is pictured here officiating in a match between Holland and Germany at the European Championships at Amstelveen in 1984.

elected to the Umpires Council in 1964 and has a proud record of continuous dedicated service to Ulster Umpiring for almost thirty years.

Another faithful servant WP (Billy) Jordan was first elected to the Umpires Council in 1958, and served in the following positions; 1959-68 Assistant Secretary; 1977-85 International Umpires Selector; 1986-88 President; 1978-85 and since 1989 as a Vice-President - a truly remarkable record of almost forty years service.

Within a year the positive results of the new structure were noticeable. The new Grading Committee, under George Blower, had met and upgraded Mike Parsons, Eddie Coulter and Derek Stanbridge to Grade 1 and Freddie Burns and Brian Gilroy to Grade 2. Billy Stewart, Paisley Watson, Basil Singleton, Alan Moore and John Blythe had passed a written test and were placed in Grade 3.

However, the coaching and grading system was slow to develop, and it was not until Mike Parsons took over as the Coaching and Grading Convenor, in 1982, that progress was made. With the help of FIH Umpires, he held annual Induction Courses with written Rules tests for new Umpires, and regular and popular Rules meetings for 'seasoned' Umpires. A proper grading system was set up and every Umpire was graded and on request could be re-assessed over a series of games.

When Mike stood down at the end of the 1985-86 Season, the foundation had been laid, but it was soon realised that if progress was to continue the responsibility for grading and coaching had to be divided up. In 1989 the Selection Committee took over the arrangements for regular grading and a Coaching and Development Committee was formed, under the leadership of Michael Jackson. The brief was to organise coaching sessions, hold development and Club meetings, and to try to recruit Umpires.

After two year's work, a Revised Constitution was finally implemented at a Special Meeting in September 1991. Michael Jackson agreed to become the Umpires' Coach, mainly to assist younger umpires with a more personal approach, and giving the necessary guidance, help and advice. Unfortunately in 1993 Michael had to resign this post because of Club commitments and it

Francis Baird was a member of the Antrim First XI for many years and indeed in 1955 was the first-ever RBAI pupil to win an Irish Schoolboy Hockey International Cap. Francis first came into the Council in 1966 and his contribution to Ulster Hockey has been well documented. Before his untimely death on 25 September 1993, Francis had served hockey as a Player, Selector, Administrator and International Umpire. He will long be remembered as a dedicated Ulster Branch Hockey Administrator who had a deep interest in the affairs of the Ulster Branch. He criticised when the occasion arose, but was equally generous in his praise of a job well done. Francis was a character - a good friend - first and foremost a proud Antrim man and a true Ulsterman. His passing has been a great loss to Ulster Hockey.

was not until early in 1996 that Nigel McCullough agreed to take on this difficult and indeed thankless task.

In 1989 Nigel had become the Convenor of the Grading Committee. The increasing availability of synthetic pitches which led to many matches being played under floodlights on Friday nights, allowed that extra flexibility for Umpires to be seen and graded. Tom Morrison, the present Grading Committee Convenor, took over when Nigel stood down to become the Ulster Branch President in the 1992-93 Season. Nigel was first elected on to the Executive Committee in 1981 and served as an Umpires representative on the Branch Council from 1982-89 and as the Association's Vice-Chairman from 1989 until the present time. His is yet another tremendous record of active involvement in the Association.

Although several fine young umpires are coming through the system, building up their experience and developing the skills required, there is still a great need for more recruits. Since the formation of the Umpires Association there has always been a shortage and in the Centenary year the number of active Umpires has fallen, unfortunately, to 35, an all-time low.

However, this is no new phenomenon!

A section from the 1949 Secretary's Report states "with a total of 36 members we were able to cover a small percentage only of the matches played. With a few exceptions the Clubs appear apathetic and so long as this spirit permeates, our Association is helpless. It is surely not beyond the capacity of each Club to nominate members as Umpires equal in number to their playing teams."

Although these same words could have been written today, the situation is now even worse because of the much-increased umpiring demands on the members.

This need for more help must be properly addressed by the Clubs and the Branch. They must actively assist the Association, to find recruits and provide proper funding, so Ulster can continue to produce some of the best Umpires in Ireland.

Ulster umpires have figured prominently in the list of International honours over the years. Pride of place goes to Richard Kendrick, who umpired the Final of the Second Inter-continental Cup in Kuala Lumpur in 1981 and was awarded his FIH Class 1 Badge in the same year; and he umpired the Inter-continental Cup at Madison, USA in 1989. He also officiated at the European Cup Finals in Amsterdam in 1983 and in Moscow in 1987; the Champions Trophy in Karachi in 1984; the Under-21 World Cup Finals in Vancouver in 1985 and at Terrassa in 1994; the World Cup Finals in London in 1986 and many more, all over the world. The popular Dr Kendrick became the first Irish Umpire to be selected for the Olympic Games and World Cup Panels. Richard retired from the International scene after he had umpired his one hundredth game in 1995.

Fifteen other Ulster umpires have been awarded the FIH International Umpire Class 2 Badge. They include OW Peacock; Dr JCS Ritchie; AF Hayes; HD Simon; FA Glasby; WRC Clarke; F Baird; A Moore; W Gillespie; P Marshall; W Stewart (Indoor); M Jackson; P Watson; S Clarke; and A Carson.

The success and standing of hockey in the past Century is a reflection of the efforts of the small pool of Umpires who faithfully give their services so that others might enjoy the game. As such, the Umpires deserve the sincere thanks of all concerned.

Schools Hockey

Schools hockey was given an early boost by the presentation in 1920 of the 'Burney Cup' by the Ulster Branch President 'Andy' Burney of East Antrim[1]. Over the years, the popularity of hockey grew steadily in the Schools, and not least because of the dedication of individual schoolmasters, coaches and administrators.

The early period was administered by a Schools Committee of four elected by the Ulster Branch. In the Sixties the key administrators were Cecil Pearson and George Blower together with the two others who varied from time to time. A Schoolmasters' Advisory Committee was formed with WK Lowry (Wallace), Hugh Taggart (Cookstown), Ronnie McNamee (Annadale) and John Smyth (Bangor) who worked with Cecil and George, eventually becoming the Committee. John Smyth chaired this from 1969-89, Ronnie McNamee from 1989-95, and the current Chairman is John Waring.

The competitions in the Sixties were limited to the Burney Cup - the premier competition - the Richardson Cup for the U-15s and the more recent introduction of the McCullough Cup. In contrast to the others which are

An early picture of a Friends' School team who won the Richardson Cup at Bladon Drive, in 1950. The team had to borrow Rugby First XV jerseys for the game, and most players returned to the oval ball game. The team, left to right, was Stanley Howard, David Boyd, Norman Cromie, David Hutchinson, Brian Moreland, Frank Patterson, Alan Finlay, Jackie Reid, Glyn Douglas, Jackie Ferguson, and Captain John Kennedy.

---

[1] See Chapter Two.

Bob Poots, of Newry Grammar School, Newry Olympic and later of Queen's University. He was one of the youngest players to represent Ireland, and won the first of his four Caps in 1957, at 18, when he was still at School. The Headmaster James Greenlees gave the pupils a day off in his honour.

knockout Cups, the McCullough Cup was played on a League basis in the Christmas Term. The strength of the schools game at this stage lay mainly in the periphery of Ulster, in the smaller rural schools - Bushmills Grammar, Ballycastle, Banbridge, Cookstown, Newry, Friends, Wallace, Royal School Raphoe, Prior School Lifford and others. The spread of the game in strength into the 'city' schools was important - to RBAI, Methodist College, Annadale, Belfast Royal Academy, Campbell College and Sullivan Upper, and further afield to Bangor Grammar.

The greater numbers playing in the late 1960's and early 1970's reflected the change from grass to the porous 'all-weather' surface which ensured a more regular game. The introduction of the Taylor Cup in 1962-63 stimulated the game in the Secondary non-Grammar School sector, but it was in the 1970-80 period that the basis of the present system was established. A range of new Cups was introduced to challenge the various age groups both outdoors and indoors and the standing of the game within schools was raised.

In 1982 the Irish Hockey Union was asked to send an U-19 Club side to an invitation competition in Holland the next Easter. As a result the Irish Schools Championship was inaugurated to find an appropriate team. The first event was held at Bangor at Halloween in 1982, and this has become a highlight of the schools year moving round the Provinces in turn, with invitations to 8 Ulster, 4 Leinster and 4 Munster schools.

At representative level the Ulster side was selected following a trial between Belfast and District schools and the North West. This format was unfair on the weaker North West as the Belfast schools improved radically. The Ulster side then played (on successive Saturdays), Leinster and Munster and the South East.

The Inter-pros themselves - then for U-19 - moved in 1976-77 to a single weekend event and in 1983-84 was expanded to U-16 as well as the re-named U-18 event. The extension to U-16 was in response to the International demands for such a team. The U-19 Quadrangular Internationals were started in 1964 and in 1984 Ireland joined the U-16 event as well as the U-18 event (replacing U-19).

RBAI, who won the first Burney Cup in 1920 by beating BRA 4-0 have made a major contribution to Schools hockey. In this picture Ralph Spearman, who did so much to consolidate and to develop hockey in the School, is seen in a typical pose with some of his young charges. The likely event is the Final of the Schools Cup, and the venue is the old Blaris. Part of the Lisnagarvey name can be seen in the background.

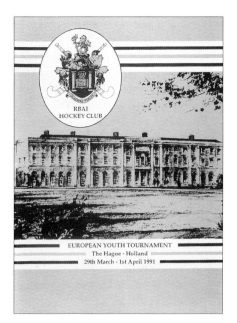

European Horizons - Copies of the Programmes for the RBAI Tour to Holland in 1991, and to Barcelona in 1995.

Playing surfaces changed gradually from grass to all-weather and then to synthetic surfaces. This was reflected in the Burney Cup Final venues - grass remained in favour well after the majority has ceased to play on grass. The last grass pitch Final of the Burney Cup was played in 1983 between Bangor and Wallace High School, and the last all-weather surface Final was in 1987 between Bangor Grammar School and RBAI. The first Final on the synthetic surface at Blaris was in 1988 again between Bangor Grammar School and RBAI. Blaris indeed has become the home and ground-setting for all the Schools Finals - even though it is a unique challenge to all players unused to the water-based surface. The spread of synthetic pitches means that not only Cookstown High School, with a pitch on site, but many other schools, are now taking advantage of the ever-increasing availability of the synthetic pitches, thus making the game and its skills unrecognisable from thirty years ago.

Whilst this rapid expansion of the secondary schools activities was proceeding, the Ulster Branch Development Committee under the late Francis Baird proposed the introduction of primary school hockey with mini hockey. John Smyth was asked to organise a Tournament and the Inaugural event took place at Ward Park, Bangor in April 1976. The event, after twelve years in Bangor, moved to Blaris where its skills help to open up the game to so many under elevens. A dominant force has been Strandtown Primary School under the knowledgeable leadership of Ronnie Dowdall. Much of the early work in the Primary School Committee was undertaken by Frank Dowdall, Eddie Megaw, Larry Stirling and Ronnie Harkness.

Individual schools had periods of dominance as well as the normal ebbs and flows one would expect. Many International players started in schools hockey, and a number of key figures in the development of the game also came from the Schools. Friends School, a traditional centre of excellence, under the many years of leadership of Brown Shaw had in the mid-1970's a four-year Burney Cup winning run and it remains the top Burney Cup winner with 19 successes. Two of their most notable recent players include Jim Kirkwood, gold medal Olympian, and the late Frank Green whose name is remembered in the Frank Green Trophy for the U-16 Inter-pros. Cookstown High School under firstly

Hugh Taggart and more recently Alan Ferguson have had a long period of continuing success. Its most notable players included Martin Sloan, former Irish Captain and the most-capped Irish player with 149 Caps and David Larmour in goal. In the Fifties and Sixties, RBAI owed much to Ralph Spearman, who challenged the bastion of rugby in the School, and he was followed by Ian Steepe whose teams reached five successive Burney Finals. After a period in the doldrums Inst re-emerged with a united front with its Old Boys. They owed much to Simon Bell, Colin Gault and David Scott, dominating the Schools' events including the six wins in the Irish Schools Championships. They took early advantage of the synthetic pitches to set standards for the other schools.

Further back Newry High School relied on two lively coaches David Kay whose U-14 sides made 12 of the first 14 Ferris Cup Finals and Lennie McCaigue. Lennie led Newry to the first three Irish Schools Championships, and coached Ulster and Ireland at both U-16 and U-18 level before going on to coach the USA Olympic Squad for the 1996 Atlanta games. His academy of hockey produced such gifted players as Billy McConnell, Robbie Taylor, Alan Dowd, Frankie McGladdery and John McKee. No match with Lennie was ever quiet!

One of Newry's great challengers was Wallace High School under Howard Thompson. After losing three successive Finals of the Irish Schools, their success in 1987 was a well-deserved reward for this popular Coach. Two of the small schools produced two of the most successful Ulster and Ireland coaches - from Ballycastle Brian Dillon and from Cairnmartin Ronnie Smyth. The Schools were very lucky to share two such gifted and sympathetic schoolboy coaches. Banbridge Academy, following the Banbridge Club with its basic forthright hard-hitting style, and led vociferously by Fergie Cosgrove, gained a sparkling win in the Irish Schools, with the Tumilty brothers temperamental stars of that era.

Not all sides were major winners, yet many made major contributions to the game. Kilkeel under firstly Bobby Boyd and latterly John Bird produced the Morris brothers, Ivan and Kenny, from a ground on which no game ever seemed to be cancelled - icy wind was no reason for cancellation apparently! Raphoe (the Royal and Prior amalgamation of the former Royal School Raphoe and Prior School Lifford) was a thriving academy in the hockey-starved North West. Much credit is due to Ray Dunne who for over twenty years has quietly kept the

The RBAI success has continued down the years and in this picture, the First XI are displaying an impressive array of silverware won in the 1986-87 Season. It includes the McCullough Cup, the Tasmanian Trophy (Irish Schools Champions), the Lisnagarvey Schools Tournament Salver, the European Youth/Schools Trophy (Runners-up), the Burney Cup, and the Hamilton (Schools Indoor Champions).

An enlightened youth policy is vital, and Ronnie Smyth (centre) is one of the most accomplished schools and youth coaches in Ireland. He is pictured here at a ceremony recognising Annadale's Junior Development policy, which received a Royal Mail Award in 1990 from the Sports Council for Northern Ireland. The schoolboys are Matthew Allison (left) and Paul Jackson. The picture includes Danny O'Connor of the Sports Council for Northern Ireland (top right) and Andy Steele of Royal Mail.

flag flying, and has periodically reached the Junior Finals.

Campbell College too has retained its reputation - not of the strength of the 1930's when Campbell played the rest of Ulster in a trial! - but following in the footsteps of Kenneth Armour, and Ted Agnew, Ted Cooke did sterling work including a Burney Cup win. Sullivan also had a Burney Cup win. The former Annadale Grammar School, masterminded initially by Ronnie McNamee, and its successor Wellington College won the Irish Schools Championship and McCullough Cup under Frank Thompson, another long servant of the game. The Annadale influence has spread its tentacles widely throughout Ulster hockey - including Ronnie McNamee, Michael Graham, Michael Jackson, Ronnie Smyth and others.

The Ulster Branch has appreciated the huge increase in interest in the game but was aware of the decreasing number of schoolmasters available to give their time to the game. To stimulate this interest the Branch appointed Stephen Martin as the first Development Officer. Having started his hockey at Bangor Grammar School, he moved through the ranks from U-19, U-21, Ireland and ultimately to the Great Britain Olympic Squad - bronze (1984) and then gold medallist (1988). With such a pedigree he was an excellent ambassador for the game and a model for the young players, and he used his status as an Olympic medallist to keep the game in the public eye. His successor, Alan McMurray, has continued the process introducing coaching videos, and courses, and continuing to attempt to open the game to new areas such as Omagh, Enniskillen and Londonderry.

Hockey in Ulster owes a great deal to the dedication and enthusiasm of all those who have encouraged and developed a love of the game in succeeding generations of school-boys, and it is at this level that continued dedication is vital to produce not only the Stars but also the Club stalwarts of the future.

The International Scene

International games between Ireland and England and Wales were played from 1895. In that year Ireland beat Wales 3-0 at Rhyl, in the world's first hockey International, and lost 5-0 to England in London. The first match between Ireland and Scotland was played in Belfast in 1902, with the home team winning 3-0. The first match between Ireland and England in Belfast took place at Balmoral in 1900, and the visitors won 2-1.

Despite the honour of staging such an important fixture, the Ulster Branch had a financial problem which would repeat itself in later years. The Honorary Secretary reported to the Annual General Meeting of the Branch on 21 September 1900:

> The most important fixture of the year, England v Ireland, was played in Belfast, and was admitted to have been the finest exposition of the game ever witnessed in Ulster, Ireland having the hard luck to get beaten in the last few minutes of the game. Unfortunately the match did not turn out a financial success, as a loss of £18 resulted. To meet this deficit your Council decided to ask the Ulster Clubs to subscribe £1 each, but so far only seven Clubs have sent in their subscriptions, viz, North Down, Antrim, Cliftonville, Banbridge, Ballymoney, Bangor and Malone. It is hoped that the other Clubs will see their way to send in their subscriptions as soon as possible.

With the exception of a match against France in 1923, when Ireland won 4-1 in Paris, the International fixture list until after the Second World War was a variation on a familiar theme of games against England, Wales and Scotland. The scorelines were familiar too, with Ireland dominating Wales and Scotland, but managing to beat England on few enough occasions.

In fact in the first 90 years or so of Internationals since 1895, excluding the periods covering both World Wars, Ireland beat England only 11 times, drew 17 games and lost 49. In the same period Ireland beat Wales 59 times, drew 9 games and lost 10. Against Scotland the fixtures began later, in 1902, with Ireland winning 43 games, losing 9 and drawing 19. After the Second World War the growing importance of the International game was underlined by the wide range of Irish fixtures, with games against many countries including Argentina, Australia, Austria, Belgium, Canada, Russia, Denmark, France, Great Britain, Italy, Japan, Malawi, Malaysia, Malta, Mexico, The Netherlands, New Zealand, Nigeria, Pakistan, Poland, Portugal, Rhodesia, Singapore, South Africa, Spain, Sweden, Switzerland, West Germany and Yugoslavia.

The story of Ireland's progress in International hockey is also the story of advances in coaching and administration, and during the second half of this century the Ulster Branch made an outstanding contribution to the game in general.

International "Caps" were treasured possessions from the earliest days of representative hockey. This Blazer Badge was worn by WH (Harry) Greenfield of 'Garvey who won 9 Irish Caps between 1928 and 1931.

*Banbridge stalwart Eric Walker
with a 1920 Cap and shirt
belonging to RF McKnight.*

The 1947 Education Act in Northern Ireland heralded the provision for specialist Physical Education in new Secondary Schools: Gymnasia were built, playing pitches were provided, and there was a supply of specialist Physical Education Teachers, trained initially at Loughborough College. Understandably these specialists were themselves sportsmen and they brought back to their sports knowledge of physical fitness, skill techniques and coaching. As well, the Central Council of Physical Recreation, the forerunner of the current Sports Council, opened a NI Office in 1949, to encourage the development of sport amongst the post-school population. This they did mainly by encouraging the provision of sports facilities, and by promoting coaching and development. Both of these developments ensured strong communication links with progressive thinking in Great Britain as well as providing training opportunities at National Sports Centres and Loughborough.

Three of the local PE specialists sent for training at Loughborough in the early Fifties were, by a happy coincidence, senior standard hockey players - Bob Fawcett, Albert Lucas and George Glasgow. Glasgow's thesis on 'Hockey' at Loughborough had sparked a keen interest in the techniques and tactics of the game and after teaching and introducing hockey at the new Kilkeel High School he was appointed in 1955 as one of three technical staff of the relatively new CCPR in Belfast.

On the facilities side hockey faced a grave problem in the public sector with poorly-draining grass pitches. The need for a harder wearing, faster draining, surface for games coaching had seen the introduction of 'Redgra' (crushed red brick) pitches in Scotland. Two were laid at Stranmillis College but import costs were prohibitive and after an abortive attempt to use local crushed stone at Cookstown High School experiments with 6 other local sources of supply were undertaken at the Ulster College of Physical Education. A locally available stone dust which bound well to form a firm playing surface, yet drained quickly was selected and promoted. This breakthrough in the 1950's and the laying of hard porous (misnamed all weather) pitches at schools such as Inst, Friends, Methody, Cookstown and at Queen's University gave a tremendous fillip to the skill level of Ulster's schoolboy players amongst whom Terry Gregg, Ian Raphael, Alan Tolerton, Noel and Reg Quinn were some of a flush of new talent ready in time for Ireland's participation in the first European Championships.

In the Fifties hockey coaching, other than in schools, was unknown and until Ian Steepe arrived at Inst relatively few of the hockey playing schools found themselves with a hockey player on the staff. In his early liaison work with the Ulster Branch, George Glasgow prepared a comprehensive set of development proposals. Members such as Owen Peacock (Honorary Secretary), Gerry Edwards, George Blower and Col Shooter of the Ulster Branch supported their acceptance. As a result Robin Bailey, a cultured Queen's/YMCA International full-back, was selected to attend a Hockey Association Coaching Course at Lilleshall - a new development under an evolving coaching scheme in England - and he returned enthused to help spread the word. A coaching panel which included Bailey, Jack Carroll, Stevie Johnson, George McElroy and various umpires was formed to give a series of winter evening demonstrations at hockey Club centres where they showed skills techniques (sometimes with a string ball), fitness training methods and also discussed umpiring.

There was a further breakthrough when the Schools Committee and the CCPR organised a coaching weekend for hockey school masters to coincide

*George Glasgow, who as Irish
Coach made an important
contribution to more professional
training, organisation
and commitment in the
International scene.*

The Irish Squad for the first European Championships, in Brussels in 1970. Ireland achieved ninth place but might have finished fourth, and on overall performance they merited a fifth/sixth ranking.

with an Ulster v Home Scots match at Cliftonville. The unique feature of the course was that after practical sessions the teachers were not only invited to watch the Home Scots game but to critically analyse it. As 'Armachia' recorded in a lengthy Newsletter review of the event "the Computist's copious notes and diagrams reveal that the ball was in play for 19 minutes in the first half, 21 minutes in the second. The whistle blew 201 times, and the ball was out of play twice for every minute it was in play!" This laid the foundation for further work with the schools sector which was more receptive to new ideas for player improvement.

"Coaching Course, Best Thing Ever Done" was the Newsletter headline on 4 January 1961. The quotation was from Denys Carnhill, three times British Olympic Team Captain and fresh from the 1960 Rome Olympics where Harry Cahill (YMCA) was the Great Britain goal-keeper. These two with Melbourne Olympian Stevie Johnson (Lisnagarvey) together with quality players drawn from Queen's University and teaching backgrounds had just completed the first three-day Christmas schoolboys coaching course for the top 57 players in Ireland - including the top players from all Ulster schools and invitees from Leinster, Munster and Connaught. Carnhill with his Olympic team-mate Tony Robinson returned the next year to establish what was to be a long-running series of courses which had far reaching effects on the game in Ireland. Not only did the best schoolboys in Ireland receive top class coaching, but schools' selectors saw the advantages of organised training. Volunteer player coaches profited a great deal too from the exposure to coaching ideas and were to play an important part in changing the culture of International affairs. The realisation that simply pitching 11 players together to play as an Ulster or Irish team was not good enough spread amongst the players, if not yet the administrators.

The successful Christmas courses format was repeated at the Orangefield Summer Courses run annually by the Belfast Education Authority under the

Harold Cahill, a Dubliner who played for Pembroke Wanderers, Belfast YMCA, Tamworth and Coventry. He won 72 Irish Caps, and represented Great Britain at three Olympics - being regarded as the world's best hockey goalkeeper at the Rome Olympics.

direction of their PE Adviser Dick Williams. Don Brownlee (Southern Counties) was a regular visiting coach and George Blower a tireless organiser. Williams and Glasgow were honoured later by the IHU with 'Awards of Merit' for their services to the development of coaching. Many of these schoolboy players and volunteer coaches went on to form the new generation of Club and National coaches, among them Ray Cantan, Ian Steepe, Terry Gregg and Philip Anderson at Irish level and Lennie McCaigue, the USA National Coach.

From the mid-Fifties the Belfast YMCA Club became a focal point for many of the developments. In Bladon Drive it had the best pitch of the day; two of its Officers were Branch officials - George Blower had joined from England in 1947 and Cecil Pearson, who as Branch Secretary never missed an Ulster Branch meeting in over 30 years. Glasgow joined on his move to Belfast in 1955, followed by Harry Cahill on his transfer from Dublin and by Robin Bailey, Ian Roulston, Tony McMillan, Ronnie Wilson, Ronnie McManus, Roy Thornton and Albert Lucas. Club training was rare, and without floodlights outdoor training was impossible. Glasgow took the team for indoor fitness and skills circuits in a small square hall with a pole in the centre which ranked as a gym on the top floor of the City YMCA. Whether by virtue of the quality of the players, or the mid-week training, or both, a 1958 Ulster team included 9 YMCA players - 5 of them full Internationals. However, perhaps history should record that this distinguished team was beaten, embarrassingly, 1-0 in a Cup-match by lowly Second Division Holywood!

Ulster teams were selected after one or two trial matches and they played single games against the other Provinces. An appointed Captain would meet the team in the changing room and decide tactics. Inevitably, there would be changes in the team after most matches; for Selectors had to be seen to act. The Inter-provincial series allowed the Irish Selectors, nominated by each Province, to pick two Irish trial teams and then the International side which annually played single matches against England, Scotland and Wales.

However, while the schoolboy courses and the Ireland schoolboy teams enjoyed much success through the Sixties, the Senior International side was being left behind. England had appointed a full-time National Coach-Development Officer and gained from a great deal more exposure to Olympic and other International events. Ireland's system of selection and preparation was proving totally inadequate even against Scotland and Wales. A dismal 2-0 defeat by Scotland in Aberdeen in 1969 highlighted the gap.

Revolutionary changes came as a consequence of the Irish Hockey Union's courageous decision to accept an invitation to take part in the first European Hockey Championships to be staged in Brussels in 1970. Having announced a huge squad of over fifty players the IHU eventually decided to invite Glasgow, then the BBC hockey correspondent, to take on the job of 'Manager'. In, fact the move came as a result of some agitation mainly from those players who had experienced coaching courses and said they were not prepared to devote themselves to unproductive training sessions.

The concept and position were entirely new to Irish hockey and no terms of reference were outlined by the IHU. However the opportunity to establish a modern squad-coaching, management and selection system was too good to miss, and Glasgow accepted the offer in writing on the 'assumption', amongst other things, that he would be called 'Coach', that "there would be a manager to take care of travel, financial and administrative arrangements", and "that the Coach would select the teams from the agreed squad in consultation with the Selectors." That last stipulation proved extremely difficult for the IHU to accept for "the constitution provided that the Selectors picked the International teams", that "they had always done so" and "of course the Selectors would take the Coach's advice." In that case, said Glasgow, they might just as well accept the terms as written, for no Coach could be expected to spend weekends training a squad in new tactics and special plays only to have the Selectors converge from the four Provinces to pick the Ireland team - inevitably representative of the four Provinces. The IHU accepted. And thereafter the Selectors were content to have their say, especially on the marginal final positions in the squad, and to unearth new talent from their own Provinces.

Con Lynch (Corinthians and Leinster) was an excellent Manager, gaining the confidence of players and learning quickly the art of liaising with the IHU, and ensuring that Tournament hosts flew the IHU's Four Provinces flag which he always packed at the top of his case. The IHU also agreed to the setting up of an International Committee which included the Manager and Coach together with people such as Bill Haughton, George McElroy and George Blower, who had valuable experience of the International scene. This 'horses for courses' Committee was able to give informed and detailed attention to the International aspects of the IHU's work, and ensured that recommendations on future programme, finance and policy issues were given due attention and carried weight.

With the system in place, the work of cutting down the unwieldy squad of over 50 to manageable proportions of 25-28 (2 teams plus reserves) began. The Inter-pro series was suspended to allow Provinces v Irish XI matches. Squad training weekends were programmed. The Fokestone Festival and Orangefield Summer Coaching Camps were included.

The first International match under the new regime was in fact the 75th Anniversary of the oldest International Hockey fixture in the world. Ireland beat Wales at Llandudno on 14 March 1970 and after playing Scotland in Limerick, they held England to a scoreless draw at Bristol in April. This was

Martin Sloan, left, the dynamic Cookstown player who represented Ireland 149 times and was Captain in more than 100 games.

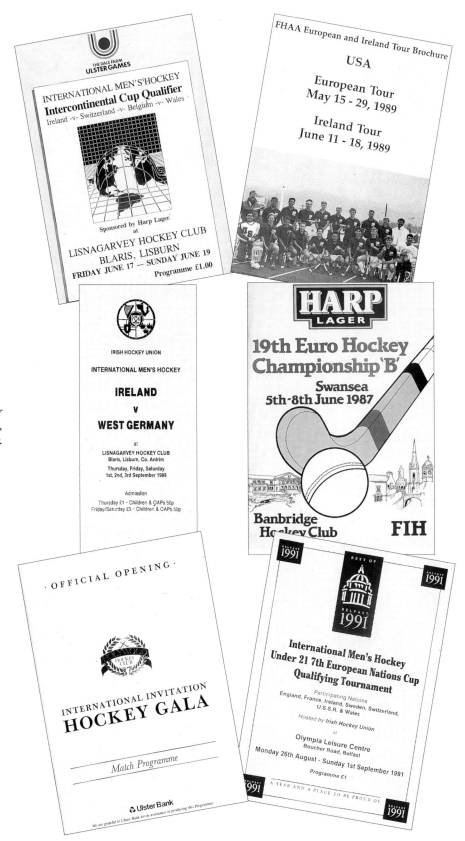

*International Hockey on a wider
scale has blossomed at all levels,
as these Match Programmes show.*

almost the end of the era of one-off International matches, and the Home Countries Championship, from which England had decided to withdraw. (Sadly soccer and rugby have followed.)

Finance was, of course, a great problem for the IHU which had little income from gates or grants, and depended largely on Club fees. The squad was organised mainly on a self-financing basis with everybody contributing a few pounds per session to help with travel costs. International Caps were not always free either. For example, the squad waited patiently to hear the 'good news' of who was to play against England in Bristol and then hear the 'bad news' that it would cost £80 a head. No one cried off! Finance may not have been a great problem for lawyers and company directors in the squad, but it was a considerable embarrassment for young students. However, informally the Ulster Umpires Association (Andy Hayes and Gerry Edwards) would sometimes have wiped out a student debt to the IHU. (One enterprising squad member was known to have broken a bitter strike in the Republic by driving a van load of cement along the back roads to Dublin for profitable sale. He, too, got to Brussels!)

The 1970 summer Season required special measures to keep the momentum until the European Championships in September. Wales came for a double-header at Trinity College when they tried out a strict man-for-man marking system, only to be out-foxed by the Irish players lining up out of position! Earlier England had been made very uncomfortable by Ireland overloading the right wing and then by posting a forward on their sweeper. Final preparation for Europe included a long weekend at Tollymore Mt Centre (a primus stove, self catering establishment) where Orienteering, Rock Climbing, Canoeing and fiendish beach games on Dundrum strand presented more awesome challenges than the toughest International opposition. A final week at Orangefield, where John Robertson also joined the staff, set the stage for the final selection.

In Brussels, Ireland was grouped with Spain, France, Czechoslovakia and Malta, an unfortunate draw since only 2 from each of the four pools could go through to the top eight play-offs. An excellent 1-1 draw with Spain was a bonus. Malta was beaten 5-0 (disappointing since goals were to count and the second half was scoreless). Czechoslovakia was beaten 2-0 in the Heysel stadium itself. The result against France was to cost Ireland a possible top-four placing, for they squandered chances to lose 1-0 through a short corner deflection past Cahill's right ear. A win would have given Ireland a relatively easy top-eight match.

Ireland then faced Scotland whose bad results were spreading Anglo/Scottish dissension in their camp but they now relished the chance to rescue a ninth-twelfth place finish at Ireland's expense. In the event extra time saw Ireland get the winning goal (2-1) in the sudden death period after a howl of anguish from Stewart McNulty during a scrummage had seen the Umpire dispatch an infamous Scot to the side lines.

That was a vital victory, and Ireland went on to win the next two games - claiming ninth place by beating Czechoslovakia again. Ireland might well have finished fourth and on overall performance merited a fifth/sixth place ranking. Eight matches were played in nine days, 6 won, one lost, and one drawn with only three goals against (2 from corners and one scrappy field goal by Scotland). This was a fine result from Ireland's first venture into the burgeoning International arena in which World Cups, Inter-Continental Cups, International Tournaments and Olympic Qualifying events were to become regular fare.

The Programme for the first European Championships, which were staged in Brussels in 1970.

Ireland v England in 1968, the last Home Countries Championship, which was won by Ireland.

Dick Williams (Limerick), an excellent President, told the Union back home that Ireland had graduated from Ford car to a Mercedes. Glasgow's report similarly exhorted the IHU to stay with the new challenges for "the lessons learned in one Tournament provided the homework for the next."

What for an encore? Government grants were available in Northern Ireland for International Competition, but in the Republic such grants were made via the Irish Olympic Council - and only to sports preparing for Olympic participation. The Irish Hockey Union had long been deterred from making an Olympic entry on the grounds that in the Olympics, Northern Ireland was British and consequently Ulster could neither support nor allow the Union to enter. When, post-Brussels, a Leinster motion in support of the entry of an Ireland team for the Olympics came forward to the Irish Hockey Union Annual Meeting, the Ulster Branch delegates, whose voting strength was substantial, were mandated to vote against. In the event the desire not to split the Union was strong enough to ensure the motion was heavily defeated.

As ever the debate in Ulster had more to do with flags, passports and anthems than hockey. Irish as well as Northern Irish players had played for British Olympic teams; Stevie Johnson 1956, Harold Cahill 1960, David Judge 1964 and Terry Gregg 1972. As far as the players were concerned, anthems were of concern only at medal ceremonies, and as Harold Cahill said "when you walk out into the Olympic Stadium there are a vast number of flags flying and you can make your own choice." In practice, the views of the players as a group and the International Committee were never sought.

The dual-nationality problem for players such as Terry Gregg facing conflicting calls was harmoniously solved at that time by the Ireland International Committee taking responsibility. In effect, Ireland had first call but was by no means selfish about requests for Gregg's release to win his Great Britain place at Munich in 1972. There were few serious conflicts of interest until later when Ireland and Great Britain both accepted an invitation to a Tournament in Spain. John Robertson, the then Coach, and the IHU decided to retain Gregg's services. To add insult to injury, Ireland had an inspired Tournament, beating Great Britain in the Final. Gregg was not merely an International class player but, like Cahill who was rated the best goal-keeper in the world at Rome, he was undoubtedly 'world class' and it was a tragic loss when ill-health curtailed his playing career. In more recent times the FIH have banned dual-nationality and now Irish International players may not play for Great Britain.[1]

After the European Cup, George Glasgow, who had become Chief Officer of the CCPR in Northern Ireland and was engaged in the process for establishing the Sports Council in 1974, decided to retire as National Coach. On the International Committee's recommendation, English County Coach John Robertson, who had been involved at Orangefield, was appointed. He took charge during another highly-successful period which included a tour to South Africa as well as Santander in Spain, before ill-health forced a short-term recall of Glasgow. This coincided with Ireland's first Indoor Tournament in Perth. Ireland, incidentally, covered themselves with glory in Spain, and beat Great Britain in the Final, with Terry Gregg scoring the only goal in magnificent style, and also making certain of his British place in the Munich Olympics.

Sadly, John Robertson's illness proved terminal and Ian Steepe, a former teacher of hockey at RBAI, a coaching enthusiast and core member of the 1970 European Championship team, was appointed in 1975. Under his guidance Ireland progressed further. They lost the Final of the First Inter-Continental Cup 2-1 to Poland in Rome, but more importantly, they qualified for the 12-Nation World Cup Finals in Argentina - in 1978 - another first! A very creditable eleventh place finish was achieved, but Steepe's appointment was not renewed and several of the established players decided to retire, including David Judge (124 Caps), Ian Raphael (70), Noel Quinn (62), John Douglas (35), and Neil Dunlop (33).

For the next few years Ireland paid dearly for allowing some of the 1970 systems and principles to lapse - although Ireland did well to achieve fourth place, behind Russia, Malaysia and New Zealand in the 1981 Inter-Continental Cup in Malaysia. It was not until Ireland looked abroad for a new Coach and appointed Cees Koppelaar from Holland in 1987 to succeed Ray Cantan that the system began to work again. Koppelaar remains the Irish National Coach, very ably supported by the popular Team Manager, George Compston, who was appointed in 1989.

In the Eighties Ireland continued to play in the European Cup, but it was not until 1988 that they again qualified for the Inter-Continental Cup and from it, a place in the 1990 World Cup. This result started Ireland on a six year run of FIH and EHF competition, as follows: 1989 Inter-Continental Cup in USA (fifth place); 1990 World Cup in Pakistan (twelfth place); 1991 European Cup in France (seventh place); 1991 Olympic Qualifier in New Zealand (tenth place); 1993 Inter-Continental Cup in Poland (ninth place); and the 1995 European Cup in Dublin (fifth place).

Koppelaar's influence, and the increased demands of playing in International competitions, increased the regularity and intensity of squad training sessions. Because of Koppelaar's Dutch connections, regular training trips to Holland became part of the International preparation, resulting in improved skill levels and tactical awareness in Ireland's players.

The top players are now engaged in International preparation for almost 12 months of the year. When they are not directly involved in preparing for a specific Tournament, squad training in the Provinces followed by regular Trial

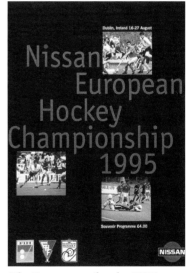

The Programme for the 1995 European Championships in Dublin which were a triumph for Ireland. The Squad reached an unprecedented fifth ranking, and the organisation of the Tournament by the Irish Hockey Union, under the leadership of Dixon Rose, was widely acclaimed.

---

[1] This aspect of the International game is also discussed in Chapter Four.

The Irish Coach Cees Koppelaar,
pictured left, and Team Manager
George Compston have played a
vital role in Ireland's success.

matches, was introduced in 1992, to keep the players operating at a higher level than they would normally do with their Clubs.

Players of the pre-1970 era would find it difficult to understand the level of commitment which is demanded from today's players. For example, preparation for the European Cup in 1995 began with Trial matches in Dublin in December 1994. Thereafter, from February until August 1995, the players in the Training Squad attended nine weekend session of 6-10 hours each; a five-day session of 25 hours; a week in Holland with 12 hours of training and 4 matches, including 2 Internationals; and three weekend International Tournaments, culminating in 7 matches in 10 days in the European Cup. All told, from 12 June until 26 August, the Ireland squad had played 20 matches, in addition to all the organised training sessions and their own personal training. This is what is required of today's young player to survive at the top level and to keep Ireland as one of the top nations in World hockey.

By common consent the Irish Hockey Union staged a highly-successful European Nations Cup at University College Dublin from 16 to 27 August 1995. For this seventh such European Championship the sun shone, large crowds watched the hockey and enjoyed the social scene, and Ireland ended the Tournament in its highest-ever place by finishing fifth. No Irish squad ever entered a major Championship in better physical and mental shape than the one prepared for this Competition by Cees Koppelaar, and no greater administrative and organisational effort was ever demanded from the Irish Hockey Union. Under Dixon Rose's leadership as Chairman of the Organising Committee, it was delivered by many willing and enthusiastic helpers. Euripedes once famously remarked that "toil is the sire of fame". Both Cees and Dixon toiled hard and their fame is assured in the annals of Irish Hockey.

An impressive Opening Ceremony took place on Tuesday, 15 August in the O'Reilly Hall at UCD, and President Mary Robinson, presiding with both grace and dignity, formally opened the Championship. Regrettably, the Belarussians were stranded in France, although they arrived later in the day to be greeted with both champagne and relief by their hosts. Their determination to take part was clear for all to see, but Ireland's narrow win over Belarus (2-1) provided a valuable start. England beat Germany the next day in a major upset while on the Friday, Ireland had its own disaster by losing to Switzerland. The loss of Ireland's best player, Jimmy Kirkwood, through injury proved to be too great a burden to an Ireland team which seemed both listless and directionless.

Thus the psychological balance had tilted away from Ireland and towards England. It was now vital not to lose the Sunday game with England. The return of Jimmy Kirkwood was the tonic the team needed. It is in such circumstances that the mettle of sportsmen is tested. The Irish team came back strongly on the Sunday and when Daniel Clarke scored first, the cheer could have been heard at Blaris. England was not to be outdone, however, and equalised just before half-time. A tense second half ensued with Ireland the happier of the two teams to hear the final whistle.

Ominously Ireland's next game on Tuesday, 22 August was against an old and formidable adversary, Poland. The game proved difficult and a less than impressive performance saw Ireland drawing 1-1.

The prospect of getting anything out of the final Pool game against Germany was remote. Psychologically, however, it was important to play well, so that the final cross-over games could be approached with a degree of confidence and optimism.

Ireland played as well as it is possible to play against the Olympic Champions and while a 2-0 defeat was probably inevitable, it left the squad intact both physically and mentally. The pool games had ended and Ireland had finished fourth. The third team in the other pool was Spain who had been edged out of a Semi-Final position by the surprise team of the Tournament, Belgium.

The Irish objective of finishing either fifth or sixth, and thus pre-qualifying for the next European Championships, was set to receive a stern test against Spain, a hockey-playing country of world renown.

The teams met on Friday, 25 August. The early morning start clearly suited Ireland and those fortunate enough to be present saw one of the best-ever Irish

The Irish International Squad whose determination and inventiveness in the European Championships in Dublin in 1995 brought them their best-ever European ranking of fifth place.

performances. A 3-1 win with goals from Clarke (2) and Canning did not flatter Ireland, and the physical energy of the team and its clear sense of purpose spoke volumes for all the hard work and preparation. It also indicated great strength of character from players who had stuck at their task even when things seemed desperate.

A major objective had now been realised. Ireland would finish, at worst, sixth and thus a place in the next Championships in Italy was assured.

This set up a fifth/sixth play-off with Poland on Saturday, 26 August, but this time, with the pressure off both teams, one of the best games of the Tournament took place.

Ireland beat Poland 4-3 (Taylor 2, Canning 2) in a game which may not have reached the technical heights of German or Dutch hockey, but for sheer excitement and drama was a game second to none in the Championships. Thus Ireland finished fifth, its best ever result in a European Nations Championship.

It was a classic Final between two of the oldest International hockey rivals - Germany and The Netherlands, and Germany deservedly won the Championship on penalty strokes.

One final Irish success, however, remained. Ivan Bateman was voted the best goal-keeper in the Tournament and so followed in the footsteps of Sandra O'Gorman who received a similar award the previous summer for her efforts for Ireland in the Women's World Cup.

The end of the Tournament also saw the retirement of the Irish Captain, Martin Sloan, whose leadership of the squad was crucial to the team's ultimate success.

He retired as Ireland's most-capped player with the unique distinction of having played for, and captained, his country over one hundred times.

The European Championships, fittingly held in Dublin, underlined Ireland's remarkable achievements and development in International hockey in which Ulster players and officials played a significant role. The International side, both in terms of talent and in back-up coaching, and managerial and administrative ability, has come a long way since that first game against Wales in 1895. It is a collective achievement of which hockey players, coaches, managers and administrators in Ulster can feel justifiably proud.

The Olympians

Ulster has produced many outstanding players who had distinguished Inter-provincial, National and International careers. However, only a handful have had the distinction of playing in the Olympics, and the following Ulster players have brought great honour to their Clubs and to Ulster hockey in general. No history would be complete without a pen-portrait of their achievements.

Just The Ticket! - Baggage label for Stevie Johnson en route to the 1956 Olympic Games.

Steven Johnson

Steven Johnson, the popular former Lisnagarvey player and Club stalwart was a member of the Great Britain team at the Melbourne Olympics in 1956 when they won a Bronze Medal. Stevie, unfortunately, injured his hand and ended up by playing only one game - against Australia. However, the trip, and the build-up, were experiences of a lifetime. Only 16 were allowed in the squad, and Stevie was taken as an all-round 'utility' player who could provide cover at left-half, centre-half, though principally as a full-back. Though pre-Olympic training was vital, the preparation in the Fifties was not as pressurised or as intense as in modern times. There were training sessions in London, but Stevie had to train on his own, with the help of a fairly rudimentary manual sent by the Hockey Association. He was kitted out in the finest style by Simpson's of Piccadilly, and his bounty included 3 sticks of his choice from Gray's, the noted manufacturers.

An action shot from the Great Britain v Australia game in Melbourne. Stevie Johnson (left) keeps a watchful eye on the ball.

Stevie Johnson in Melbourne with (left) Thelma Hopkins who won a Silver Medal in the High Jump.

The journey to Melbourne, in the days of the old turbo-prop aircraft was memorable. They had stops at New York and San Francisco and the team stayed in the famous Raffles Hotel in Singapore. Discipline was strict but not strict enough to prevent certain players stealing out of the New York hotel to sample some night life in that vibrant city!

The Olympics was the highlight of Stevie Johnson's International career which included 20 Irish Caps from 1952-57, the first being against Wales. He captained both Ulster and Ireland, and at Club level he played for Friends School Old Boys before joining Lisnagarvey where he gave long and distinguished service on and off the field. His major recollections centre around the Olympics where he witnessed Ulster's Thelma Hopkins win a Silver Medal in the High Jump, and Ron Delaney win the 1,500 metres for Ireland. His abiding memory was that of walking into the Melbourne arena at the Opening Ceremony. "Hockey players were not used to that level of world exposure. All of a sudden you walked down a tunnel into the sunlight in front of many thousands of cheering people. I can recall the cheers and the comments to this very day. It was absolutely phenomenal."

Terry Gregg

Terry Gregg was an outstanding hockey player and Coach who has played a major role in Ulster and Irish hockey. He played for Ireland during his first year at Queen's,

Terry Gregg

and went on to win 103 Irish Caps. He was Captain of the Irish team from 1975-79, and Vice-Captain of the Great Britain team from 1974-80. He did not compete in the Montreal and Moscow Olympics, due to politics, but played in every game for Great Britain from 1972-80, winning 42 Caps. He did play in the Munich Olympics, when the Great Britain team came sixth.

Terry Gregg captained Queen's in 1972, when the University team won the Irish Senior Cup for the first time in 60 years. He finally stopped playing for Queen's in 1974 to join Belfast YMCA, but a serious viral illness caused his early retirement at 29. However, he then began a remarkably successful career in coaching. Under his guidance, Team Volkswagen Indoor team won the All-Ireland Championship seven years in a row, and he also coached the Ireland Indoor Team from 1983-86. He then switched to outdoor hockey with equal success and coached Lisnagarvey to six Irish Senior Cup wins in a row. He made yet another switch and successfully coached the Ireland Ladies team which took part in the 1994 World Cup Finals in Dublin.

Billy McConnell

Billy McConnell, who started his playing career with Newry Olympic, went on to win 135 Outdoor and 35 Indoor Caps for Ireland, and 51 for Great Britain. He won almost every major honour in the Game, culminating in a Bronze Medal at the 1984

Olympic Games in Los Angeles. His career, however, did not start with marked success and during his time at Newry High School from 1967-75, he lost in every major Schools Final including the Richardson, McCullough and Burney Cups!

At Queen's he won a Blue and played for the British Universities team. His representative career included Ulster and Irish U-21's and U-22's and captained the Senior side. As a Belfast YMCA player from 1978-87 he won 3 Irish Senior Cups and all the other Trophies, and with Holywood 87 he won all the Ulster Trophies but not the Irish Senior Cup. In Indoor hockey he played for Targetmen, Team Volvo, Team Volkswagen, Team Kaliber, dominating the local game and becoming highly successful in Europe.

Billy McConnell

He recalls: "The most memorable moment of my career was the feeling I experienced when I walked out into the bright sunlight at the Opening Ceremony of the Los Angeles Olympics. The atmosphere was absolutely electric, and knowing that the eyes of the world were watching, made every hair on my body stand on end. It was an experience that I will never forget."

Stephen Martin

Stephen Martin not only holds two Olympic Medals, but he is the 'most-capped player' in the Guinness Book of Records, with a total of 229 Senior Caps. He won 135 of these for Ireland and 94 with Great Britain. His first Cap for Ireland was in 1980, against France, and his first game for Great Britain was in 1983, against the USA in London. He represented Ulster and Ireland at Schools, U-21 and Senior level, and captained Ulster, Ireland and Great Britain.

At Club level he played briefly for Civil Service, and then for Bangor, YMCA, Holywood 87, and latterly for Newry Olympic.

In a career distinguished by a long list of representative honours, the highlights were the Olympic Medals - a Bronze in the 1984 Games in Los Angeles, and Gold in Seoul in 1988, and also playing for Ireland in the 1990 World Cup competition in Lahore. He also captained Great Britain in the Barcelona Olympics in 1992, when the team came sixth.

Stephen Martin

In latter years he has been the first Ulster Branch Development Officer. He is British Olympic Association Tutor helping Great Britain and Northern Ireland athletes plan for success in Sydney 2000. He is also Northern Ireland Co-ordinator of the Olympians Club, and a Technical Officer with the Sports Council for Northern Ireland.

In 1993 Stephen was awarded the MBE in the New Year Honours List for 'services to hockey'. He recalls his most memorable hockey moment: 'When 2-1 down to Australia in the third/fourth play-off game at the Olympic Games in Los Angeles I cleared the ball off the line. Fifteen minutes later after goals by Barber and Kerly we won Olympic Bronze by beating Australia (the pre-Olympic favourites) 3-2. It has been described by players and journalists as the turning point of the game and the start of four glorious years for British hockey culminating in Gold Medal success in 1988."

Jimmy Kirkwood

Jimmy Kirkwood, one of the most exciting forwards of his generation, won 130 Caps for Ireland and scored 36 goals. He also won 40 Caps for Great Britain, scoring 5 goals. His representative career was most distinguished, and he played for Ulster and Irish Schools, and for Ulster and Ireland at Senior level.

His career virtually spanned the globe and his appearances include those at the European Cup in Moscow in 1987, Paris in 1991, and Dublin in 1995, as well as Inter-continental Cups in Malaysia in 1981, Barcelona in 1985, the USA in 1989 and Poland in 1993. He took part in the World Cup in Pakistan in 1990, and the Olympic Qualifier against New Zealand a year later.

Jimmy also played in the Champions Trophy at Amsterdam in 1987, and Melbourne in 1990. One of the highlights of his career was taking part in the Seoul Olympics in 1988, when he won a Gold Medal with the Great Britain team.

At Club level he played for Friends School Old Boys from 1976-80, for Queen's (where he won a Blue) from 1980-83 and then with YMCA from 1983-86. He joined Lisnagarvey in 1986 and played a major role in their outstanding successes over the next few years, including seven consecutive Irish Senior Cups, four consecutive Senior League Titles, and many other honours. He also has the distinction of winning nine Irish Senior Cup Medals. He recalls, among his most memorable events, the Seoul Olympics, the World Cup in Pakistan in 1990, and in 1995 the European Cup in Dublin where he helped Ireland to reach an unprecedented fifth place.

A delighted Jimmy Kirkwood displaying his Olympic Gold Medal, with his father Cecil.

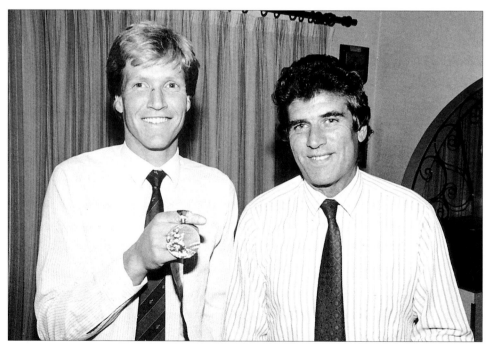

Indoor Hockey

Abbreviated forms of hockey have been in existence since hockey, as we know it today, became a sport in its own right. In the British Isles, for example, tournaments featuring teams of, say, six players have been, and still are, regularly played. Deck hockey with teams of four to six players was one of the highlights of sporting activities on the great passenger liners of the first three decades of this Century. As hockey spread from the British Isles to Europe there are records of the game having been played indoors in 1910 in Berlin in an exhibition hall, in a ballroom, and, in the concert hall of the Philharmonia. Students played hockey indoors in those early days in the Franz Joseph army barracks in Vienna.

The above are instances of hockey being played indoors on an irregular basis before the Second World War. Essentially it was outdoor hockey played indoors to provide practice where outdoor practice was impossible, due to adverse weather conditions so prevalent in the European winters. There is little doubt that the frustrations caused by heavy snow and frost eventually led to the game of indoor hockey as we know it today. Before the Second World War, indoor sports halls were few and far between and those that did exist were gymnasia rather than the multi-purpose halls we know now. Consequently hockey played indoors was in a comparatively-restricted environment.

After the Second World War indoor hockey restarted in Hamburg in a hall in the Post Office. The game also recommenced in Leipzig, Berlin, Cologne and Vienna, and in 1947 in Copenhagen. There is little doubt that German players were the first to exploit the possibilities of indoor hockey and to lead the way to the modern game. In the 1950s and 1960s the game spread to Belgium, Switzerland, The Netherlands, Spain, France, Poland and Czechoslovakia. In the 1970s and 1980s indoor hockey spread outside Europe to places like Australia, New Zealand, Argentina, Canada and Jamaica. A census carried out by the International Hockey Federation in the mid-Eighties showed that there were approximately 135,000 people playing indoor hockey throughout the world, of which about 90,000 were in Europe.

Initially indoor hockey was played only at Club level but fairly rapidly the game became administered by the National Associations of the outdoor game who wanted to control this new version of hockey. In due course this led to International Tournaments which immediately presented problems, as in different areas there were different rules and non-standardised goals and sideboards in the halls in which the game was played. In 1952 the International Hockey Federation formed a Sub-committee to manage indoor hockey for the game as a whole, and before the start of

Brian George, President of the Irish Hockey Union, presents the Inter-provincial Indoor Championship Trophy to Ulster Branch President, Dixon Rose, after Ulster 'A' had beaten Leinster 'A' 10-5 in the Final at the Valley Leisure Centre. Pictured (Back row); the late Gordon McIlroy (Coach), Paul Cooke, Billy McConnell, Neil Dunlop, Norman Crawford, Trevor Gowan, Harold Burns, George Compston, John McKinstry, Philip Anderson, Joe Silcock (NI Milk Marketing Board). Front row; Gerry McWilliams, Philip Marshall (Captain), Colin Shields.

the 1952-53 Season this Committee produced in German the first book of rules which was later translated into French and English. Needless to say those rules have been revised many times since then.

In the British Isles in the 1960s some forms of hockey indoors were being played but it was not until the 1970s that the authentic indoor game became established. The first official League game in Britain was played in the Meadowbank Stadium in Edinburgh in September 1970. The League in Scotland quickly flourished and it is interesting to note that Scotland was by far the most enthusiastic of the four Home Countries for indoor hockey. In the early 1970s, official Leagues commenced in England, and in the mid-Seventies also started in Wales.

It is believed that the first Tournament to be played in Ireland was a women's event in the former Ulster Polytechnic (now the University of Ulster at Jordanstown) at Easter 1974. A short time later, Antrim Forum was host to the first Tournament for men, and in December 1975 the first of a series of Annual Tournaments organised by the Queen's University Club got under way. The Irish Hockey Union accepted an invitation for an Irish International team to play for the first time in a Home Countries Tournament in Perth, Scotland in 1976. The first official League in Ireland began in Dublin during the 1976-77 Season and in 1978 the first League in Ulster began. The first Inter-provincial Championship followed soon afterwards, and the first National Club Championship both took place in the 1979-80 Season.

The game in Ulster rapidly expanded from one League to include two Leagues, a Knock-out Cup competition and a Schools Tournament. The success of the indoor game was marred by personal tragedy when Frank Green collapsed and died while taking part in a weekend training session with the Ireland Indoor squad. At its peak in the early and middle Eighties indoor hockey in Ulster was played by sixteen Clubs, and others wished to play but could not be accommodated. In latter years interest tended to diminish mainly due to the high costs to Clubs arising from the hire of halls and perhaps also due to the advent of artificial surfaces.

In the Branch Minutes of 20 August 1992, George Blower reported that only four teams had applied to play in the Indoor League, and it was unlikely that there would be an Under-20 League. A meeting was held on 7 September to consider the situation, and it was decided that it would be impractical to proceed, with such a small number. Attempts were made by Eddie Coulter, the Honorary Secretary, along with Leinster Indoor officials to form an All-Ireland Indoor League, but the difficulties could not be surmounted.

The writing was on the wall, and at the AGM of 5 May 1993, Eddie Coulter reported that no Indoor Hockey, except the ever-successful Schools Tournament was held the previous Season. He felt that the meeting was left with two options, either to attempt to form some sort of League with Leinster or to wind up the Association. A proposal to wind up the affairs of the Ulster Branch Indoor Hockey Association and to cease to exist from midnight on 27 May 1993 was passed unanimously.

However, indoor hockey remains an exciting game and provides an excellent vehicle for young players to develop many of the skills required to play outdoors on artificial surfaces. It is no coincidence that most of the top International players outdoors are also accomplished indoor players.

ULSTER HOCKEY CLUBS

This Section contains the short histories of the Clubs affiliated to the Ulster Branch. The details have been supplied by representatives from each Club and have been checked, as far as possible, for accuracy in relation to the quality of information obtained - although a number of inaccuracies may have inadvertently crept in. Some source material is sketchy or cannot be found, but it is the hope that this Section will give a sufficiently broad picture of the development of Club life in Ulster over the past 100 years.

ANNADALE

Annadale Hockey Club, formerly Annadale Grammar School Former Pupils, made its debut in 1968. Ken Bradbury (inaugural Secretary) was the main driving force in the formation of the Club, supported by Ronnie McNamee, Michael Graham (inaugural Chairman) and David Bennison.

The majority of the members had played for Cliftonville, and the close association then established between the two Clubs remains strong. Whilst Annadale is now an open Club, the bonds with Annadale Grammar School, now Wellington College, are firmly maintained through coaching and use of the school playing facilities.

The Club commenced with two teams and is now represented by six teams in addition to its successful mini and youth squads.

The First XI gained promotion and cup victories every year until 1974. In 1976 advancement to Senior League I was achieved. In 1977, the First XI won its way to the Ulster Section Final of the Irish Senior Cup, losing to YMCA but later that year overcame Lisnagarvey to win the Anderson Cup. In 1984, Annadale reached the Final of the Irish Senior Cup being narrowly defeated by Banbridge.

Annadale was the first Club, in 1982, to introduce a structured youth development programme, initiated and managed by Ronnie Smyth. A number of players, products of this youth policy, have recently gained International selection at Under 15, 16, 18 and 21 level - with Chris Jackson, Andrew Smyth, David Smyth and Andy McBride gaining honours at three levels. Ronnie Smyth has been the major influence in the club throughout the years

The Annadale First XI Squad at Upper Braniel in 1988, with Coach Ronnie Smyth (Back row, second left), Manager Michael Graham (Back row, second from right), and Club President Ronnie McNamee (Back row, extreme right).

*Home Competition -
Annadale Fourth XI who defeated
their Third XI to win the Ulster
Junior Shield, in 1994.*

as Club Captain and Coach. He has continued to develop the coaching programme which now attracts 90-100 children aged 6-14 years every Saturday morning at the artificial pitches at Olympia and Queen's.

In 1975, Annadale's Harp Lager Breakthrough Festival was launched as the pipe-opener for the Season. This introduced Sunday hockey to Ulster and Ireland for the first time. Now known as The Harp Masters, this continues to be the major invitation tournament in Ireland, attracting teams from Britain and overseas.

On the social side, the Annadale Annual Dinner is one of the highlights of the Season. It has gained a high reputation for hospitality and the quality of the speeches. Representatives from the Irish Hockey Union, The Ulster Branch and Clubs throughout Ireland are always welcome guests at the Dinner.

The Club has made a valuable contribution to Ulster and Irish Hockey in Umpiring and Administration. Michael Jackson, Alan Moore and Billy Stewart have gained International umpiring honours, with other members gaining Inter-provincial appointments. Ronnie McNamee was elected President of the Ulster Branch in 1988 which was a just reward for his tremendous contribution to Annadale and Ulster Hockey.

Ronnie Smyth has made an immense contribution to coaching and development in Ulster and is presently Chairman of the Ulster Coaching Committee. He has also held appointments as Coach to the Ulster Seniors, Ireland Under 16, Under 18 and Under 21 sides.

Michael Graham who was Treasurer of the Ulster Branch 1981-95, Manager of the Ulster Senior Team 1987-94, and Manager of Ireland Under 21 1994-95, has been elected President of the Ulster Branch for the Centenary Year.

The Club will be celebrating the Branch Centenary Year with the opening of its new artificial pitch, in conjunction with Castlereagh Borough Council, at Lough Moss Leisure Centre.

ANTRIM

Antrim Hockey Club was established sometime in 1894, but despite extensive research the first recorded mention of Antrim appears in a Press report of a match against Ballymena on 19 November 1896. So the truth lies somewhere in between.

It is known that the Club was formed by professional gentlemen - land owners, linen barons, mill managers, solicitors and others. These were the reasonably well-off people who, at that time, had the influence to obtain a playing pitch and were able to provide or pay for transport to away games.

Antrim sent Thomas Lyle McElderry and George Bromwell Parke as delegates to a General Meeting of the Ulster Hockey Union, held on 15 October 1897 in the Royal Avenue Hotel Belfast, where proposals were accepted to form an Ulster Hockey League along with League Rules, and to affiliate with the Irish Hockey Union.

At the meeting on 29 October 1897, Mr John Kirk JP, presented the Ulster Union with the Ulster Challenge Cup (now the Kirk Cup). The Antrim Club is justifiably proud that this old and prestigious trophy was presented by a local man.

Antrim was a prominent Club from its beginnings and into the early 1900's, when its two Club teams won the Senior and Junior League and Cup competitions on many occasions.

At the end of the 1907-08 Season, in the scramble to play off postponed fixtures before grounds became unavailable at the end of April, the Press reported "that the Branch Secretary refused a request by the Club to arrange a play-off for the League with Malone, who were equal on points with two games to play. Antrim travelled to Banbridge and played a draw, but won the game on a protest over Banbridge playing an ineligible player. Malone finished second with one game unplayed. Antrim were 'handed the Cup' for that Season". These events must have been very controversial because Antrim withdrew from the Senior League in the 1908-09 Season, claiming "to have fulfilled their fixtures since 1897 in a way that compared with any other club. Last Season, out of 17 games, they played 11 away, and were not prepared to do a similar amount of travelling this year."

Although Antrim returned to the Senior League for the 1910-11 Season, many of their best players had left to join other senior clubs and it was seven Seasons before they were able to again win the League. One year later, in the 1921-22 Season, the Anderson Cup was won for the first time.

For the next eight years the Club was very successful, winning the Senior League three times, the Anderson Cup twice, and the Kirk Cup once. The Second XI won their League three times, and the Braddell Shield once.

Antrim have never won the Irish Senior Cup, losing in their first Final to LYPMA by 2-1, in Dublin in March 1928. Bitterly disappointed, a protest was lodged against one of the umpires, but to no avail. (The team on that day was W Burrows, John McKillop, D Quigley, W Morrison, H Curry, A McKee, G Clarke, WJ Wallace, L Campbell, J Hannon and James McKillop.)

Through the Thirties Antrim struggled to survive, seldom being able to field two teams during this period. During this time Antrim played their hockey at various locations - first at the Bush, then the Agricultural Showgrounds before moving to a pitch which was then in the Massereene Estate below the Easter Hill (now the seventh fairway of Massereene Golf Club). In 1922 a Clubhouse was built beside the pitch. It was sold off in 1942 for £70 to David Rea's Sawmill, Castle Street, Antrim.

After Antrim won the Anderson Cup in the 1938-39 Season, the Second World War intervened and the Hockey Club did not restart until 1945. (Due to a misunderstanding over a Resolution not to reform the Club until the war was over, Antrim Olympic Hockey Club played the 1944-45 Season!)

By now, a new era had dawned, younger men had taken over, and despite the struggle to restart, this period was to become one of the Club's most successful ever. The playing pitches were now located in the Castle Grounds, a magnificent arena which was surrounded by high hedges. Access was only available, about an hour before bully-off time, through a gateway in Castle Street. A large stone sink with a cold water tap was even then considered reasonable for cleaning up after matches!

The Second XI moved up to the Intermediate League and a Third XI, formed in 1947, entered the Junior League. The Second XI won the Irish Junior Cup twice in successive years - in 1947, beating Roscrea, from Co Tipperary, 2-1; and 1948, beating Pembroke Wanderers Second XI, by the odd goal in five.

The First XI won the Anderson Cup four times in six years, between 1947 and 1952. In 1955 the First XI lost another Irish Cup Final to Dublin YMCA and in the 1956 Semi-Final lost again to the same Club. Prominent players at that time were Billy Jarden, Billy Allen, Bob Fawcett, Billy and Ronnie Ludlow, Bob Gordon, Billy Crawford, Bobby Peacocke, Tom Allen, George McBurney, Sam Wallace, Joe Lavery, Robert McNally, Stanley Young and Morris Hilland.

In 1953 Paddy Marks joined the Club and, with his abundant enthusiasm, hockey was started in Antrim Primary School, where he was a teacher. With the help of other energetic members, the Club gradually grew in numbers, fielding a Fourth XI in 1958 and a Fifth XI in 1976. The First XI again won the Kirk Cup in 1966 under the captaincy of the late Billy Harkness and in the 1971-72 Season shared the Kirk Cup with Instonians after two replays. Incidentally the Cup, which had been on display in Hall's Hotel, survived a terrorist bomb which exploded outside, severely damaging the building.

In 1970 another pitch was acquired at the Lough shore on ground owned by the Club President, Herbie McCabe and in 1973 a new gravel pitch was available when the Antrim Forum opened. After protracted negotiations, the Club joined with Antrim Rugby Club in 1972. An old stable in the Castle grounds was converted into a Clubhouse and the drive was on to realise the dream of the Club's own pitches and premises at Allen Park, the site allocated for sport in the Antrim New Town Plan.

Changing accommodation with three hockey pitches, two grass and one gravel, along with three rugby pitches were constructed and first used in 1979. Although the Ireland v Scotland International was played on the grass pitch in 1980, very little hockey was played on that surface and with hindsight the laying of another gravel pitch would have been more sensible. The building of a Clubhouse was completed in 1985, and for some people a dream was realised.

Antrim Second XI - Winners of the McCabe Cup and the Irish Junior Cup 1975-76.

The Second XI won the Irish Junior Cup in 1976, defeating LPYMA by two goals to one. The four Mailey brothers, Robert, Derek, Dougie and Stevie, along with Jimmy Gleghorne, Jackson Fleming, John McMeekin, Jimmy Orr, Michael Campbell, John McKee and Crawford Carson were the victorious team that day.

In 1961 the Antrim Six-a-Side Tournament was born. It was the brain child of Bobby Peacocke, together with Paddy Marks, Bob Fawcett and Drew Francey, and with the strong support of all the members and their wives and girl friends, it developed to become a permanent fixture in the Ulster hockey calendar.

The First XI survived three relegation Senior League play-offs, against Bangor in 1963-64, Queen's in 1982-83, and Cliftonville in 1984-85.

In the 1985-86 Season the First XI, built around experienced players like David Haugh, Jimmy Orr, John McMeekin and Andy Gleghorne headed the League until well into the new year, finally finishing third, behind YMCA and Banbridge, with 22 points. They were very unlucky to lose 1-0, in extra time, to Banbridge in the Final of the Anderson Cup.

With one of Antrim's best-ever Seasons behind them, tragedy struck on 27 September 1986. In an horrific road accident, not far from the Club, Jimmy Orr, Colin Rainey, and Harry Young, three First team players, died. The loss to Antrim Hockey Club was immense but it was nothing compared to the loss to the families. A Memorial Fund was set up in their memory and contributions from the Fund still go to help the coaching and development of promising young players.

Despite these traumatic events, the Club struggled on, but with the loss of such talented players it was no surprise that the First XI were relegated in 1988.

Although Antrim have finished second in Senior League II in five of the last six Seasons, the prize of regaining Senior I status remains elusive. However, due to the coaching of Andy Gleghorne, George Houston and David Haugh a good supply of young players is coming up through the Junior teams. The Fourth XI has won its knock-out competition, the Strabane Cup, four out of the last five years.

In 1991 Antrim Borough Council constructed a new sand filled artificial plastic pitch at Antrim Forum. The Club Annual General Meeting in June decided that, in order to compete at the top level, all five of the Club teams had no option but to play as much as possible on the new pitch.

The joint Club had incurred considerable debt in completing the facilities at Allen Park and although this was slowly being reduced, the strained relationship between the two sections over the years had drained the loyalty of most of the hockey members.

At a Special Meeting in April 1995 the majority of those present decided that they should concentrate all the efforts and resources into hockey, and membership of Antrim Hockey and Rugby Club was not renewed.

Meetings and after-match socialising now takes place in Muckamore Cricket Club.

The Club has had six players who have played for Ireland:-

H Armitage Moore - 3 Caps, 18-3-1899 against England at Richmond, 17-2-1900 against Wales at Llandudno and 10-3-1900 against England in the first ever International played in Belfast at Balmoral. Mr H Armitage Moore inherited the Rowallene Estate in Saintfield which was bequeathed to the National Trust after his death; **TL McElderry** - 1 Cap against England on 10-3-1900; **Sam Rea** - 1 Cap, 8-3-1902 in the first ever International against Scotland played in Belfast at Balmoral; **JG Entwhistle** - 1 Cap in 1904; **Francis L Robinson** - 2 caps in 1914 against Scotland and England. He also played 11 other games for Ireland from 1908-11 as a member of Malone H.C; and **George Clarke** - 3 Caps - 1932-36. One of the most distinguished of all was **Alvin Carson**.

Seven Antrim Hockey Club members have served as Ulster Branch President:-

George Hurst in 1900; **William Heney** from 1911-20; **Robert H Coulter** in 1924; **Nathaniel M Clarke** in 1938; **WRJ (Bob) Fawcett** in 1973; **Francis Baird** in 1980 and **George Houston** in 1993 - honoured in the Club's Centenary Season, and the youngest-ever President to be elected.

Antrim Winners of the Lisnagarvey "Sixes" - Easter 1985.

ARMAGH

There is a record in the Ulster Branch Minute Book of 1901-02 of an Armagh Club becoming a member, but little is now known of those early days. However, a new hockey Club was founded on 23 February 1994. Hockey was played at The Royal School, Armagh until 1966. When Armagh Secondary School opened in 1965, George Compston, in charge of PE, introduced hockey into the PE programme and some friendly games were played.

In 1973 Ronnie Harkness (Cookstown HC), joined the staff and assisted with hockey. At the same time Wesley Ferris, Markethill High School, initiated the Mid-Ulster Schools' Hockey Leagues, creating a greater interest in hockey in the area.

The Secondary School entered these Leagues, as did the Armstrong Primary School, under the influence of Eddie Megaw (Portadown HC), thus laying the foundations and interest for the game in the Armagh area. Eventually the Secondary School entered the Ulster Schools Leagues/Cups, and this development produced many good players at 16-plus, with no outlet when they left school.

Some were encouraged by Portadown Hockey Club to join. Of these, the late Alan Dixon, who was selected to play for Junior Ulster, and Mark Davidson, a Junior Ulster trialist, made the most impact. Later Richard Compston, whilst attending The Royal School, played a Season for the Portadown First XI, as a goalkeeper, before going to University.

Armagh Cricket Club had considered the idea of having a hockey section but it was only when David McManus, Cookstown Hockey Club, decided to stop playing at Cookstown, and to make himself available to a proposed Armagh team, based at the Cricket Club, that the idea became a possibility. George Compston had been approached many times by past pupils to start a Club but was still too heavily committed to playing, and latterly to the management of the Irish Senior Squad, to be able to make a full commitment to the idea.

Under the influence of David McManus, and supported by other Cricket Club members, the late Seamus Duffy, Phil Homan, and Michael Best, a meeting was called on 23 February 1994 to explore the idea of starting a hockey team. Alan McMurray, Ulster Branch Development Officer, attended to give advice. Others who were there were George Compston, Armagh Secondary School, and prospective players, Colin Wilson, Jonathan Doherty and Mark Elliott.

As a result of this meeting it was decided that there was enough support amongst the young people in the City to start a Hockey Club, attached to, and supported by the Cricket Club. One team was to be entered in the Intermediate League.

A programme of training and practice was set up under the guidance of George Compston. David McManus used his contacts to arrange a series of friendly matches against neighbouring clubs. So much interest was generated that by September 1994 it was evident that a second team was needed and one was entered in Junior League 8.

In September 1994, Cees Koppelaar, the National Coach, who was visiting in Armagh, agreed to take a coaching session for the new Club, an exercise which he repeated in February 1995.

In May 1995 a first tour was undertaken to the Isle of Man Festival and in June 1995, a Six-a-Side Tournament was held on the Mall for Intermediate Teams.

At the end of the first Season, the First XI had played well and held their own again most opposition but still finished last in the League. However, experience was being gained and Colin Wilson, the First Club Captain, was proving to be an able leader.

Armagh First XI in 1994, when the new Club was Founded. There was an Armagh Club around 1901-02, but little is now known about it.

The Second XI surprised everyone, including most of their opposition, to become runners-up in Junior League 8, and to gain promotion. Kenneth Spence was their Captain and played a large part in their success.

During the Season Laurence Homan, Colin Wilson, Colin Clarke, Hilton Parr and Howard Quinn attended Junior Ulster trials, with Howard Quinn being selected, to become the Club's first Representative player.

Colin Wilson, Jonathan Doherty, David McManus and Mark Elliott completed Preliminary Coaching Awards.

During 1995-96, a Third XI was introduced at the start of the Season to accommodate the increasing number of young people who wanted to play hockey. This team was entered in Junior League 8, with the Second XI now in Junior League 7.

Saturday morning coaching was held by Club members for schoolboys to help ensure the future progress of the Club.

In December 1995, the first Club Dinner and Awards Presentation was held at the Cricket Club with the Guest of Honour being the Ulster Branch President, Mr Frank Young.

Some promising young players are emerging, notably, Julian Davidson, an Ulster Under 15 player in 1995 and an Under 16 trialist in 1996, and Karl Clarke who was just over the age for these teams. At present the future looks good for the Club.

BALLYNAHINCH

There are records of Men's Hockey being played in the Ballynahinch area back as early as the 1920s and 1930's, and later playing as Ballynahinch Recreation Club up to the 1960's.

The present Club, however, was not formed until 1971 when a group of people who were playing their hockey outside the town mainly for Shorts in Belfast called a meeting. When twelve players and four previous players turned up they decided that a team should be formed. Their application to the Ulster Branch was accepted after much help from hockey stalwart George Blower, who was instrumental in helping the Club to obtain a pitch, and they entered Intermediate League II in 1971-72.

Home matches were played at Somerdale School in Belfast and in the first Season the team won their League undefeated, and gained promotion. As interest grew, a Second XI was formed and for two Seasons both teams travelled to Belfast for their home fixtures.

In 1974 the Club moved back to home soil when they were granted permission to play at the Assumption Grammar School in Ballynahinch, which was to remain their home until new playing fields were opened in 1977. The First XI continued to play in the Intermediate League, missing out on promotion on several occasions and also reaching the Intermediate Cup Final in 1985-86.

The Ballynahinch Club in the 1985-86 Season when they reached the Intermediate Cup Final.

The first signs of school hockey in the area began at this time when the local High School started to play boys' hockey and interest in the game at Primary level became apparent.

This interest quickly paid dividends as the Second XI won promotion from Junior 6 to Junior 3 in consecutive years, and in 1990-91 the First XI gained promotion to Senior hockey for the first time in their history.

The Club were now fielding a total of four Men's teams and at this time formed a Ladies' section who gained promotion each year from their League until the 1994-95 Season.

The First XI have consolidated their promotion in Senior II and in 1995-96 the Second XI gained promotion to Junior I for the first time.

Since 1993-94 the First XI have been playing on artificial pitches at various venues, hoping to encourage the youth of the area and at the time of writing plans are afoot to lay a sand-filled pitch in the Town.

BANBRIDGE

Banbridge Hockey Club, which is one of the most distinguished in these islands, began in 1897 when a group of local young men met on a Saturday afternoon to knock a ball about at Millmount Green beside the River Bann, just off the Lurgan Road. Little did they know then that they were in the process of creating a club which would become an outstanding contributor to the game of hockey in Ulster, throughout Ireland and beyond.

In 1900 Edgar McCall became the first Banbridge player to be awarded an International cap when he represented Ireland against Wales. He was the first of thirty to be honoured by the Irish Hockey Union. Outstanding among these great players were Jack Harvey and Rodney Malcolmson, each of whom gained fourteen caps, and also George McElroy and Aubrey Allister with thirty-nine and twenty-four respectively. These were remarkable achievements as Ireland normally played only three games each Season - against England, Scotland and Wales.

When the format of International hockey changed and the Irish side qualified to play overseas more often, Mark Sinnamon, Norman McGladdery, Colin Allister and David McAnulty brought further honour to the Club when they passed the fifty-cap milestone in their hockey careers.

Throughout their history Banbridge teams have won all the Irish Hockey Union and Ulster Branch trophies on numerous occasions and in recent times have qualified to represent Ireland in European competitions. The Club has won the Senior League 18 times, the Irish Senior Cup 9 times, the Kirk Cup 17 times and the Anderson Cup 13 times, and also had noted success in the European B Division.

In 1906 Banbridge won the Kirk Cup for the first time and, in the next Season, the Irish Senior cup. Simply stated on the base of the Cup is the fact, 'Banbridge H C 1907'. This is but a small unemotional picture of that event. When the all-Ireland hockey champions came back home, the first time the Cup came North of the border, a band was waiting at the station, a lorry stood ready to tour the streets of the town and show Cup and team off, and the population stood on the streets to cheer!

The years 1909-11 were impressive, for (on these three successive years) the Club won the Senior League and the Kirk Cup. As a recognition of the players' consistent form, it is recorded that the Ulster team of 1911 which defeated Connaught 9-nil had six Banbridge players! They contributed seven of the goals, Smyth scoring five and Simms two - a fitting climax to those great pre-war years of local hockey.

A sad event was commemorated by the presentation for annual competition of the Anderson

Banbridge First XI 1925-26, who won the Senior League, the Irish Senior Cup and the Kirk Cup. It is interesting to note that the highly-successful teams of that time featured only eleven players in the Team Picture, and not a larger squad as they do today.

BANBRIDGE HOCKEY TEAM, 1925-26.
Winners of Keightley Cup (Senior League), Irish Senior Cup and Kirk Cup

T. N. Anderson   T. Stanage   *J. H. Harvey   W. N. M'William   *R. S. Malcolmson   A. Call   S. Preston   Jas. M'Keown   J. C. Wray   *J. Morton
W. A. Shooter (Hon. Sec.)   *H. C. Call   G. Greenfield   *D. N. Coburn [Capt.]   J. Hughes   *J. Coburn,   J. U. Finney (President).
*Denotes International.   Inset   *R. A. Banbridge   F. J. Davis.

Cup. The Cup was presented by TN Anderson in memory of his brother, Capt George Anderson, an International player who was killed on active service in France during the First World War. Strangely, George himself represented Scotland in 1910 - gaining recognition during his studies at Edinburgh University. The Cup was first played for in 1920, and won by Banbridge.

During the Great War, twenty-seven members served with the Forces and eight were killed in action, four of whom were Internationals.

The Club's remarkable success continued throughout the decades, and the first team squad travelled to Yugoslavia in 1983, and to Wales in 1987, securing the runner-up spot each time. In 1990 they finished third in Germany, but in 1985 they had their greatest success when they hosted the European Cup B at the Castlewellan Road Grounds. After a super-human effort, they emerged as Champions, defeating the Italian representatives Anniscora Alisarda after trailing by three goals to one with just twelve minutes remaining in the Final. It was truly a 'Boys' Own' ending, and there were great scenes of emotion at the finish.

No Club exists through the efforts of players alone, and Banbridge has always been blessed with a team of non-playing enthusiasts who have given unstintingly of their time and talents to assist the furtherance of the game in the area. Space only permits reference to a few but this in no way detracts from all those who have served over the past ninety nine years.

Jack Hagan has been an outstanding cornerstone of the Club, having served as President for twenty-five years, and at the same time officiating as an umpire at games throughout Ireland. His generosity to Banbridge Hockey Club will always be remembered with gratitude.

The late Billy Cupples will for ever be held in the highest esteem for his encouragement of young players. It was he who formed the successful Colts' Section of the Club which endeavoured to introduce young schoolboys to the game, especially those from schools where hockey was not on the curriculum, and this is continuing - thus providing a nursery of young players - many of whom have graduated to the top teams.

Over the past half century, the name of Eric Walker has been synonymous with hockey and with Banbridge in particular. In his earlier years he had the distinction of playing for Ulster and Leinster, and today he is as well-known throughout Ireland and further afield as he was then. An outstanding organiser of social functions and a source of encouragement to all, his greatest contribution to the successes of Banbridge in recent years has been his planning and support of trips throughout Ireland, the United Kingdom and Europe. No-one will ever know how much time and effort this demanded but the successes of the teams were fitting rewards for his contributions to this aspect of Club life.

In 1949 the members of the Club had the foresight to purchase the present grounds situated in a wonderful setting within easy reach of the centre of Banbridge. Over the years these have been developed to provide a pavilion and social centre, two grass pitches and an outstanding shale surface which, until recently, was the envy of many visiting Clubs.

However the progress of the game and the demands of the Federation of International Hockey and the Irish Hockey Union have placed an urgent priority on the need for a synthetic grass surface, if senior hockey is to continue in the Banbridge area. To this end Banbridge District Council has agreed to provide such a pitch and other necessary facilities at Havelock Park, which incidentally is close to Millmount Green. These should be in place in

BANBRIDGE HOCKEY CLUB
European Cup Finals, Swansea, 1987

Back—D. McMASTER (Assist. Team Manager), N. ANDERSON (Team Manager), C. ALLISTER, M. McDOWELL, J. BELL, M. SINNAMON, A. GRAHAM, R. CARSON, B. LOCKHART, M. SCULLION, N. ALLISTER, I. STEEPE (Coach), E. WALKER (Tour Manager).

Front—N. MADELEY, R. CROZIER, L. WEIR, H. McDOWELL (President), N. McGLADDERY (Capt.), P. MALCOLMSON, J. McKNIGHT, J. WALKER.

The Banbridge Club at the European Cup Finals in Swansea, 1987, when they were Runners-up.

time to ensure that the Club's Centenary will mark not just the end of an era, but a new beginning when hopefully many will enjoy the game of hockey and, equally important, create life-long friendships, as generations have done since those humble beginnings in 1897.

In a sense the story of Banbridge has come full circle - beginning with a group of local men playing at Millmount Green, and a century later the brand new facilities will be established in the same area. In the past 100 years or so the Banbridge Club has given a great deal to the game - on and off the field. It remains one of the most-respected Clubs in these islands.

BANGOR

A Bangor Club was formed at the turn of the Century and re-formed in 1921. Reference is made in Irish Hockey records to Bangor's AD McIlwaine playing for Ulster against Leinster in 1902-03 and SA Bullock (Bangor, Malone and Marino) playing for Ireland against Scotland in 1903, 1907 and 1909, as well as a number of times for Ulster. It is interesting to note that it was not until the early Seventies that another Bangor player represented his country - Davy McManus, who gained his First Cap against West Germany and who, with Frank Young, another young Bangor player in his early days, was selected to play against England. Nothing further appears to be known about the Bangor Club after 1910 or 1911 until it was re-formed in 1921.

A meeting was then held in the Dufferin Hall and the sponsors were B Bell and J Breeze. It was decided to re-form the local Hockey Club and that a team should be entered in the Minor League for the 1921-22 Season. J Breeze was elected Honorary Secretary and SR Bell, Honorary Treasurer.

Since then, with the exception of the War years, Bangor have fielded several teams each Season. The first pitch was in Church Street, and 'Miss Hanna's Hall' was used as a pavilion. The first game was played against a team known as Anglo-American whom Bangor beat by three goals to one. The Bangor Club, in its first Season, finished well up in the League.

After two Seasons at Church Street the Club obtained a pitch beside Godfrey Avenue near Ballyholme show grounds. This was one of the best pitches the Club ever had - being sandy, flat and well drained. Here a pavilion was built and the membership became so strong that it was possible to field three teams, one in the Senior Qualifying, one in Junior and one in Minor League hockey.

Here the Club remained for approximately five years and during the summer months it organised Five-a-Side competitions which were very popular. (An interesting feature of the Club in those days was that the subscription was 10 Shillings and the charge for catering was 1 Shilling per member!)

Around 1927, the Club moved to the Ashley Park district, and later to Silverstream, Belfast Road, where two teams were fielded, one in the Intermediate League and the other in the Junior League. After a sojourn at Silverstream, the Club moved to Ward Park, and then in 1957 to the new Castle Park Playing fields, where they remained until the return to Ward Park in 1975.

The most successful Seasons in the early days were 1933-36 when Bangor won the Junior, Intermediate and Senior Qualifying League in three successive Seasons. Immediately prior to this Bangor had the fine record of five Seasons (1928-32) on the Ashley Park ground without a single home defeat. During this period the trophies won were - Junior Charity Cup 1932-33; Braddell Shield 1933-34; Intermediate Charity Cup 1934-35; Junior League 1932-33-34; Intermediate League 1934-35; Senior Qualifying League 1935-36.

The most successful years were 1960-61 when Bangor won promotion to

The Bangor First Team Squad who won promotion to Senior League I in April 1977, with the Ireland's Saturday Night Cup. Included is Walter Dowdall, a long-time member of the Bangor Club, and President of the Irish Hockey Union in that year.

Section A Qualifying League and 1961-62, when the First XI, captained by Harry McDonagh, won promotion to the Senior League - having gained promotion on two successive years and having gone two Seasons without a League defeat. In 1962-63 they maintained their place in Senior Hockey but were relegated to Senior League II the following Season. In the 1963-64 Season Davy McManus brought honour to the Club by being selected for the Ulster Senior team as well as the Ulster Under-23 team.

In 1955, to mark the town's 1,400th Anniversary, the Hockey Club inaugurated a Six-a-Side Tournament. From small beginnings of a mere 20 teams it has grown over the years and at one time was thought to have been the largest tournament of its kind in the British Isles, attracting a record 150 teams. Now in its forty-third year, it still attracts considerable numbers, its longevity being testimony not only to the format of the event but also to the quality of the organisation.

Since the Club began to use Ward Park there has been a lengthy period of stability as regards a playing venue, but this degree of consistency has not necessarily been matched on the field! The First XI have endured a lengthy flirtation with Senior I status, the most successful spell coming in the mid-Eighties when a League position of 4th was gained. The annual exodus of schoolboys to more successful Clubs is a major factor. As a consequence the First XI have sat frustratingly in limbo, always having a squad too strong for Senior II but not able to compete effectively over a period of time at Senior I level. However, the Second XI have been playing at top Junior level and the Club now boasts seven teams, one of the largest complements in Ulster hockey. The First XI reached its first-ever Senior Cup Final in 1990, failing narrowly at the final hurdle.

Turning to Schools hockey Bangor Grammar have enjoyed consistent success in the past two decades, the school system producing teams which have won the Burney and McCullough Cup double in 1983, and the McCullough Championship in 1989. Recognition for the schools success in developing hockey talent has come in the form of representative honours for a considerable number of schoolboys over the years, the most notable success being Stephen Martin, the Olympic player.

As the Club enters its 75th Anniversary Year there is both a sense of achievement and expectation. From September 1996 the Club has a new playing home at the Ballykillaire complex, providing two artificial pitches. This will bring benefits on many levels - modern facilities will encourage local talent to remain at the Club which will strengthen the playing pool and therefore hopefully help achieve sustainable playing success.

CIVIL SERVICE

The Ulster United Services Club became affiliated to the Ulster Branch at the AGM of 6 September 1923. Six days later, at a Special Meeting, they changed their name to Civil Service Hockey Club. The First XI are recorded as competing in the Intermediate League in 1923-24, a Second XI entered the Minor League in 1925-26, and a further ten years passed before a Third XI was formed in 1935-36.

The Club's first Trophy success was in 1936-37 when the First XI won the Intermediate League. The following Season they competed in the Qualifying League. During these early years FS Skillen represented Civil Service on the Ulster Branch Council. All hockey in Ulster was suspended on 12 September 1939 due to the outbreak of the Second World War but, for reasons unknown, Civil Service did not re-form when the War ended.

In the mid-1950s 'Wanderers Hockey Club' who played Senior Hockey off the Comber Road in Newtownards were about to fold. An approach was made to the Civil Service Sports Council to consider forming a hockey Club at Stormont. As about a dozen of the Wanderers players at that time were Civil Servants and the remainder school teachers, their request was granted. The players involved had the immediate use of a superb grass pitch and changing facilities with showers, (in the famous green shed). The First XI competed in the old Qualifying B League against such opposition as Old Bleach, Saintfield, Ballymena, East Antrim, Crossgar and King's Scholars. The Second XI competed in the Junior League. Soon a Third XI was formed playing in the Junior League.

The year 1957 saw the opening of the magnificent Maynard Sinclair Pavilion which included modern, up-to-date changing facilities, TV lounge with function-rooms, bar and catering services. This new Club House was the

The Civil Service Club, 1970.

'Come on the 'Ten Men'!' - Civil Service Second XI managed to field only 10 men v Convoy in Donegal, in the First Round of the Irish Junior Cup, in the early Sixties! It was a common short-coming of many Junior sides.

envy of every local sportsman. In the early years, the Hockey Club existed financially by means of annual subscriptions and - incredibly - through the profits on the sale of Christmas cards, sold by members during November and December.

Originally, schoolboys were encouraged to play at Civil Service by Jimmy Parke - a dashing 'Right Inner' who taught French at Annadale Grammar School. A few years later Campbell College became the nursery for Civil Service through the then First XI Captain 'Titch' McDonald, who also taught at Methodist College.

The 1964-65 Season saw perhaps one of Civil Service's best ever players emerge. A fifteen-year-old schoolboy, Norman Crawford, played for the First XI for two seasons. He went on to gain 42 Caps for Ireland as well as playing in 60 Indoor Internationals and gaining, of course, numerous Ulster Caps.

During the mid-1960's to mid-1970's the numbers grew and Civil Service were fielding four teams on Saturday afternoons. In 1974 another rising star emerged - a fourteen-year-old school-boy from Bangor named Stephen Martin who played for the Third XI before gaining his place on the First XI. Stephen then decided to join Bangor, and Service's loss was Bangor's gain! Stephen went on to represent Great Britain on 94 occasions, Ireland 135 times and to win Olympic Gold and Bronze Medals.

In 1975 the First XI were promoted from Intermediate League to Senior League II, and in 1978 the First XI won Section II, but unfortunately there was no promotion that year, due to Ireland's participation in the World Cup. In September 1980 the superb new extension to the Maynard Sinclair Pavilion was opened, and continues to be one of the best of its kind in Ireland. Soon afterwards, in 1983, the Club laid its own 'shale' pitch at Stormont to complement the two existing grass surfaces.

On the pitch, the Club had a 'roller-coaster' ride through the 1980s. After reaching the Anderson Cup Final in 1985 (losing 1-0 to Belfast YMCA), the Club had a disastrous Season in 1985-86 which saw the First XI relegated to Intermediate hockey. They won the Intermediate Cup in 1987 and the following year, 1987-88, recorded an Intermediate League and Cup double, and promotion back to Senior hockey. This achievement was made greater by the fact that the team won the League without dropping a single point (Played 18, Won 18) - the first and only time this has ever been achieved in Ulster hockey. NICS was also awarded 'Ulster Hockey Team of the Year' for 1987-88.

During this time, the Club also increased in membership and it now fields seven teams each week, with over one hundred playing members. Between 1988 and 1991 the First XI never finished outside the top three in Senior II, but could never quite achieve its goal of promotion.

In the 1990-91 Season the NICS Prentice Indoor team finished runners-up in the Ulster League and reached the Semi-Final of the All-Ireland Championships. On 3 September 1994 NICS officially opened its new £500,000 artificial pitch with a game between the Civil Service and Ireland. The new pitch beautifully complements the facilities at the Club and many finals and 'show case' matches are now staged at Stormont. The Club has a flourishing Youth policy with many teams and individual honours won during the early 1990's. Over half of the First XI squad are now teenagers, and the future indeed looks bright for the Club.

CLIFTONVILLE

Cliftonville is one of the founding Clubs of the Ulster Hockey Branch, and it has had a distinguished record on and off the field. It has supplied many outstanding players and hockey officials, and despite losing its famous ground during the Troubles, it has shown enormous tenacity in not only surviving but in winning promotion back to the Senior League Section I in its Centenary year.

The first Annual General Meeting was held on 12 October 1896 but unfortunately the Minute books prior to 1903 have been lost, so the early details of the club are not available. However, the first recorded match was played against North Down at Comber in November 1896 which Cliftonville lost 8-0! (Cliftonville only had thirteen members, but they all went to Comber with one acting as a linesman and another as an umpire.)

For the first six years of the Ulster Branch, formed in 1896, John Moore of Cliftonville was the Honorary Secretary and other members of the club who have held this post since then were A Rose, DD Persse, AC Montgomery, J Wilton and HD Simon.

In 1897, quite remarkably, the Club reached the Final of the Irish Senior Cup in Dublin but lost against Dundrum, one of the founding and leading clubs of the Leinster Branch. In 1898 a Second XI went to Dublin for the Semi-Final of the Irish Junior Cup, but having won, could not field a team to travel to Dublin to play in the Final seven days later!

In the early years of the century the membership of the Club increased sufficiently to run three regular teams and also a Zingari XI and this level of membership has generally remained ever since.

The Club was suspended during the 1914-18 World War when 31 members joined the forces, six of them losing their lives, and eight being wounded.

Following an informal meeting on 20 February 1919, the Club was revived but not officially until the Annual General Meeting on 24 September 1919. Mr JC Picken (a prominent Cliftonville Cricket Club member, later President of the Cricket Club and the Irish Cricket Union and the first President of the joint Cricket and Hockey Club) assisted in the re-starting of the Club, by helping to bring the goal posts from a timber yard in Corporation Street!

Until 1914 the colours of the Club were myrtle and maize, the shirt being myrtle with a monogram in maize on the pocket. On the revival of the Club, black, red and green jerseys were worn but in 1925 the present shirts of black and red quarters with green sleeves were adopted.

During the 1939-45 World War when competitive hockey in the Ulster Branch was suspended, Cliftonville formed an Association to organise games on a friendly basis and in doing so helped to keep the game going in the Province. Jimmy Wilton, a stalwart of the Club as Captain and Honorary Secretary, took a leading part in this initiative. Between 1945, when competitive hockey resumed, and 1962, the Club did not win any Senior Trophies but was still one of the leading Clubs running four and on occasions five teams each Saturday.

In the Sixties hockey in Ulster began to change, with a more serious and

Andrew Rose, left, and Des Simon, both former Cliftonville players and Presidents of the Irish Hockey Union who had the rare distinction of handing over, as President of the IHU, the Irish Senior Cup to their winning Club sides. Andy Rose was President in 1932 when Cliftonville won the Cup for the first time, and Des Simon was President the next time Cliftonville won, in 1975. The Club also won the Irish Senior Cup in 1976. In 1990 Bobby Howard of Lisnagarvey was IHU President when he had the unique distinction of handing over the Irish Senior and Junior Cups to his 'Garvey colleagues. And in 1995 Instonians' Brian Hanna, as IHU President handed over the Irish Senior Cup to Instonians' Captain Paul Hollway.

professional approach to training and tactics, and with an influx of new young players adding to the experience of the older members, Cliftonville, over the next twenty years enjoyed its best and most consistent period of success in its hundred years existence.

In 1963-64 the Second XI won the Irish Junior Cup against all the odds, beating very strong Lisnagarvey and Three Rock Rovers teams in the process. So far this is its only success in this competition. In 1966-67 the First XI were losing Irish Senior Cup finalists against Cork Church of Ireland but won the Corken Cup awarded to the Ulster team which went the furthest in the competition.

Between 1966 and 1976 the Senior League was won seven times including a hat trick of victories from 1966 to 1968, and runners up positions in 1965-66, 1969-70 and 1974-75. The Anderson and Kirk Cups were also won in this period, and with the two successive Irish Senior Cup victories in 1974-75 and 1975-76 both leading to qualification to play in the European Cup Winners Competition, it was truly a golden era for the Club.

The only time the Club previously won the Irish Senior Cup was in 1931-32 when it was presented by President of the Irish Hockey Union Andrew Rose who was also a member of the Club. It was a unique coincidence that the next time the Club was successful in 1974-75, the Cup was presented by Des Simon another stalwart of the Cliftonville Club and also in that year President of the Irish Hockey Union.

The Eighties unfortunately did not yield similar success although the First XI made an Irish Cup Final appearance in 1982 against a very strong Banbridge team who won 2-0 after extra time.

In 1985 the Club was relegated from Section I of the Senior League, for only the second time in its history after a play-off with Antrim. The previous relegation was in 1959 but they quickly returned the next year to the top section.

This time the stay in Section II was much longer and it was not until 1992 with again an influx of young players that the Club returned to Section I. Regrettably they were relegated again at the end of Season 1994-95 even though they performed well against the top teams but very poorly against the lower order. However, they returned to Senior I again in 1996.

Up to 1968 the relationship between the Cricket and Hockey Clubs had been as landlord and tenant although prior to the 1914-18 War, Cricket Club members could join the hockey club at reduced fees. Traditionally there has been a co-relationship between cricket and hockey at Cliftonville. However, it was not until 1968 that the two Clubs agreed to amalgamate for their mutual benefit.

Sadly in late August 1972 hostile elements in the area set fire to and eventually looted the club-house and then by physical intimidation prevented the members from entering the grounds. No assurances were forthcoming from either local or government authorities that the Club would be protected and assisted in the continuance of their sporting activities. As a result the Club had no option but to abandon the ground and take up a nomadic existence.

Ironically and by necessity the cricket and the hockey clubs had to again become separate entities, with the cricket players using the Council grounds at Mossley and the hockey players using the Girls Model School pitches at Dunkeld Gardens, the social facilities kindly offered by the Academy Club in Salisbury Avenue, and holding Committee Meetings in Castleton Bowling Club in Skegoneill Avenue.

The destruction of the JC Picken Pavilion in 1972 was very sad as it had been erected in 1959 on the site of the original pavilion destroyed by the German bombing in 1941 and replaced the Nissen huts which had served as a club-house since then. Today the ground, now the property of the Belfast City Council, is used by the local community but sadly not for cricket or hockey.

In 1981 the Club moved to Boucher Road Playing Fields and obtained the use of the changing facilities, social amenities and Committee rooms at the Queen's University premises at the Dub.

Then in 1986, arising from the Belfast City Council's objection to the Anglo-Irish Agreement, the Boucher Playing Fields were closed and once again Cliftonville was adversely affected by the political climate in Northern Ireland. They returned to the Queen's University pitches until taking over the tenancy of Belfast YMCA all-weather pitch at Bladon Drive in 1987 when the YMCA Hockey Club left and re-formed as Holywood '87.

In 1992 YMCA sold part of the ground for housing, and while the junior teams continued to play there for one more season before using the Queen's University pitches, the First XI played on the artificial pitch at the Olympia Leisure Centre in conjunction with other Clubs under the auspices of the Ulster Branch.

While the First XI are still at Olympia Leisure Centre the Junior elevens are using the new artificial pitch at the Ballysillan Leisure Centre. This is an expensive operation but it is giving the players the opportunity to use a modern hockey surface.

The Club has a reputation for loyal and long-serving players and officials notable amongst whom are the present Honorary Secretary Dixon Rose in office since 1960 and the current Chairman of the Committee, Carson Rose, since 1977.

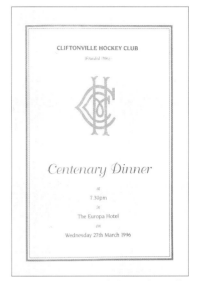

The Programme of the Cliftonville Centenary Dinner in the Europa Hotel, Belfast on 27 March 1996.

The Club has provided a steady stream of Inter-provincial and International players - Walter Dick (1926-34) with 32 Caps was the most-capped Irish player well into the 1950s. Currently Gregg Sterritt has passed this number, with 39 to date.

Cliftonville has supplied thirteen Presidents of the Ulster Branch - Rev Prof Dick, AM Adams, A Rose, A Lowe, AC Montgomery, JS Templeton, J Wilton, WP Jordan, G Edwards, HD Simon, FA Glasby, AD Rose and FDB Young; six Honorary Secretaries - J Moore, DD Persse, A Rose, AC Montgomery, J Wilton and HD Simon; three Honorary Treasurers - J Wilton, WH Mayes and GR Colvin as well as six Presidents of the Irish Hockey Union - A Rose, AC Montgomery, WP Jordan, HD Simon, FA Glasby and AD Rose. WP Jordan, HD Simon and FA Glasby have been honoured by the Ulster Branch with Honorary Life Membership.

These are achievements of which the Club is justifiably proud and despite the enforced moves over the years and a somewhat nomadic existence the resilience and progress of Cliftonville are still very much in evidence.

COLLEGIANS

Collegians is effectively an old boys Cub of Methodist College, Belfast, although it has been 'open' for some years. Although hockey has been played at Methody since the mid-1940s, it is perhaps surprising that it was not until 1967 that the school finally produced its hockey Club for former male pupils.

The first match was in September 1967 - a 1-0 win against Gallahers, Lisnafillan. All 16 League matches in the first Season were won and promotion to the Intermediate League was secured. This success was carried over to the 1968-69 Season and the Intermediate League was again won. However, a restructuring of the Leagues meant that the First XI had to win the League for the second year in succession to receive promotion to Senior League II.

A Second XI was now playing League hockey, and the Club have had as many as six teams in Ulster Branch competitions. The 1970's and 1980's saw the First XI being promoted (and relegated) with monotonous regularity, but Senior hockey was always the preference. The two occasions on which the Senior League II were secured will live long in the memory of those who

Collegians First XI, Winners of Senior League Section II, 1987-88, which the Club previously won in 1971-72.

Alan Green, the well-known BBC Sports Commentator, who distinguished himself with Collegians - in more ways than one!

witnessed them, as both promotion titles were won on the final day of the Season with large crowds in attendance! The 1971-72 title was won after an exciting play-off victory against Annadale and included a goal by Ian Kirk-Smith. Ian was undoubtedly the most talented player produced by the Collegians Club, his tally of Irish Caps being tragically few in a hockey career blighted by illness.

The sojourn to Section I lasted for just one Season and the Club returned to a less exacting standard of hockey until 1987-88 when the Section II Trophy was won for a second time. Unfortunately the Club again failed to make any impact in the higher division and there was a quick return to Section II, where they have remained ever since.

The Junior teams have tended to mirror the successes (and failures) of the First XI. It could be said that the Club has also reflected the fortunes of Methody School teams who, despite producing some players of the highest standard, have failed to win either the Burney or McCullough Cups over the last 30 years.

In addition the grounds used by the Club have continued to change. The MCB facilities at Pirrie Park have been used since the outset while the pitches at Deramore Park were opened in 1978. In recent Seasons the First XI have joined with several other neighbouring Clubs in using the artificial pitch at Olympia Leisure Centre. An artificial grass surface is urgently required to service the Club's 12 hockey teams, although the Deramore Park pitches remain the traditional centre of summer mixed hockey, with the Club hosting its popular summer League and Tournament.

Deramore also hosted a special match in 1990 to celebrate the Centenary of the Collegians Club. The First XI managed to beat an Ulster Presidents XI containing several current and future Internationals. In addition several of the Great Britain Olympic Gold Medallists from 1988 were in attendance.

Collegians have found themselves in a position similar to many others who play outside Senior League I in that it supplies players to other Clubs. People such as Geoff Clarke (Holywood 87), John Stephens, Ian Weatherup and Andrew McBride (Annadale) all commenced their hockey careers at the Club while other quality players such as former Ireland Under-21 goalkeeper Iain Kelly have remained. Many players have shown true commitment and those deserving long-service awards include Cecil Andrews, Ivan Kerr, Alan Smith and especially Kevin Ryan, who alone has played for the Club in every Season since its foundation.

In coaching, Jim Carlisle made a great contribution to both Club and Province in the 1980's, while Brian Cairns and Stephen Clarke became International Umpires. In administration Peter Wood was Ulster Branch Fixtures Secretary from 1989-93 and has been elected Junior Vice-President of the Branch for its Centenary Season.

Finally Alan Green of BBC radio fame spent several Seasons at left half for the First XI and also holds one irrevocable record - he was the first player for Collegians ever to be sent off!

COOKSTOWN

The Cookstown Hockey Club was founded in 1951, under the captaincy of Paddy Marks, with Dickie Harkness as Vice-captain. The Club showed determination and skill from the start, and steadily moved up all the Leagues to become one of the leading forces in Ulster hockey.

In the 1954-55 Season, Cookstown won the Intermediate League Section B title under the captaincy of Gordon Henderson. Their success continued in the Sixties, with Captain Gordon Donaghy leading the Club into Senior League II, having won the Intermediate League Section A title the previous year. Given such consistency and determination, it seemed inevitable that Cookstown would reach Senior League I, and this they did in 1975.

Since then, the Club has won every Senior honour at least once. During the Eighties, its most successful period, Cookstown won Senior League I, the Anderson Cup, the Kirk Cup and the Irish Senior Cup. In 1983 Raymond Acheson, the Club's most successful Captain during these golden years, led Cookstown to a Senior League I and Anderson Cup double. Then, in an epic 1987 Irish Senior Cup Final, Cookstown again led by Raymond Acheson beat the much-fancied Banbridge side 4-0 at Blaris, in what proved to be the last such Final played there on a grass pitch.

There were also disappointments for Cookstown in these years, and in 1980 they lost to Belfast YMCA in the Irish Senior Cup Final. However the clouds of defeat had a silver lining, and when YM were unable to represent Ireland in a European competition, Cookstown accepted the invitation with alacrity.

Cookstown Club members, helping to lay, in 1994, the new sand-based astroturf pitch at the local High School, which has produced many first-rate Club and Schoolboy players.

Cookstown's Geoffrey Hamilton, right, in full control.

Fund-raising by the Club and the local community began in earnest, but Cookstown were taken aback to learn that they would have to participate in a Qualifying Tournament in Zagreb, and if successful they could then proceed to the European competition in Rome.

In the event, Cookstown won the qualifying tournament and went on to Rome where they won the Final after a series of nerve-wracking penalty-flicks! Martin Sloan scored the first, goalie David Larmour saved a flick and with the score at 3-1 in Cookstown's favour, Bobby Hamilton coolly stepped forward to make it 4-1 for Cookstown, who thus became the first Club in Ireland to win a major European competition. In 1988 Cookstown were again in a European competition and finished 7th in Holland - the highest position that an Irish team had thus far achieved in the premier division of European Hockey.

A bed-rock of the Club's success has been its close connection with the local High School which has supplied many gifted hockey players. In 1994 the School opened its sand-based astroturf pitch, and was the first Ulster school to do so. This facility will be an advantage for the Cookstown pupils, and the School's victory in the 1996 Burney Cup may well be a portent of things to come.

Like many another Club, Cookstown has its personalities and distinguished players including Martin Sloan, who has played for Ireland 149 times and was Captain in more than 100 games; Internationals David McManus, Mark Burns, Geoff Hamilton, and accomplished goal-keeper David Larmour; and stalwarts Dickie Harkness and Davy Black. Sadly, the Club has suffered loss as well, and in October 1994, Nigel Cheevers died. An Annual Tournament for Clubs from North and South has been instituted in his memory, and it was fitting that the first winners of the Nigel Cheevers Memorial Tournament were his home Club.

The Club has a proud record since its foundation in 1951 and over the past 45 years it has made an important contribution to the game in Ulster and much further afield.

CROSSGAR

The Club was founded in 1932 by A Jaye, J Bell, W Whyte and J Ferris (Snr). The Club played in the Minor League for many years and was successful in League and Cup competitions, winning both the Braddell Shield on a number of occasions and the Mulholland Shield.

Hockey was played on a pitch which is presently used by Kilmore Rec Football Club in the grounds of the monastery in Crossgar, and in a field belonging to a Mr Harris on the Kilmore Road until 1945! The Club was in a very good financial position, and it purchased land on the Downpatrick Road, where hockey was played until 1947. This was the year in which hockey in the village was brought to a temporary end by a sine die suspension placed upon the Crossgar Club. This was eventually lifted in 1967.

In the years between 1947 and 1967 some of the players who were involved in the original suspension were allowed to play for other Clubs and as a result Down, Ballynahinch and Montalto benefited. In the early 1950s under the auspices of the local Church and its Minister, the late Rev Sam Finley, himself a former Lisnagarvey player, Lissara Hockey Club came into existence. They played hockey on what was the old cricket ground on the Saintfield Road, now a housing development (Lissara Close), and in a meadow in Kilmore owned by the late Mr John Patterson.

In 1967, when the Club was reinstated into the Ulster Branch, the original trustees handed the land and the accumulated funds to the new Committee

The Crossgar Second XI circa 1967, with the Mulholland Shield. (Copyright Newtownards Chronicle)

chaired by Mr Jim Ferris, a son of one of the founder members. The land was very low-lying and the East Down Rural Council had been given permission to use the ground as a dump on the condition that it was reinstated as a playing field on completion of the infill. Unfortunately the dump was returned to the Club in an unsuitable condition. This was not rectified until 1985.

The new Crossgar Club played its hockey in a field belonging to Mr Tom Orr at Ballytrim. After this first Season in the Intermediate League, and as a result of the re-arrangement of the Leagues, Crossgar found itself in Senior Hockey for the first time. However, with four other Clubs in the district and no feeder schools, the Club remained small and it struggled. Sometimes in good years it fielded three teams, and in bad years it was barely able to field one team. It was eventually relegated from Senior to Intermediate League.

In 1995 the Club decided that it was necessary to move from the grass pitch to an all-weather surface to try to improve its standard of hockey. Arrangements were made to play home games on the Down High School pitches. It is hoped to continue this arrangement for the Second XI, but it is the intention to play all First XI matches in the coming Season on the new Astroturf pitch at Lough Moss in Carryduff.

Over the years hockey has been maintained in Crossgar by the sterling efforts of a few so that the game could provide a sporting outlet for the youth of the district.

DOWN

Hockey came to Downpatrick in 1900, when it was played at Saul Camp at the Saul Road. In 1901 the Club was admitted to membership of the Ulster Branch of the Irish Hockey Union, together with Randalstown.

Down Hockey Club first made the headlines in the 1905-06 Season when they won the Junior League by beating Lisburn 8-5 at Saul Camp.

In 1910 Down had a remarkable victory, by defeating Lisnagarvey 7-1 in a Senior League match. However, 'Garvey were not at full strength!

In 1911 JH Acheson played at left back for Ulster against Leinster, and a year later W McCormick played for Ireland against Wales. This was the only occasion in the history of the Club when a member played for Ireland. In the same year W McCormick also played for Ulster.

During the First World War hockey was not played in Downpatrick. In 1923-24 the First XI was still in the Senior League, but they had a poor Season, and were relegated to the Junior League A section. The Second XI met with considerable success winning the A Division of the Minor League, the Minor League Championship and the Mulholland Shield. By now the Club was using the Asylum Ground and had also applied to use the cricket ground.

The Club was also £6 in debt - a not inconsiderable amount in those days and at the AGM there was a lengthy debate on ways and means of raising funds. Finally the Committee decided to run a ballot for a Golden Sovereign, the winner to be declared on the night of the dance - a very acceptable prize!

Next Season, 1924-25, the fortunes of the Club revived. The First XI had a lengthy tussle with CPA in the second round of the Irish Junior Cup finally losing after the third replay. However, they won the Braddell Shield - last won by Down Hockey Club in 1904-05 - when they beat Parkview after a replay and they also won the A Division of the Junior League but lost the League decider to Parkview (Winners of the B Division).

The Club's next successful Season was in the year 1926-27, when James Clements was Captain and J Morrison was Vice-Captain. The First XI beat Banbridge in the Intermediate Charity Cup Final at the Downshire Hospital and they also beat Antrim Second XI in the Intermediate League Cup (Linden Cup). Unfortunately the night before the match Jim Clements was rushed to hospital for removal of his appendix! In the Irish Junior Cup the Club had an eventful match in Clones on 1 January 1927 when they drew 1-1 after two periods of extra time. On 8 January in Downpatrick, Down won 3-2. However in the next round Down was defeated by YMCA. The two Cups won by the Club were proudly displayed in McBride's shop. RJ Morrison was selected for the Ulster Junior Inter-provincial XI.

April 14, 1928 was a black day for the Club. The First XI were beaten 2-0 in the Intermediate Charity Cup Final and the Second XI were beaten by Ards (the eventual winners) in the Semi-Final of the Irish Junior Cup.

In the 1929 Season the Captain of the Second XI was Mr Sam Cunningham and in that year Jim Clements was selected for the Junior Inter-provincial team and also elected a member of the Council of the Ulster Branch.

During the early 1930s the membership was small, but in the year 1931-32 the Club applied for re-admission to the Senior League. They were not accepted, but played with great success in the Intermediate League.

The Club became moribund with the onset of the Second World War when no League matches were played. On 9 September 1941, a meeting was called to revive the Club. Jim McClurg became Secretary, a position he occupied for 25 years with distinction. The hospital ground had been taken over by the Army and the cricket club kindly made their ground available.

In 1945-46 the Irish Junior Cup came to Downpatrick. The Club won 2-1 at Londonbridge Road, Dublin, by beating Craiguenamanagh of Kilkenny, after extra time. Immediately the match ended one of Down's supporters, also a pigeon-fancier, sent the result back to Downpatrick by pigeon post!

After major ground improvements in the mid-Forties, Down returned to Senior Hockey and over the next few Seasons a good team drew large crowds to Strangford Road to witness many thrilling 'battles' with senior opposition, including Lisnagarvey, Banbridge, Cliftonville, Portrush and Antrim.

For the next few Seasons the Club remained in Senior League II, and the Third XI won the Minor Cup in 1958, but once again the ground developed drainage problems. In the early 1960s, following relegation to Intermediate hockey, the Club played matches at Ballykinlar, where the ground was outstanding - but the support for hockey seriously diminished as many supporters could not make the journey there.

Miraculously however, the Club has been fortunate enough to have had good officials who have kept hockey going in Downpatrick and have also contributed to the Ulster Branch, and numerically the Club remains strong.

Since 1953, Down have won few trophies, although the Second XI won their League in 1972-73 and S Connor was selected for Junior Ulster.

From its 75th Anniversary to date, Down has remained very much in business. It maintained close links with Scotland, and with the Ayr Club in particular, who also made a number of reciprocal visits.

A milestone in the Club's history was the opening of a new ground in 1979.

Down Hockey Club 1984-85, Winners of the Intermediate Cup for the third year in succession, gained promotion to Senior League Section II. The Club has won the Cup four times in recent years.

The Club purchased land at Strangford Road, Downpatrick, from Lord Dunleath for £700. This was a rare achievement as very few hockey Clubs owned their own ground.

That year also the First XI returned to Senior Hockey, after an absence of 20 years - also an achievement as few Clubs make it to Senior Hockey without the aid of a school as a nursery. A grass pitch was laid, due to the efforts of life time members, Jim McClurg, Eddie Malone and Bob Law. The new ground was officially opened on 21 September 1979 by the President of the Ulster Branch Dixon Rose with a match between the Ulster President's XI and a Down team, strengthened by three Internationals. It ended in a 1-1 draw.

On the field, the Club performed steadily. In 1983 the First XI won the Intermediate Cup, and came close to winning promotion to Senior II. Two years later it won the Intermediate Cup for the third Season in succession, and the fourth time in the previous few years. In 1983 Down also won the Bangor Six-a-Side Tournament. In 1989 a Fourth XI was entered in the League, and the Second XI was presented with the Braddell Shield at the Ulster Branch Dinner.

A number of individuals also gained distinction, including Eddie Patterson and Stephen Malone who were selected for the Junior Irish squad in 1983, as was Alex Burgon for Junior Ulster in 1985. More recently, in 1992, John Torney played for Ulster U-18s and won an Irish U-18 Cap. Over the years a number of former players and Club administrators passed away, including former Chairman Bob Law, Eddie Malone, after whom the Club's ground was named in 1987, and Jack Brown, the Honorary Treasurer for 45 years. Eddie Malone began playing for Down as a schoolboy, becoming Vice-captain of the First XI in 1931, Captain when Down won the Hospital Cup, and Captain of the League-winning team in 1952. In 1994 work began on the laying of an all-weather pitch, and in 1995 it was officially opened by Eddie Malone's son, a Down player, and his sister Thelma.

As Down Hockey Club looks forward to its Centenary in the year 2000, its heart remains strong, and one of its primary aims is to return to Senior hockey.

Dr John Ritchie
In the early 1940s, Dr John Ritchie, who had just qualified, was appointed as a House Surgeon at Down Infirmary. He had started his hockey career with Cregagh, and had played for Queen's from 1934-40, being Captain in 1937-38. During that time he became an Ulster Inter-provincial player, and a final Irish Trialist. He was a prolific goal-scorer for Down, and in 1948 scored more than 50 goals in one Season.
When he retired from playing he became involved in administration. He was appointed to the Ulster Branch and to the Irish Hockey Union. He later represented Ireland on the International Hockey Federation and on the Federation of International Umpires. He was also an Irish selector.
In 1958 he became President of the Irish Hockey Union, the first member of Down Hockey Club to achieve the top position in Irish Hockey.
His untimely death in 1968 robbed the Irish Hockey Union of a fine administrator and Down Hockey Club of a good friend.

EAST ANTRIM

East Antrim Hockey Club was founded in 1902 by Andrew George Burney, whose name has been perpetuated by the Trophy he presented in 1920 for Ulster Schools competition. An Inaugural Meeting was held at Thompson's Place, Hydepark on 3 October 1902. Among those present was Hugh McMeekin, whose name also lives on through the Trophy he presented in 1920.

The Club fielded one team in 1902-03, playing friendly games only - the first recorded match being against Cliftonville at Hydepark in December 1902. In 1903-04, the Club was accepted into the Junior League and in 1904-05, a Second XI was formed and entered in the Minor League.

The First XI had their first success when they won the Junior League in 1905-06, winning all twelve games. In 1911-12, the League title was won again, but the Irish Junior Cup Final was lost to Trinity College. During this period, four Lyle brothers - John, Sam, Hugh and William - all played for the Club and were a cornerstone in the early days.

In the early years all home matches were played at Ballyclare Road, Glengormley. In 1912-13, East Antrim were playing in the Senior League, but with the outbreak of the First World War, all hockey ceased. When the War ended the Club re-formed and played on the Hightown Road, Glengormley. The Club was determined, however, to return to the ground it had played on since 1907. During 1921, money was raised and the ground at Ballyclare Road was purchased for £400, thus making East Antrim the first Club in Ulster to own its ground.

The Twenties were quite successful for the Club, winning the Senior League in 1924 and also reaching the Ulster Final of the Irish Senior Cup (only to lose

The East Antrim Squad which played against an Irish XI in April 1978 to mark the Club's 75th Anniversary. The Irish team won 4-0. In the line-up are Billy Williamson (second from left, back row), and Andy Hayes (fifth from left, back row), both of whom were President of the Ulster Branch. Andy Hayes was also President of the IHU.

to Banbridge after a replay). In 1925, the Second XI lost in the Semi-Final of the Irish Junior Cup and the First XI lost to Lisnagarvey in the Final of the Kirk Cup - a feat later repeated in 1928 when losing to Banbridge.

In 1932, East Antrim unsuccessfully contested the Kirk Cup but returned the following year to beat Banbridge 3-0. The winning team included no less than 8 Ulster players, 2 of whom, Hugh Leeburn and SJ Courtney, also played for Ireland.

During the Second World War hockey continued on a friendly basis until 1942, when competitions were re-introduced. One of the main problems at this time was travel, as petrol was rationed. However, thanks to Andy Hayes' apparently unlimited petrol allowance, the Club were able to fulfill all its fixtures!

The Club continued in the Senior League, but the War had taken its toll and decline was setting in. When the Senior League and Qualifying League were reconstituted in 1951, East Antrim was placed in the Qualifying League. This was the turning-point in the Club's history. Until then, it had been a powerful club and, although not the most successful, it had always played in the top grade, producing quality players for Ulster and Ireland.

During this period, the five Alexander brothers played for the Club, with four of them together on the First XI - a unique record for Ulster Senior hockey at that time.

The Fifties was a decade of struggling to keep the Club alive and, again, a strong family connection came to the fore - The Archbolds - Hugo and Wilson - virtually ran the Club at that time.

Despite the gloom, there were some highlights. Although he did not achieve glory on the hockey field, East Antrim's most famous personality played during the early Fifties. He was a local lad called Billy Millar, who went on to gain world-wide fame as the film star - Stephen Boyd! Tragically, he died in 1977, at the early age of 49. Andy Hayes, a club stalwart, became President of the Ulster Branch in 1956-57, a year in which the Club supplied no fewer than 9 umpires to the Branch.

The end of the decade brought the bitterest blow to the Club. A court case over road repairs to the adjoining Hillview Drive was fought and lost. In order to pay the debts, the Club was forced to sell the ground at Ballyclare Road. Relegated twice in quick succession, 1962-63 saw the Club playing in the Intermediate League at a ground on the Hightown Road.

This was another turning-point brought about by a nucleus of enthusiastic hard-working players. These included Jim Strange, Billy Williamson, Ken Skelton, Max Abbott and Derek Reade. At the same time the Club moved to a new all-weather pitch at Whitewell and this led to an immediate improvement in the standard of hockey.

The year 1965-66 was very successful and the Club easily won the Intermediate League. Andy Hayes was also elected President of the Irish Hockey Union. The following year saw the Club back playing at its old ground on the Ballyclare Road, which had been re-laid as an all-weather pitch by Newtownabbey Borough Council. This was such an encouragement that the Club was able to field 3 teams with the First XI again winning the League and gaining promotion to Qualifying League 'A'.

During this successful run, the First XI remained unbeaten at home for just over 3 years. Consistency was elusive and again in 1972-73, the Club suffered relegation to the Intermediate League. At least there was consolation for five Club members who were selected to play for Junior Ulster. At this time, the

The Hollywood film star Stephen Boyd who, as a local Ulster lad called Billy Millar, played for East Antrim in the Fifties.

Club made its first visit to the Whitsun Festival in the Isle of Man - a tradition which still continues.

In 1974 the Club was playing in Senior League II and performed there as a 'mid-table' Club for the remainder of the decade. The 75th Anniversary was celebrated in 1977-78 and the culmination of these celebrations was a game against the full Ireland team. A crowd of several hundred enjoyed the game in which East Antrim lost 4-0 to a team just returned from the World Cup in Argentina. In 1979 a Constitution was produced and Jim Strange was elected the first Chairman of the Club.

The early Eighties saw the familiar picture of relegation followed quickly by promotion. In 1983 the Club's first Continental tour to Holland took place and Billy Williamson became the President of the Ulster Branch. The Club suffered a double tragedy in 1986 with the deaths of Andy Hayes and Billy Williamson, two real sportsmen and stalwarts of East Antrim. Both had been committed players and outstanding administrators in Ulster and Irish Hockey.

From the mid-Eighties until the mid-Nineties, the Club played in Senior League II and whilst results were not outstanding, 5 teams were being fielded consistently. At present, however, the Club is back in the Intermediate League with 3 teams taking to the field each week.

Whilst results on the field have been mixed, the Club has vigorously pursued the social side. Always a Club which looks to the future, it became the first Hockey Club in Ireland to have its own Web-site on the Internet! With this forward-looking attitude, East Antrim faces the future with confidence as it approaches its centenary in 2002.

FRIENDS' SCHOOL OLD BOYS

On 15 March 1944, the Lisburn Old Scholars' Association visited Malone Training School, Balmoral, and it was there, just before the curtain went up, that Robin Bell, one of the players, remarked "What about this hockey Club?"

This inquiry stimulated the debate which had been simmering for some time and the idea was further debated at the LOSA Annual General Meeting later that month. By now, a sufficient number of people had indicated their enthusiasm and as a result the first Meeting of the Club took place on 4 July 1944, with the result that the Lisburn Old Boys' Hockey Club was formed. The First XI was entered in the Intermediate League for the 1944-45 Season and early enthusiasm was typified by a letter received from North Africa from Colin Doak expressing his wish to join 'on the cessation of hostilities'.

The first match was a friendly against Co Armagh Club Laurelvale, played on 16 September 1944 at Friends' School, with a 1-0 victory for the home team.

Following this heady start, competitive games in League and Cup took priority and, although not threatening to collect any silverware, in the early years the 'Lobs' gave as good as they got. The Club owed a great debt in its formative and later years to J Arnold Bennington, schoolmaster and first Club Chairman. His enthusiasm and support were an inspiration to all the members.

Encouragement and inspiration were surely needed. The first success for the Club did not come until the 1964-65 Season when promotion was won to Senior Qualifying League B. That the Club survived this twenty year period is a tribute to the dedication of those members who turned out week after week,

The FSOB team which, as a Qualifying League A Side, achieved the considerable feat of winning the Corken Cup in 1968.

on many occasions with fewer than the permitted allocation of eleven players, and played the game purely for the pleasure of taking part.

The lack of success for the Club did not reflect the quality of the schoolboys being produced by Friends' School. The School First XI regularly won the Burney Cup but the boys seldom joined the Old Boys on leaving school. Over many years the annual pipe-opener to the Ulster hockey Season, was the Friends' School Old Boys v Ulster match. For these matches the 'Lobs' could select (and then view) all the talent they had missed.

However, the 1964-65 Season changed all that, and was the start of a period of success which was to last some twelve years with promotion to Senior Qualifying League B for one Season, and promotion to the A Division at the end of 1965-66.

Success bred success. Schoolboys started joining the Club direct from school and established Senior players were attracted from other Clubs. In 1966 the name of the Club was changed to Friends' School Old Boys. Probably the high spot in the Club's history came on 9 March 1968 when, as a Qualifying League A side, the First XI became the only non Senior League team to win the Corken Cup (the Cup for the Winners of the Ulster Final of the Irish Senior Cup).

Success was gained at the expense of favourites Cliftonville who were beaten 1-0. Unfortunately this success was not continued and the provincial play-off Semi-final was lost by the same margin to Railway Union from Dublin.

After three years in Qualifying A, promotion was gained to the Senior League at the end of the 1968-69 Season. Further success was achieved that Season. In a highly-emotional Anderson Cup Final (for both players and spectators), Lisnagarvey were beaten 1-0 by FSOB in what was a 'local Derby', played at Banbridge.

However, it was not only the First XI which was successful - Junior teams also had their moments of glory, being promoted up the Junior Leagues and also gained some Cup successes.

A number of Seasons followed in the top division but at the end of the 1976 Season the Club was relegated to what had then become Senior II. Sadly, at the end of the 1994-95 Season, due to a lack of playing members, the Club was left with no option but to withdraw from the League.

Down the years, a number of members brought fame to themselves and the Club by gaining representative honours, while others honoured the Club by their years of unstinted service. However, the list of people deserving of recognition in either category would be too long to include here.

Former hockey writer Theo Snoddy noted in his booklet 'The Story of the First Two Years' published in 1946 ... "let Lisburn Old Boys' play hockey in such a sportsmanlike manner that when they lose even the opposition will be sorry." The feeling was not always reciprocated by the opposition but this general attitude to the game was the main reason, many feel, that playing hockey for The Old Boys was always an enjoyable, if sometimes a forgettable experience!

HOLYWOOD 87
(Incorporating YMCA)

Holywood 87 was formed in 1987 when the members of Belfast YMCA decided unanimously to relocate to Holywood and form a new Club. The reasons behind this move were financial. Over the previous years the central YMCA had been reducing its financial support for the grounds at Bladon Drive, with an increasing financial burden falling on the sports Clubs. Restrictions imposed by the ethos of the YMCA organisation made fund-raising very difficult and there was also the threat of development of the grounds for housing, which has since taken place.

The decision to move was made with great regret in view of the long and successful history of Belfast YMCA Hockey Club, and also because of the fact that Bladon Drive had in years past been the home of many representative matches - although this had changed with the advent of non-grass pitches.

Thus the history of Holywood 87 Hockey Club is inextricably tied up with that YMCA, although the link becomes more tenuous as time goes on. It is appropriate therefore to take a brief look at the YMCA story.

The first minuted meeting, the fourteenth AGM, took place in 1934, so the YMCA Club can be assumed to have been formed in 1920. In 1935 the Senior team was entered in the Qualifying League with members including Cecil Pearson, John Stirling and George White. In 1937 Goalkeeper Jack Carroll became the first YMCA player to represent Ireland. In 1944 the Club entered the Senior League and shortly after this George Blower, who over the next 45 years was to contribute so much to Ulster and Irish Hockey, joined the Club from England.

YMCA won the Senior League in 1955-56 at which time the great Harry Cahill was in goal, playing with fellow Internationals Ian Rouston, Tony McMillan and Robin Baillie. Subsequently, in spite of fielding five Internationals and several Inter-provincials, the only success on the pitch was a win in the Kirk Cup in 1960.

Harry Cahill went on to represent Great Britain in the Rome Olympics in 1960, and in 1961 YMCA won the Senior Cup for the first time, and this was followed by the Senior League in 1963-64 and the Anderson Cup in 1967-68. However, this team was ageing and the Club eventually slipped into Section II in 1971.

The situation started to improve again in 1972, with the laying down of a new all-weather, floodlit pitch and these excellent facilities were vital in attracting seven players from the Queen's University team that had won the Senior Cup in 1972. In this year George Blower also umpired his first International match, and Cecil Pearson retired.

Promotion back to Division I was achieved in 1974, and this was followed by a successful period for the Club. In 1975 the Ulster section of the Senior Cup was won convincingly, but it had to be forfeited on a technical ruling. However, in 1977 the Irish Senior Cup was won along with the Kirk Cup, and in the following ten years the Irish Cup was won three more times, the Senior

The YMCA First XI Squad of 1984-85 which won the Irish Senior Cup and Corken Cup, the Ulster Senior League Cup, and the Kirk and Anderson Cups. In the front row, third from the right, is George Blower, the last President of YMCA and the first President of Holywood 87.

Belfast Y.M.C.A. Hockey Club
Season 1984—85

League five times, the Kirk Cup two more times and the Anderson Cup twice. The Second XI also won the Irish Junior Cup in 1981. In 1984-85 the Club achieved the first modern day 'Grand Slam' of domestic competitions.

In the Seventies Terry Gregg achieved great success for both Ireland and Great Britain, receiving his one hundredth Cap for Ireland in 1981. Other Internationals were John Clarke and Stewart McNulty (who both captained Ireland), Norman Crawford, and Philip Anderson. In the late Seventies and Eighties these Internationals were joined by Billy McConnell, John McKee, Sam Martin and Kenny Morris, and Billy McConnell went on to become the most-capped player in Irish Hockey until overtaken by Martin Sloan. Along with Sam Martin he represented Great Britain on numerous occasions, winning a Bronze Medal in the 1984 Olympic Games in Los Angeles.

YMCA also represented Ireland twice in the First Division of the European Cup, a competition of the very highest standard. On both occasions relegation to Division Two was the result, though finishing sixth out of eight in Utrecht in 1986 was a satisfying achievement.

The link from Belfast YMCA to Holywood 87 is through the last President of YMCA, George Blower, who became the first President of Holywood 87. George, who had contributed so much to hockey for forty years, as President UBIHU in 1978, President IHU in 1982 and Fixtures Secretary for many years, actually developed a fresh enthusiasm which was vital for the new Club's success. Virtually all the members of YMCA moved to Holywood and the

Ulster Branch showed great understanding by allowing the four existing teams to retain their status in the Ulster Leagues.

The launch of the new Club was heralded by an Opening Gala with a match between a Holywood 87 XI and a Kaliber International XI at Holywood on 12 September 1987, followed in the evening by a Reception at the Folk Museum. The aim was to achieve sporting excellence, and this was given substance when the TSB presented a beautiful cut glass trophy in memory of Frank Green who was a member of the YMCA First XI in its last years, and who had died tragically at an Irish Indoor training session. This trophy is presented each year to honour sporting excellence.

Holywood 87 achieved success in their first Season under John McKee as Captain, winning the Anderson Cup. However, even with players of international quality such as Stephen Martin, Billy McConnell, John McKee, Kenny Morris (Ireland and GB), Mark Burns, Norman Crawford and Philip Anderson (Ireland), success was limited to Kirk Cup victories in three consecutive years, 1990-91, 1991-92, 1992-93. Unfortunately for many of the more important matches, the Great Britain commitments robbed the club of top players.

However the achievement by Stephen Martin in winning a Gold Medal as part of the Great Britain team in the 1988 Olympics in Seoul, brought great honour to the Club, and many people believe that Billy McConnell should have been part of that team as well.

The Club membership increased with the move to Holywood and soon a Fifth XI was being fielded. This team has won leagues twice as it moves up the junior ranks. The Second XI produced the first all-Ireland success winning the Irish Junior Cup in 1990-91 and then again in 1991-92. In 1992-93 with Norman Crawford as Coach the Club finally won one of the major competitions - Senior League I. However this success will always be tinged with sad memories - on the afternoon when the First XI beat Lisnagarvey at Olympia Leisure Centre to virtually win the League, George Blower collapsed and died from a heart attack at the side of the pitch. George's moment of delight as the final whistle went, just before he collapsed, showed how important Holywood 87 Hockey Club was to him, and how important he was to Holywood.

Recent years have been involved with re-building, and under the guidance of John Clarke as Coach, there are hopes that the Club will continue to aspire to sporting excellence.

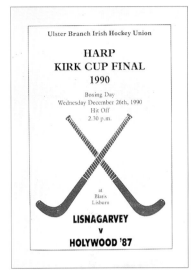

Programme for the 1990 Kirk Cup Final which was won by Holywood 87, for the first time since the Club was formed, largely from the former YMCA Club. Holywood also won the Cup the next two Seasons.

INSTONIANS

One of the inspirations behind the formation of Instonians Mens Hockey Club was Ralph Spearman, a Mathematics Teacher at RBAI. He was one of those who had developed hockey at the school in the late Forties. The Club was formed in September 1959 and is still a 'closed' Club in that only former pupils or teachers at the school are eligible to join.

Instonians started playing in the Intermediate League with only 14 players and struggled to survive. The following Season saw the arrival of old boys from other Clubs, and Instonians began to prosper with the addition of a Second XI. In the space of 4 years the Club was knocking on the door of Senior League hockey and this was finally achieved in the 1965-66 Season, when a goal scored by Tommy Reid against Parkview gained Instonians promotion. Since then the First XI has never been relegated. Although runners-up on five occasions, the League title has been won only twice - the latest being in the 1995-96 Season when the First XI squad went on to win the Irish Club Championship and gain entry as Ireland's representatives in Europe and the European Cup. The previous year they had played in Europe as Ireland's representatives in the Cup Winners Cup in Gibraltar and finished runners-up. This was due to winning the Irish Senior Cup, for the first time, in Cork against Cork Harlequins.

Despite being finalists in Kirk Cups previously, the first major Cup won by the Club was the Anderson Cup in 1969 when Kenny Lee scored the only goal against Antrim at Banbridge. Since then the Club won many more Ulster Cups but had to wait until 1995 before winning the big one - the Irish Senior Cup.

The Second XI won the Irish Junior Cup in 1978, against Cork Church of Ireland. They went on to win the Cup again in 1980 and were beaten finalists in 1981 when they also won Junior League I for the first and only time.

One of the mainstays of the Club has been Haydn Taylor who captained the team when they gained promotion to the Senior League in 1965-66 and also when they won the League title for the first time in the 1974-75 Season. Fittingly he was also Team Manager during the Club's most recent success, including winning the Irish Senior Cup and Irish Club Championships in successive years.

Another stalwart has been Brian Hanna, one of the founder members of the Club. He went on to become a leading umpire and Ulster Branch Council member before becoming the first Instonians Hockey Club member to become the Ulster Branch President. He then went on to become President of the Irish Hockey Union and one of his final acts was to present the Irish Senior Cup to the Instonians Captain Paul Hollway in Cork in April 1995 - a very proud day for both.

Many players have made their mark in representative hockey, but for a long time only Ian Steepe, a teacher at RBAI, had played for Ireland while at the Club. He was Vice-Captain of Ireland, Captain of Munster and later became Coach to the Senior Ireland team.

Terry Gregg, one of Ireland's greatest hockey players, played for the Club

The Instonians First XI Squad which won the Ulster Senior League 1995-96 and were Runners-up in the European Cup Winners' Cup 'B' Division in Gibraltar.

while still at school and represented Ulster and Ireland's U-21's. While at Queen's University and then Belfast YMCA, Terry represented Ireland over 100 times and played many times for Great Britain for whom he was also Vice-Captain. Since he 'retired' he has become a distinguished Coach, steering Lisnagarvey to many League and Cup wins, and now coaching Ireland's Ladies Senior International team.

Philip Anderson was a member of the First XI while still at school. He also played many times for Ireland at Senior level both Indoor and Outdoor. More recently he has returned to the Club as Coach and guided the squad to their first Irish Club Championship and also in their first trip to Europe.

Other Irish Internationals include Paul Cooke, Neil Cooke, John Atkins, Paul Hollway (also Captain of Ulster), Mark Irwin and Patrick Brown.

Andy Kershaw, a member of the team who first won the Senior League title is now the Secretary of the Irish Hockey Union. Ernie Brown has been President of the Ulster Umpires Association. Kenny Lee is a member of the Ulster Branch Council and a member of the Disciplinary Committee.

The Club which started off with only 14 players now has 5 teams enabling 15-20 schoolboys to play each week and also fields a U-13 and U-15 Colt XIs. This is very important for a 'closed' Club which can only recruit players from RBAI. With such a sound youth policy, the future success of Instonians seems assured.

GORDON McILROY
1944-96
Gordon McIlroy's death at Easter 1996 at the early age of 52 was a great blow to his many hockey friends especially within the Instonians Club. It was ironic that the Club to which he had contributed so much learned of his death in London as the Senior squad were travelling home from Gibraltar following a major success in winning Silver medals in the 1996 European Cup Winners' Cup Competition.

It was fitting tribute to him that in the last two years of his life Instonians had finally won the Irish Senior Cup in 1995 and was beginning to scale the

The late Gordon McIlroy of Instonians (left) with Colin Russell, playing against Portrush in a Kirk Cup match.

European heights in 1996. Indeed only a few short weeks later Instonians claimed another major success in winning the Irish Hockey Union's All-Ireland Club Championship thus ensuring European hockey in 1997.

Gordon McIlroy was one of a small band of people who made all this possible. He made his initial debut as a 15 year old in the Inst school hockey team in 1959 at the Oxford Public School Hockey Festival. This was at a time when Ralph Spearman's hard work in building up Inst hockey was beginning to pay off. No one present in Oxford in 1959 could have guessed that this slightly chubby and studious boy would have such a profound effect on Instonians' Ulster and Irish hockey.

Two years later in 1961 Gordon delivered the first of many 'future' Inst victories when he captained the school team to success in schoolboy hockey's greatest prize - the Burney Cup. Success over Banbridge Academy at the old Cliftonville ground was a major achievement, given that the Banbridge team contained such fine players as Errol Grafton and Ray Quinn.

At Queen's University Gordon's hockey education was considerably developed. The Queen's team of the early Sixties included many good players. Reg Quinn - surely one of Ireland's most cultured players - Alf McCreary, Ray Quinn, Crawford Bell and Instonians contemporaries Colin Russell and Terry Jacques.

While Queen's were playing in the Senior League, the recently-formed Instonians Club (1959) was attempting to rise from the depths of Intermediate hockey to a similar level. Two promotions were attained (1962 and 1963) and by the time Gordon, Colin and Terry rejoined Instonians from Queen's (1966) the Club was only one promotion away from its objective of Senior hockey.

There is no doubt that the injection of experience and quality brought by the three Queen's 'Blues' made all the difference and Instonians duly won promotion to the Ulster Senior League in 1967, a position which has been maintained ever since.

In those days Gordon in many ways 'was' Instonians. He captained the team on many occasions, was Match Secretary for many years and indeed his mother played a major role in feeding generations of Instonians en route between school and old boys games!

Gordon was a good although, not a great, player. He recognised this himself, but was strong and had considerable stamina though he certainly could not lay claim to being the quickest player around!

He was a great Captain, being able to see the total picture without sacrificing attention to detail. His team talks were collectors' items and it is a pity that some of them were not recorded for posterity. There was no player on an Instonians team who did not gain from Gordon's individual attention, and the collective effort always improved. In many ways and for many years he was the psychological cement which held the fledgling Club together. He played on the Instonians team which won the Senior League in 1975 and he lived to see that feat repeated in the Spring of 1996 shortly before his death.

As his Senior career came to an end, he played in the Instonians Second XI which won the Irish Junior Cup (1978) and he began a long coaching career which involved him at Club, Inter-provincial and Ireland levels - both Outdoor and Indoor.

It was at this stage that he also began a long association as a Coach with Knock Ladies Hockey Club. This involvement was clearly a joy to him and his affection for the Knock Ladies Club was returned many times over.

Gordon McIlroy was a gentleman. He loved music, literature, good food and wine but most of all the company of his hockey friends. The Ulster Branch of the Irish Hockey Union made him its President in 1991. The highest Office and the greatest tribute his hockey friends had within their gift was gladly bestowed upon him. He discharged his duties as President with both style and dignity. He and his wife Hilary graced many hockey occasions and clearly enjoyed every minute.

In his last few years of life when illness over-took him he faced it as he had faced all difficult situations with both resolution and courage.

KILKEEL

The first records of a Kilkeel Hockey Club can be traced back to the 1920s. Indeed, the Northern Whig newspaper, in their edition of 23 September 1924 announced: "At the Annual General Meeting of the Kilkeel Hockey Club, Mr JB McKeown presiding, the following appointments were made:- Captain - Mr M Healey, Vice-Captain - Mr Smyth, Secretary - Mr TH Ferguson, Treasurer - Mr RJ Ferguson, Committee - Messrs McKeown, Givens, Hanna, Russell, O'Riordan, Walsh and Dr Henderson." Unfortunately, current research into this early Kilkeel Club has been unable to shed any more light on the formation, structure and success of this Club.

Kilkeel High School Old Boys' Hockey Club, today commonly abbreviated to Kilkeel Hockey Club, is one of the younger Clubs within the Ulster Branch. The 'current Club' had its Inaugural meeting on 10 September 1971 in the gymnasium of Kilkeel High School, to determine whether there was sufficient support for the formation of a competitive hockey Club in the area. An early affinity with the local High School, from which the Club has taken its name, has continued through the Club's history and is still as strong today, with the vast majority of past and current players having come through the ranks of the school.

At the Inaugural meeting, the local headmaster, Moore McCauley, was elected President - a position he held for 16 years. CR Boyd, a past member of Lisnagarvey Hockey Club and the Sports Master responsible for the development of hockey in Kilkeel High School, was elected as Chairman, with B McMullen and J Charleton (both of whom are still associated with the Club) taking the roles of Treasurer and Secretary respectively. SC McBride accepted the role of Captain for the Club's Inaugural Season, 1971-72. It was significant that one of the founder members of the Club was Chris Harte

The Kilkeel Squad in 1976-77 when they lost the Ulster Final of the Irish Junior Cup 1-3 to Lisnagarvey Second XI, after extra time.

from Bangor, more famous for his exploits at cricket. However, Chris' membership did not last long, as the early Club Constitution only allowed for ex-members of the local school to become members of the Club.

In their Inaugural Season, Kilkeel finished runners-up to Michelin in Intermediate League II and gained their first piece of Ulster Branch silverware when they won the Mulholland Shield. The early years were a period of consolidation rather than immediate success. Throughout the Seventies, Kilkeel rarely featured for promotion to Senior League II, but continued to hold mid-table respectability in most Seasons. For a brief spell, the Club flirted with a Second XI, but initial interest was poor and the Second XI folded after two years. It was resurrected more successfully in the 1980's, when it began to climb the Junior League tables at regular intervals, until the team reached Junior League I during 1993.

It was not until the mid-Eighties that Kilkeel began to prosper and develop, both as a team and a Club. With the Second XI providing a larger team base than was available during previous years, Kilkeel's fortunes took an upward turn, with the Club finishing runners-up in both the 1984-85 and 1985-86 Seasons. However, the ambition to attain Senior status was finally reached after a successful 1986-87 Season, in which they went undefeated, by winning 18 and drawing 2 of their League matches and eventually finishing five points clear of the second-place team.

The Club's first Season in Senior League Section II was successful, in that their objective to be in the top half of the table was achieved, finally finishing in fifth, with 23 points. This early success, coupled with the continuing climb up the tables by the Second XI and the success of the GB Hockey team at the 1984 and 1988 Olympic Games, saw an increase in the interest in hockey in the Mourne area. Such was the demand from the local population to play regular and competitive hockey that the Club had to form a Third XI and Fourth XI to satisfy the demands from its increasing membership.

At present, Kilkeel fields four teams, with the Second XI maintaining their Junior League I status, and the Third XI now looking forward to their first Season in Junior League 3 after a successful promotion campaign during 1995-96. The Fourth XI is more focused on youth development, rather than geared to winning trophies. It is the Club's hope that the Fourth XI will produce the players who will provide the nucleus for Senior Kilkeel teams in future.

In 1995, a decision was taken to invest in a synthetic pitch, subject to the availability of capital assistance. At present the application is with the relevant funding bodies for decision. The AGM, in May 1996, gave approval for the creation of a Junior Club, aimed at 8-14 year-old schoolchildren in an attempt to develop their skills and enthusiasm for the game at an earlier stage than present. It is hoped that the development of a synthetic pitch, the creation of the Junior Club and increased commitment and ambition of players will see Kilkeel push for Senior I status within the next few years.

Kilkeel has produced players of exceptional ability, namely Irish Internationals Kenny and Ivan Morris, plus Club stalwarts Clive Russell, Trevor Russell, William Quinn and Ashley Stevenson - undoubtedly all players who could easily have played at a much higher level, only for their loyalty to their local Club. Kilkeel's development plans should ensure that players of exceptional talent do not feel that they must leave to develop their personal skills, but rather strive for Senior I hockey through their local Club.

LARNE

Hockey was played in Larne in the early 1900's, but there is little record available until the 1940's. At that time, the Club played regularly at Greenland Park, now the grounds of Larne High School, where the Second XI and Third XI play their home games. The Club then faded until it was re-formed in 1963, with the first competitive game being played against Dunmurry on the grass pitch at Sandy Bay.

In 1964, a Second XI was entered in the Minor League, and in 1968 Larne was promoted to the Intermediate League and reached the Semi-Final of the Intermediate Cup. In a successful Season, the Second XI played in the Semi-Final of the Minor Charity Cup and finished third in their League.

The late Mr William Long, Postmaster of Larne, chaired the Club for ten years, until his retirement in 1973, while William Young (Senior), has served as Secretary, Umpire and player and is a Past President and Life Member. His son Billy, and grandson William are players in Club teams. The current Club President, Michael Telford who played in the first 1963 match, still turns out for Larne Third XI in Junior League 8.

Larne players who made their mark at Senior League level include David Hull and Wilson Lilley who moved to Mossley in the 1980's. Both returned to play for Larne, gaining Intermediate Cup Medals in the 1993 win over Saintfield, and in 1994 against Wanderers.

The Club made great strides in 1993, when Kieran McGoldrick re-joined as Captain and the First XI began to play its home games on the astroturf at Mossley Hockey Club. This, combined with an emphasis on Junior coaching, has enabled a young, talented team to emerge.

Larne Hockey Club - Winners of the Intermediate Cup 1992-93 and 1993-94.

Several Larne players have represented Ulster Hockey at Junior Inter-provincial Level - Seamus Agnew, David Hull, Leslie King Jnr, Leslie King Snr, Kieran McGoldrick, Michael Telford, Billy Young and William Young, while Larne Manager, Ronnie Blair, has been Ulster Junior Manager since 1993, and he and Noel McAlister are members of the Ulster Branch Council. Ronnie Blair and Kieran McGoldrick are graded Irish Hockey Union Badge Coaches.

With its three league teams and thriving Junior coaching, Larne is in a healthy position and should be able to build on the advances made in the 90s well into the new century.

LISNAGARVEY

In September 1901, three young Lisburn men met in the local Temperance Institute and talked about starting a Club. They canvassed support and it was decided to form Lisnagarvey. The three founder-members were RC Bannister, who became Captain, EE Wilson, the Honorary Treasurer and WS Duncan, the Honorary Secretary. The annual subscription for playing members was five shillings, and the original colours were light and dark blue. Thus began the history of one of the most illustrious hockey Clubs in these islands.

'Garvey, as they are known universally, began with friendly matches, and the first competitive games took place in the 1903-04 Season. The next year the club won its first trophy, the Mulholland Shield. During this period 'Garvey played at different venues, and eventually found premises off the Antrim Road. Members themselves built a pavilion, complete with toilet facilities.

From 1905-10, Lisnagarvey played Junior hockey, reaching the Final of the Irish Junior Cup, but losing the replay 5-0 to Monkstown. They also won the Junior League and the Braddell Shield. Their steady progress was confirmed by admission to the Senior League, and in 1908 Fred Hull won an International Cap - the first by a 'Garvey player. During the First World War 43 club members served with the armed forces, of whom four were killed and four wounded. Four others received the Military Cross for bravery.

After the War, the membership increased to over 100 by 1922, and in the Season 1924-25 Lisnagarvey won the Irish Senior Cup for the first time, beating Limerick PMYA. The captain JL Alderdice gave each member of the team a suitably engraved miniature cup. In 1926-27 'Garvey again won the Irish Senior Cup, under the captaincy of RTS Bailey. This was the era of the famous Gregor McGregor, an international player who was described as "the most dangerous forward in Ireland".

All the Talents - The Lisnagarvey Senior Squad and Officials 1993-94, with the Corken Cup, the All-Ireland Trophy, the Irish Senior Cup, and the Anderson Cup. Also included is the Harp Lager "Team of the Year Shield". 'Garvey sides dominated Irish hockey from the late Eighties onwards, winning seven consecutive Irish Senior Cup victories, four consecutive Senior League Titles, and many other trophies.

A lean spell followed, but this was offset by the introduction of fifteen-year-old Jack Bowden who began a most distinguished International and Club career, and his partnership with 'Garvey's Brian Raphael was outstanding. During the Second World War competitive hockey was suspended, not least because Clubs found travelling difficult, due to petrol rationing. The post-war period heralded a new era of success for Lisnagarvey, during which the Irish Junior Cup came to Lisnagarvey for the first time - incidentally 'Garvey has won this trophy 15 times, more times than any other club, since their first win in the Season 1954-55.

Dan Clarke, foreground, and Jimmy Kirkwood, background - two of the Irish Internationals who contributed significantly to Lisnagarvey's success.

The Fifties was a significant period in 'Garvey's history. The Club moved to its famous Blaris pitches, under the shadow of the huge BBC transmitter, and the club won 9 out of 14 trophies in 1957-58. In the decade 1950-60 'Garvey won 43 Trophies. There was also great individual success, with Steven Johnson playing with the British Squad at the 1956 Melbourne Olympics, but there was also personal tragedy, with the death of club stalwart Jimmy Corken in a drowning accident at San Remo in Italy. The Corken Cup was instituted in his memory in 1958. It is awarded to the Ulster team which reaches the furthest stage of the Irish Senior Cup. In the first three years it was won by Lisnagarvey who have held it 19 times to date.

The decades from the early Sixties to the mid-Eighties witnessed most commendable achievements by the Club both on and off the field. During the 1961-62 Season 'Garvey recorded their third 'Double' by winning the Irish Senior and Junior Cups. The next Season Brown Shaw and Wally Mercer won their first Irish Caps, to maintain a long tradition of international success by Club players, 39 of whom have been capped so far. Indeed Wally Mercer had the distinction of leading Ireland to success in the Home International Championships of 1968, the first time they won the series since 1949.

Meanwhile Michael Bowden, a mercurial winger maintained the close family link with 'Garvey, and - not surprisingly - gained International honours.

Off the field, the 'Garvey back-room helpers worked ceaselessly to establish for the Club an enviable social and financial base. They included people such as John Kennedy, the first Chairman (who became President of the Ulster Branch in 1986-87), David McClements, Jim Lappin, Billy Lowry, Ronnie Jess, Bobby Richardson, Jim Clarke, Howard 'Howdy' Clarke, Jim Reid, John Waring, and many others. Bobby Howard was the first 'Garvey man to become Ulster Branch President in 1977-78, an honour richly deserved. Bobby went on to become President of the Irish Hockey Union, in 1989-90, and he had the unique honour of presenting both the Irish Cups - Senior and Junior - to his 'Garvey colleagues during his term of office.

One of the hall-marks of 'Garvey has been the length of service undertaken by Club officials and supporters. For example Bobby Totten captained the Third XI from 1948-57, and was a committe member until 1965. Ken Hood, who wrote the Lisnagarvey history was Honorary Secretary from 1949-65, which was another record. The lack of space prevents a mention of all who helped, but clearly the success of 'Garvey on the field has been underpinned by first-class financial guidance, and a good social network - for example, the

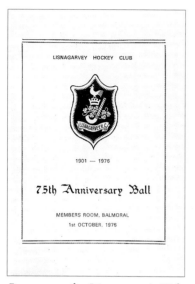

LISNAGARVEY HOCKEY CLUB

1901 — 1976

75th Anniversary Ball

MEMBERS ROOM, BALMORAL
1st OCTOBER, 1976

Programme for Lisnagarvey's 75th Anniversary Ball at the Members' Rooms, Balmoral in 1976.

establishment of a Lisnagarvey Social Club (the brainchild of Bobby Richardson) not only gave 'Garvey a reputation for good hospitality, but also helped the finances as well.

The Club made various structural changes to their premises at Blaris, but in the mid-Eighties they took a quantum leap by establishing a new artificial pitch complex at a completely new venue nearby, and set the direction for others to follow. This significant move was made possible by the sale of the 'old' Blaris grounds to a private developer, Marks & Spencer.

The transfer to the new premises and the building of a splendid pavilion led the way for a remarkable resurgence of Lisnagarvey's success on the field. Under the guidance of Coach Terry Gregg and others, a formidable squad virtually dominated Irish hockey for several years, and achieved the unequalled (and probably unsurpassable) record of winning the Irish Senior Cup seven years in succession. When 'Garvey approached Terry Gregg in 1987 to take the position of Coach, the Club had not won the Irish Senior Cup for 17 years, despite reaching two Finals and two Semi-Finals. The next years witnessed a glorious chapter of success overall which few if any other Irish clubs will emulate. As well as seven consecutive Senior Cup victories, 'Garvey won four consecutive Senior League titles, seven Corken Cups, two European B Division trophies, sixth place in the A Division of the European Cup in Frankfurt, plus one Anderson Cup, one Kirk Cup, two All-Ireland League titles, and two All-Ireland Flood-lit Cups. As well, the Second XI won two Irish Junior Cups, two McCabe Cups, and four Junior League I titles.

The resultant boost to the Club's national reputation has been enormous, and such continued success has inspired many younger players to try to emulate their elders - with a resultant range and depth to Garvey's youth sides which augurs well for the future. Arguably the outstanding 'Garvey player and role-model for the young has been Jimmy Kirkwood, Olympic Gold Medallist, and a modest and brilliant player and tactician.

Despite the Club's remarkable record 'Garvey players and officials have carried their great success with a relative modesty and dignity that is itself impressive. On the field 'Garvey are formidable opponents but off the field Blaris is a by-word for friendliness and hospitality.

The spirit of the Lisnagarvey Club was well-summarised by Captain Robbie Taylor in his speech after the memorable 1996 Final of the Irish Senior Cup which was won by Avoca.

He quoted part of the 1909 Annual Report of the then Honorary Secretary RC Bannister, a founder-member, and said: "We hope to have a better Season than last, but whether good or bad, it is to be hoped that fair play and good sportsmanship may ever characterise the Lisnagarvey Hockey Club." This most distinguished Club continues to be a winner, and in more ways than one.

MOSSLEY

Mossley Hockey Club was formed in 1929 following a meeting of employees of Henry Campbells, Mossley. A few friendly matches were played including several against near neighbours East Antrim. The original ground was opened by Cliftonville, the top team at that time, and included quite a few players who had played for Ulster and Ireland. Gradually more experienced players joined the Club and it began competing in Junior Hockey. Regular league matches were played against Clubs such as Parkview, Crossgar and Duncraig from Cullybackey.

During the Thirties the Club enjoyed great success in the Intermediate and Junior League, and in 1944 History was made when Mossley became the first Club to bring home five trophies in one Season. With such talent the Club continued to flourish, and a Third and Fourth XI were formed. Soon the First XI were promoted to Qualifying League B, winning that section in 1951. In 1952 the first International honour came to Mossley when Bryan Gilroy was chosen to play for Ireland. During the following years, however, few Senior trophies came to the Club, the exception being the Kirk Cup in 1954; but the Second, Third and Fourth XI's were still successful!

In 1966 the Second XI won the Irish Junior Cup with a superb record of scoring 23 goals and conceding only 2. This surpassed the performance of the First XI who were beaten in the Ulster Final of the Irish Senior Cup in 1965 by Portrush. The Anderson Cup was won by the First XI in 1967 and this heralded promotion back to Senior status in 1968 where the Club has remained despite a few flirtations with relegation.

Champions -
A sun-drenched Mossley Squad who won the Club Championship of Great Britain and Ireland, in the Isle of Man, May 1982.

During the 70's the team was built around Bert McBroom, a good old-style 'centre half', and John McKinstry, a most accomplished player who represented Ireland at Under 23 level.

The Burns family always played a leading role in Mossley, and when Harry Burns Jnr made his debut in the First XI in 1969 a new era had arrived. He became the mainstay of the Mossley defence and was the second member of the Club to gain full International honours, in 1978. He toured Australia in 1979 as a regular member of the team.

In 1973 Mossley made a second appearance in the Kirk Cup Final, losing to Lisnagarvey after a replay. Two Anderson Cup Final appearances followed that success, and in 1982 the Club won the British Club Championship in the Isle of Man. This was followed in 1983 by a third Kirk Cup Final appearance, again against Lisnagarvey. On this occasion Mossley won 2-0,

The Mossley team, with officials, in the 1943-44 Season when the Club won the Irish Junior Cup and Intermediate League A.

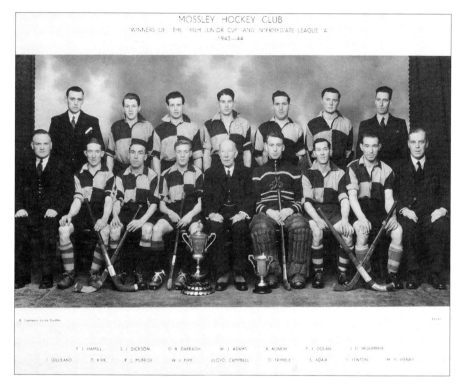

inspired by the brilliance of Paul Cooke. Shortly afterwards, to no one's surprise, Paul Cooke made his first appearance in the Irish Squad, along with two other Club members David Gordon and Richard Willis.

The Second XI were successful in the 1986 Junior Cup, defeating old friends and rivals Pembroke in the Semi-Final and Banbridge Second XI in the Final. Remarkably, the team was Captained by David McKinstry, who was also a member of the 1966 Cup winning team!

Another International honour worth noting is that of Harry McNeill, a successful manager of the Ireland team. Off the field Derek Watt was an able Ulster Branch President in 1985, and brought honour to the Club by his service to the Branch and in his year of office.

The old grass pitches at Mossley were abandoned in 1976 and the Club was forced to play at the City of Belfast Playing Fields at Mallusk. It was during this nomadic period that the Club celebrated its 50th Anniversary in 1979. After a long and at times frustrating search the present site at The Glade was purchased in 1984, and in 1991 the Club installed a synthetic surface at a cost of approximately £250,000. This decision has been instrumental in attracting a large number of junior members, and in 1994 the Club won a prestigious coaching award in recognition of its work with young players. The Club continues to provide a service to the local community and, with plans for further development, looks forward to a successful future.

NEWRY OLYMPIC

On 5 October 1911, an advert was published in the Newry Reporter asking anyone interested in forming a hockey Club in the area to attend a meeting the next evening in the Victoria Hotel at 8.00 pm. It took place with twelve in attendance, and RC McGrath was appointed as Captain. The membership was open to both ladies and gentlemen and an opening practice was held at Newry Show Grounds.

In February 1913 Newry Olympic Hockey Club proper was established by the Newry Methodist Guild for those belonging to the Church, but membership was widened to include any young people interested in playing the game. At the first AGM held in the Methodist Church Lecture Hall, it was stated that the aim of Newry Olympic was not to play in competitive matches, but friendly matches to provide enjoyment for young people and their friends.

These two Clubs functioned side by side, with the town team playing at the Show Grounds and the Olympic team playing on a field kindly donated by a member of the Methodist Congregation.

The Newry Club arranged mainly mixed matches, but in 1914 the men and ladies formed their own teams. Mixed hockey was still a large part of the game in the area with an inter-Club League being run at the Show Grounds in the middle of the week. Just before war broke out challenge matches between Newry HC and Newry Olympic HC took place at the Show Grounds, the town Ladies winning by 5-0 and the Men by 12-0.

It was September 1919 before Newry Hockey Club was revived from a state of abeyance during the war, with the men's and ladies' sections playing non-competitive matches as well as mixed hockey for several years. At the AGM in September 1921 it was agreed that a new ground should be sought and this was established at the St Colemans College gate house in November.

In 1922 the McWilliam Cup was revived, with Newry having held the trophy since 1914, although it had not been contested since then. The Newry team lost in the Semi-Final.

The Club, at this stage, had the use of three grounds - the Gate House on the Armagh Road, the Intermediate School on Downshire Road and the Show Grounds pitch at the Marshes.

At the start of the 1923-24 Season, a Second XI was formed and was entered in the McMeekin Cup, with the First XI competing in the Braddell Shield. Club colours at this stage were white and green halves! A regular fixture at this time was a Town v Visitors match on Christmas Day and on the social front the Club ran dances on Saturday nights to raise funds. These were much-appreciated by the local community.

In 1924-25, the First XI were admitted to the Intermediate League 'A' Division where they remained until 1930-31, but the Second XI were disbanded due to lack of numbers. In 1928 the Newry Olympic name was revived and used for the Mixed team. In November 1931 the Mens XI became South Down HC and made their competitive debut in the Athletic Stores Cup. The Newry Olympic name was also used by the Men's XI when playing

H DOWNEY   D WHITTEN   J COWAN
R CRAIG   A ROGAN   J GRACEY   S ROGAN.   P HUGHES
J SMYTH   A REILLY   S GRAHAM   G O'HARE   W HEATHER
G ORR   (CAPT)   W NICHOLL

The Newry Olympic team of 1934-35, who won the Irish Junior Cup and the Braddell Shield. They also won the Irish Junior Cup the next year.

friendly matches across the border in Dundalk.

In 1933 the Newry Olympic name was used for all the teams with the 'A' team men, 'B' team mixed and 'C' team ladies. The mens' XI were admitted to the 'B' Division of the Junior League and by 1934 they were in the 'A' Division. A Second XI was re-formed for the 1934-35 season, which was a memorable one for the club. The First XI won the Braddell Shield, the Irish Junior Cup and were undefeated in Junior League Division 'A'. Their victory over Corinthians Second XI by 2-0 in the Junior Cup at Londonbridge Road made them only the fifth Ulster team to bring the trophy north in 41 years. The Second XI in their first season reached the Final of the Minor Charity Cup.

In 1935-36 the First XI played in the Intermediate League, and in March 1936 made the journey to Dublin again for the Irish Junior Cup Final, this time beating Althinkard of Limerick 2-0, to become the only Ulster Club at that time to have won successive titles!

In 1936-37 the First XI made their debut in the Senior Qualifying League and in an effort to obtain a ground suitable for senior hockey played on the pitch at the Show Grounds enclosed by the Greyhound Track. The Second XI continued to function as the nursery for the senior team using players from Newry Intermediate School, and played in the Junior League in 1938-39.

With the outbreak of the Second World War, the Ulster Branch suspended all hockey, but a number of Clubs (including Newry) played friendly games. In December 1939 the first competitive match between Newry Olympic and Banbridge First XI's took place in the 'A' Division of this wartime league programme.

Newry took part in the competitions over the 1939-45 period and were kept in the Senior League when it was divided into two divisions in 1945. A Second XI was again revived and entered in Cup competitions. A problem with the use of the Newry Town pitch was resolved by moving back to one previously used by the Club on the football club grounds.

From 1946, the First XI competed in the Senior League 'B' Division and the Second XI in the Intermediate League. In 1948 the Club lost the use of the Newry Town pitch and moved down the road to another field at the 'Marshes'.

In 1948-49 T Whitten brought honour to the Club in being selected to Captain the Ulster Senior Squad against Leinster at Bladon Drive. In the early 1950's the Club competed in the newly-formed Qualifying League and several players gained representative honours. The most notable was E Walnutt, who was selected for Ulster, having previously played for Munster.

In April 1957 Bob Poots became the first Newry Olympic player to be capped by Ireland, at the tender age of 18. By now the Club had moved its base to Carnbane but the construction of a new Tandragee Road meant the pitch had to be re-sited. Two teams continued to function without much success until 1963 when due to a lack of numbers the Second XI was disbanded. As if this was not bad enough, the lease on the Tandragee Road ground had expired, but fortunately another pitch was found nearby.

The next few years saw the Club struggle to field even one team, but fresh talent began to emerge from Newry High School in the shape of Ulster and Ireland schoolboys Freddie Martin and Noel Mears. In 1966 the Club was granted permission to use the new all-weather pitch at Newry High School and a year later with players having returned from other clubs the Second XI was again re-formed. Such was the enthusiasm of the Second XI that in 1967-68 they won the Braddell Shield, the first Olympic side to reach a knock-out Final since 1936.

During the 1970's the First XI were relegated from and promoted to Senior League II on several occasions, but by this stage a Third XI had been formed with the influx of new members, mainly Newry High School pupils.

In 1977 a decision was taken to start fund-raising to purchase the Club's own premises which would contain a club-house and a playing surface. By 1978 the Men's and Ladies' clubs had joined forces, and a Fourth XI mens' team was started.

The early Eighties saw the Club win the Irish Junior Cup, Intermediate League and Intermediate Cup, all in 1981-82. The Junior Cup win was the first in 46 years, with Brian Lockhart scoring all 4 goals in a 4-2 victory over Monkstown Second XI at Banbridge. The Second XI made it to Junior League 1 for the first time in 1982 and after 5 years of fund-raising the land on the Belfast Road was eventually purchased.

In 1983 the foundations of the club-house were laid and with a tremendous effort from a number of members the club-house was opened in June the following year. An official opening was held in September 1984 when an Ulster Presidents XI played Newry Olympic and the ceremony was performed by the Club President Mr Stanley Graham who travelled from New Zealand

An action shot from the match between Newry and an Ireland team to mark the opening of their new facilities in May 1993.

for the occasion. Stanley was the Captain of the Olympic side which first won the Junior Cup in 1935.

In 1985 a Fifth XI men's team was formed and a timely venture was the construction of another all-weather pitch by the local council at Derrylecka. By the end of the 1985-86 Season all the teams were enjoying some measure of success and the Club had 5 representatives on the Ulster U-21 team, with 2 making the Irish U-21's, 4 representatives on the Ulster Indoor U-21's and one on the Senior Ulster and Irish Squads.

The next few years saw the lower teams bring home various pieces of silverware, but in a concentrated effort in the 1989-90 Season, the First XI obtained Senior League I status for the first time in the Club's history and managed to make the Semi-Final of the Irish Senior Cup in the same year. In 1990 the possibility of a synthetic playing surface at the club-house site was first mentioned and a feasibility study was started. In June 1992 work commenced, with the first match taking place in October of that year.

An official opening match between a Newry Olympic Squad and the full Irish Squad was arranged for May 1993 with the Olympic team being boosted by Dutch Internationals Bovelander and Van den Honert and GB Internationals Stephen Martin, John Shaw and Sean Kerly. The match ended in a 5-5 draw, and the large crowd of spectators enjoyed a thrilling game.

In 1995 the First XI reached the Semi-Final of the Irish Senior Cup, and the Second XI the Semi-Final of the Junior Cup - with almost all the other Club teams making a Final or Semi-Final of some sort, or gaining promotion. In the 1995-96 Season, the First XI made further headlines by reaching the Final of the Kirk Cup, which they lost 2-0 to Lisnagarvey.

The playing and social aspects of the Club have improved immensely from both the building of the club-house and the laying of the pitch and are certainly a far cry from the first newspaper advertisement to form a Club in 1911.

NORTH DOWN

North Down Hockey Club, based at The Green in Comber was founded on 24 August 1896 by members of North Down Cricket Club, and is one of the founder-members of the Ulster Branch.

The first elected Captain was Oscar Andrews, a member of the well known Andrews family in Comber who have had a close involvement with both Clubs down the years. William Graham was elected as Secretary and Treasurer for the first Season and went on eventually to serve as President of the Ulster Branch for two years and as President of the Irish Hockey Union for sixteen years from 1905 until 1920.

During September 1896 the first hockey pitch was marked out at The Green at the Castle Lane side of the ground and, give or take a yard or two, has remained in the same position ever since. Unlike many Clubs which started in the years after 1896, North Down had the comparative luxury of a firm base from which to start - in that the Clubhouse, grounds and potential membership were already well-established.

The first Club match in Ulster was played in Comber against Cliftonville on 7 November 1896 in front of a large crowd of spectators with North Down winning 8-0. Oscar Andrews scored six of the goals.

Representatives from North Down and Cliftonville met in December 1896 to discuss the formation of an Ulster Hockey Union and the rules were formalised in April 1897. The first non-local visiting team to Comber was City of Derry who were beaten 8-2 before playing against Cliftonville on the following day. By the end of their first Season, North Down had won all of their 21 games, scoring 116 goals and conceding 23, and a Second XI also played some matches, mainly against sides from Cliftonville.

In September 1899 North Down supplied the first active President of the Ulster Branch in Herbert Andrews and in the same Season won their first two Cup competitions. In the only year when the Keightley Cup was played for on a knock-out basis, Antrim were defeated 3-2 and in the Kirk Cup Final Cliftonville were beaten 4-2. In the next twenty years the Kirk Cup was won three more times but the Club, by now with three teams, went through a poor spell in the 1920s before it was won again in 1928-29.

The Second XI's 3-1 Intermediate Cup victory over CPA in 1931 was the start of the most successful period in North Down's history. The star of the Senior team was James MacDonald, acknowledged as the finest centre-half in the Province, and the team was built around him. MacDonald went on to play 25 times for Ireland, eventually captaining the side, and he was also one of the finest cricket all-rounders ever produced in Ulster. His 159 runs not out in the 1935 NCU Cup Final is still an NCU record!

During the 1930s North Down won the Senior League five times in six years, and the Kirk Cup twice in 1935-36 and 1936-37 and would have possibly continued in the same vein had the Second World War not intervened in 1939.

The 1935-36 Season was the highpoint of North Down's achievements. The Season started with JLO Andrews being elected as President of the Ulster

*The North Down Senior Squad
1989-90, who won the
Intermediate Cup, and gained
promotion to Senior League
Section II.*

Branch, the first time that this honour had been accorded to some one who was still playing, and James MacDonald was selected as Captain of Ireland for the first time. In addition, the Club retained the Kirk Cup, won the Senior League and reached the Irish Cup Final in Dublin. At one stage the cost of purchasing and engraving shields for the plinths of trophies put such a strain on the meagre resources of the Club that an unsuccessful approach was made to have this responsibility transferred to the Ulster Branch!

When competitive fixtures resumed in 1943-44, North Down won the Kirk Cup for the eighth and last time to date by beating Banbridge 3-1 after three periods of extra time. However, as they moved into the 1950s there was a gradual decline in playing standards. This eventually resulted in the Club being placed out of Senior hockey in a Qualifying League, following a restructuring of the Branch Leagues in 1958-59 to allow for promotion and relegation.

The nature of the Club changed permanently in 1961 when North Down Ladies were formed. The Ladies were simply assimilated into North Down without the formal creation of a Ladies Section and this arrangement has continued ever since. The arrival of the ladies had two direct results. Firstly, the already pressing need for additional playing facilities was now an immediate problem and secondly, greater emphasis had to be placed on fundraising and Club administration.

North Down were relegated to Qualifying League B in 1964-65 just when there was an influx of younger players into the Club. This eventually saw them win back their place in Senior hockey in 1968-69, at a time when there was a growing momentum in the Club both on the playing side, and socially.

The next ten years saw the completion of two new Council shale pitches in Comber, but on the field the competitive nature of Senior II saw the Club sometimes struggle to maintain its position. By now, with greater emphasis on coaching and the opening of a bar at the Clubhouse, the number of teams had grown to five, would soon reach six, and the spirit and morale in the Club had never been higher, despite the difficulties on the pitch.

In 1979-80 the Club had a Season in the Intermediate League but bounced back immediately and had several more good years in Senior II before again being relegated in 1988-89. Although again returning at the first attempt, winning the Intermediate Cup in the process, the team went back down again in 1990-91 where they stayed for five long years until the 1995-96 Season, again winning the Intermediate Cup in their promotion year.

All First XI games have been played on the synthetic pitch at Glenford Park, Newtownards since 1994, and Centenary Year in 1996 was celebrated with a number of events, including a celebration game against Cliftonville at the same venue as that very first match in 1896.

North Down has had a thriving youth development strategy for some years, now based on close links with local schools which has produced, and will continue to produce, talented youngsters for the Senior team.

For one of the oldest Clubs in Ulster, the future looks rosy indeed!

OMAGH

Omagh Hockey Club or Omagh YMCA, as it was known in the early days, was formed in 1950 and played in the North West Intermediate League until 1954, before achieving Senior status in the North West from 1955 to 1961. During these years, the team won the North West Intermediate League and Cup in 1953 and 1954 and won the McAlinden Charity Cup in 1958.

Sadly, due to a shortage of players in 1962-63, the Club was forced to fold and after a gap of 20 years Omagh Hockey Club was re-formed to compete in the Intermediate League in the 1982-83 Season. The following Season a Second XI was formed and within 2 years had gained promotion from Junior 7 to Junior 5 before disbanding a year later due to lack of players.

The highlight of the Club's history was its appearance in the Intermediate Cup Final, during the 1986-87 Season, in which the team narrowly lost to Civil Service.

Presently, the First XI is still in the Intermediate League, whilst the Second XI re-formed in the 1990-91 Season and is currently in Junior 8.

The Club always has placed emphasis on the social aspects of the game and has recently revived the North West Cup Tournament with a one-day format at the end of the Season. Invitations are sent to Intermediate and Junior teams within Clubs that are 'West of the Bann' and this has proved very successful over the last few Seasons.

The Omagh First XI, 1995-96, pictured in the new strip which was introduced to mark the tenth Anniversary of the Club. (Picture courtesy of the Tyrone Constitution).

PARKVIEW

Parkview Hockey Club, one of the oldest Clubs in Ulster, was founded in 1898 and was based, as it is today, in the Co Antrim village of Doagh just a few miles from Ballyclare. The Club's founding members were workers from the many local Spinning Mills and from agriculture.

The Club's original name was Fisherwick which was changed to Parkview in 1924. As with many Clubs, the same family names can be found on the membership lists from the foundation to the present day - including the McGrugans, Kirks, and Fentons.

During the War years Parkview did not play, but in 1945 returned under the same name Parkview DMRC, an indication that once again Doagh Mill was taking an active interest in the Club. Indeed the Mill donated the present two acres of grounds to the Club. In 1952 the title of DMRC was dropped, as many more members with no connection to the spinning industry were joining the Club.

It may surprise some people to learn that Parkview have won almost every major hockey trophy in Ulster, the only exception being the Keightley Cup for the Ulster Senior League, and also the Irish Senior Cup. The Second XI has won the Irish Junior Cup several times.

Through the Fifties and Sixties the Club had many good years (winning the Kirk Cup, and Anderson Cup). However, a milestone was reached in 1970, with the opening of a club-house built by the members, and in 1974 it was renovated to include a bar. Now playing in Senior League II Parkview has been a match for any team on their pitch beside the Sixmilewater (stories still abound of opponents and even umpires ending up very wet, but no one who met this fate has ever admitted it!)

The Parkview Senior Squad for the Season 1996-97.

In 1983 the Club was relegated to the Intermediate League and it took 11 years to regain Senior status. Promoted in 1994, Parkview is now strongly established as a progressive Senior Club. It fields three teams every Saturday, though it is unfortunate that the Senior team has to play its home matches on the artificial turf at the Valley Leisure Centre. Plans are advancing for the laying of an artificial pitch at Doagh and this will hopefully be a reality in the Club's Centenary Year in 1998.

PORTADOWN

Hockey was played in Portadown before the Second World War but very little is known about this era. The Club, as it is today, was formed in 1951. The men behind the formation of the present day Club were both Leinster players - Rev DC Jameson (Trinity College) and JTN McGaffin (Pembroke Wanderers). Other men with great enthusiasm for the game were Billy Graham and Charlie Lambe.

The Inaugural meeting was held in Thom's cafe with fourteen intending members present. The Club colours chosen were, as today, Royal blue and white. The Council had promised a pitch but little else! The fees for the year were 12/6, and the first Captain was Billy Graham, later to become Club President.

Banbridge proposed and Newry seconded that Portadown become affiliated to the Ulster Branch. A bank loan enabled the Club to pay affiliation fees and provide the raw materials for making posts, backboards and other equipment. The nets were made by a local unemployed fisherman!

The first competitive match was played on October 27, 1951 in the Junior League. The Club lost but in their first Season they had a successful record: runners-up in the League, beaten in the Braddell Shield Final, and beaten in the Semi-Final of the Junior Cup.

The Club gained promotion in 1961 to the then Intermediate League, under the captaincy of Ray McKay. Three years later with Jim Barriskill as Captain Portadown won Qualifying League B. This meant that Senior hockey came to the town, just one year before the Club moved to Chambers Park and the advent of a shale pitch, a far cry from the bumpy grass pitches of the Public Park and Lurgan Road!

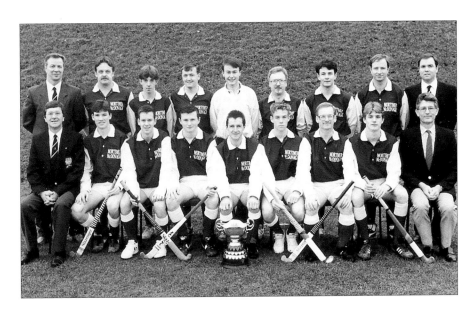

The Portadown First XI Squad, with officials, who won the Intermediate Cup in 1990-91.

WJ Lynas (Centre, with walking-stick) who captained the Ulster Senior Inter-provincial Champions of 1922. Mr Lynas, pictured here with Portadown members in 1968, awarded the Lynas Cup (a miniature of the Leinster Regiment Cup, the Inter-provincial Trophy) to the player who did most to further the name of Portadown Hockey Club, on and off the field. Since 1968 the Winners have included Bill Gillespie, Ronnie Harkness, Victor Mullen, Philip Mehaffey, Fergie Cosgrove and John Fleming.

In 1968 the Club was again relegated from Senior hockey and for many years were contenders for promotion. In 1976, Captained by current Club President Des Gregg, Portadown won the Intermediate title in a nail-biting 3-2 play-off with Raphoe to regain Senior status.

In 1981 Portadown became Senior II Champions under the captaincy of Fergie Cosgrove but unfortunately suffered relegation the next Season to the Intermediate League.

A period of re-building then took place and this resulted in winning the Intermediate Cup in 1991. There was a notable League and Cup double the following season, under the captaincy of John Fleming, to regain Senior status.

Whilst the Second and Third XIs have remained in the lower regions of the Junior Leagues they have had their share of success with League, Braddell Shield, Junior Shield and Minor Cup titles over the years.

Off the field Portadown has in recent years provided two Ulster Branch Presidents in Bill Gillespie and Sammy Jones whilst several local players made their mark with other Clubs including Fergie Cosgrove (RUC and Banbridge), John Cosgrove (RUC), Trevor Burns (Banbridge) and John Fleming (Cookstown), now happily back with his home Club.

The Club has struggled over the years in a rugby/football area, as hockey was not a recognised school sport - though this has improved in recent years due to the Club's own youth policy. With a synthetic pitch for the 1996-97 Season, due in no small measure to the work of both the Men's and Ladies' Clubs, it is hoped the game will really take off in the area.

Finally, on an historical note. One of the annual Club trophies was donated by Portadown-born WJ Lynas who captained the Ulster Senior Inter-provincial winning side in 1922. As a memento he was awarded an exact replica, in miniature, of the Leinster Regiment Cup awarded to the Inter-provincial Champions. Now known as the Lynas Trophy, it is awarded to the player who has done most to further the name of Portadown Hockey Club both on and off the field.

PORTRUSH

Portrush Hockey Club was formed in 1909, following a meeting in the town's Osborne Hotel on 29 September. The first President was F Audinwood, and the first Captain was RA Bailey, who chaired the original meeting. The Club achieved early successes, winning the Derry and Antrim League in 1913 and 1914, and the Kerr-Smiley Cup in 1912, 1913 and 1914. The Club's success was mirrored by the individual achievement of the youthful James McVicker of Portrush and Queen's who was capped for Ireland against Wales in 1914, winning 2-1 at Cardiff. That Season Ireland also beat Scotland 4-2 in Dublin and drew 1-1 with England in Birmingham.

After the First World War, during which hockey was suspended, the Portrush Club began playing again, and achieved success in 1922 by winning the Braddell Shield in the Final against Lisnagarvey Second XI, and winning the Intermediate Cup the next year - again by beating Lisnagarvey Second XI. Success continued in the Twenties, with Portrush winning the North-West Senior Cup in 1924, 1927 and 1928.

Further success was to follow, and with a new generation of players in the Thirties, Portrush won the Irish Junior Cup in 1932. One of their players that day was Fred Daly, who went on to become the Open Golf Champion. For the rest of the Thirties, Portrush played in the Senior Qualifying League, and towards the end of that decade they won the Ulster Section of the Irish Senior Cup.

The Portrush side which won the Irish Junior Cup in 1946. It was reported that bonfires were lit in the town to welcome home the victorious team. Hugh Patton, who played outfield for Ulster and later for Portrush as a goalkeeper, is pictured here in the Front row, second from left.

Fred Daly, the Open Golf Champion, was a member of the Portrush team which won the Irish Junior Cup, for the first time, in 1932.

Though hockey was suspended at the beginning of the Second World War, the all-Ireland Cup competition continued, and Portrush won the Irish Junior Cup in 1943, for the second time. Don Minihan, a member of that Cup-winning side, later played for Ireland. In 1946 Portrush again won the Irish Junior Cup, by beating Monkstown 2-0 in Dublin. It was reported that the winning team was greeted with bonfires in Portrush when they returned with the Cup.

Portrush played their home games at Randal Park from 1935-48, and since then at Seaview Park. Their first home ground, from 1911-35 was at Metropole.

After the Second World War, Portrush became a Senior side, and in 1947 won the first of the Club's three Kirk Cup victories. They also won the Ulster Section of the Irish Senior Cup in 1947 but lost in the Final to Dublin University. One of the Club's most noteworthy Anderson Cup successes was in 1949 when they beat the then all-Ireland Champions Banbridge in the Bladon Drive Final on Boxing Day. One of their outstanding players was young Howard Adams.

In the Fifties, Portrush won the North West Association's Festival Cup, and in 1958 the Senior League B Division Championship. They tied the test match 2-2 against First Division Winners Banbridge, and both names were inscribed on the Keightley Cup.

The regular supply of good young players from Bushmills Grammar School was a boon for the Club, and when Portrush beat Queen's University 2-0 in the Anderson Cup Final at Blaris in 1962, it heralded a period of sustained success. In 1964, Portrush beat Lisnagarvey 2-1 in the Ulster Final of the Irish Senior Cup, but without schoolboy players Tommy Woods and Stan McCurdy who were on duty for the Ulster Schools XI, they lost the Final in Dublin.

The next Season Portrush won the Anderson Cup for the third time, by beating Lisnagarvey 4-1. They also beat Banbridge 2-1 in the Kirk Cup Final, and they again reached the Final of the Irish Senior Cup, in 1965; but after a 1-1 draw in Belfast against Dublin YMCA they were beaten 1-0 in the Dublin replay after extra time.

The halcyon days of the Sixties have not been repeated, though they won the Kirk cup again in 1970. The closure of Bushmills Grammar School was a heavy blow to the Club, as it cut off the supply of young players. Portrush were relegated to the Intermediate League in 1988, and won the Intermediate Cup in 1989, for the second time in their history. Unfortunately, they lost successive Intermediate Cup Finals - 1-3 to North Down in 1990, and 2-7 to Portadown a year later. However, Portrush's recent history is more encouraging, and in 1993 they became Intermediate League Champions, with an unbeaten programme in which only six points were dropped and only seven goals conceded in regaining Senior status for the first time in five Seasons.

Over the years many people have worked hard to keep hockey alive in the Portrush area. As well as noted success as a Club, Portrush have had a number of outstanding individuals including in recent years Ronnie McManus, also of Queen's, and the peerless Jimmy Shanks, both of whom played for Ireland.

QUEEN'S

A Men's Hockey Club was formed at Queen's in the latter part of last Century. The Belfast News Letter reported the Ulster Branch AGM of 19 September 1898, and recorded that "a committee meeting was held afterwards when Queen's College Hockey Club was admitted to membership." Queen's was known as a 'College' until it was granted its Charter as a University in 1908.

The early Queen's team struggled in the newly-formed Senior League, and during the 1900-01 Season the Club finished at the bottom, with only 2 points. Its dismal record was: Played 11, Won 1, Lost 10, Goals for 5, Against 48!

Incidentally, Antrim pipped Banbridge by one point to win the League, with the other teams ranked as follows: Cliftonville, North Down, Lisburn, Ulster, Bangor, and, of course, poor old Queen's College.

With a new generation of students, the Club's fortunes improved dramatically, and in 1912 Queen's won the Irish Senior Cup and the Keightley Cup. It may have been no coincidence that the University around that time boasted several Internationals, including (and mainly) the Rentoul family - AT Rentoul gained the first of his three Caps in 1909 as did JL Rentoul, also with three Caps, while RWR Rentoul won his single Cap in 1911. Yet another Rentoul, this time WW, won the first of his four Irish Caps in 1920.

There were three other Caps in those years prior to the outbreak of World War I - EM Dillon and E Purce in 1913, and S McVicker in 1914. Such evidence points to a University pool of good players who helped the Club to

This picture of the Queen's College hockey team dates from 1904-05. The changing facilities consisted of the shed in the background!

Queen's University First XI 1959-60, Winners of the Mauritius Cup, the Irish Universities Championships. Included are Internationals Bob Poots (Front row, second from right), and Ken Shooter (Front row, extreme right), who died tragically at an early age.

win the Irish Senior Cup, and the Keightley Cup in 1912 but as with all University teams, the students left and the continuity was lost.

After the War, Queen's fielded other International players, including SR Malcolmson who won 14 Caps with Queen's and Banbridge between 1921 and 1930, and SC Courtney who won his single Irish Cap in 1926. In the Season 1927-28, Queen's won the Priory Cup which was at that time awarded to the top team in the Wednesday League.

Queen's won the Anderson Cup in 1935-36, for the first of three times - the others being in 1941-42, and again in 1956-57. Queen's also lost 0-2 in the Anderson Cup Final in 1962 to Portrush.

During its long history the Club had some notable successes, and produced many first class players, but Queen's - unlike most other Clubs - was never in control of its own destiny because students stayed at the University for only a few years, and then moved on - taking their skills with them. The list of Queen's International players is extensive and includes, as well as those mentioned earlier, Philip Anderson, Robin Bailey, J Browne, WA Browne, JC Carson, John Clarke, Norman Crawford, Neil Dunlop, Terry Gregg, Jimmy Kirkwood, John McCartney, Billy McConnell, Ronnie McManus, Tony McMillan, Wally Mercer, Ivan Morris, Bob Poots, Reg Quinn, Noel Quinn, Ian Raphael, Ken Shooter, Ronnie Wilson, Frank Young, and many others.

Perhaps Queen's outstanding achievement in recent years was in winning the Irish Senior Cup (and Corken Cup) in 1972, for the second time in its history and again in 1981 when the team was captained by Peter McCabe, later of Lisnagarvey. The Club literally lives from year to year and somehow manages to blend each batch of new undergraduates with more experienced campaigners, to form sides which vary from being 'useful' to 'formidable'. None was more so than the 1972 team which beat Monkstown 3-0 in the Irish Senior Cup Final, with a goal by Philip Anderson and two by Terry Gregg, including one characteristically brilliant solo effort.

Queen's has rigorously maintained its standards for awarding Hockey and other 'Blues', which remain a prized possession. The Club has played its own significant role in Ulster hockey over the years, not only in keeping the game alive in University circles, but also in acting as a training ground and as an unofficial nursery for some of the best players in the history of Ulster and Irish hockey. Some old 'Blues' at times think of what it might have been like if a solid pool of former 'Blues' had been encouraged to form a Club down the years, but that, unfortunately, is another story.

Queen's Old Boys

The Club was formed in 1994 by students who had mainly played in the Queen's Junior teams. The intention was to provide a vehicle for those who wished to maintain their connection with University hockey and were not committed to other Clubs or who might otherwise have stopped playing altogether.

They began playing in the Intermediate League and in the first Season 1994-95 they finished sixth and joint fifth the next year.

At present the Club is unable to field a Second XI but numbers are increasing. David Mitchell and Martin Scott have both represented Junior Ulster, as members of the new Club.

RUC

The RUC Men's Hockey Club was established in 1935 and its first Captain was REG Shillington. The Club played at Newtownards beside the old RUC Training School. In the 1938-39 Season the Club won the Braddell Shield.

There are very few records in existence from the early days of the Club. However, it is known that the Club took a very active part in all competitions throughout Ireland, winning the Irish Junior Cup in 1952 against Monkstown (2-1). The match was played at Cliftonville, and the team on that occasion was Armstrong, Shaw, Graham, Reid, Russell, Fleming, Cowan, Bradley, Tweedie, Higginson, and McDowell.

The first RUC Officer to be elected to the Ulster Branch was John Graham in 1953. In 1956 the RUC Athletic Association bought grounds, from the old CPA at Newforge Lane on the edge of the River Lagan in South Belfast. Following the purchase, RUC gradually moved towards Senior League status.

During the 60s and 70s the RUC played with two teams in Ulster hockey, finding it extremely difficult to maintain sides and compete against growing opposition. Not that the players were apathetic, but circumstances were such with regard to the civil unrest that duty commitments often prevented their availability for selection.

In 1971 the RUC clubhouse at Newforge Lane was damaged in a terrorist attack and the Hockey Club then played at Shore Road, Church Road, and latterly at Manse Road for some years.

In 1982 they entered the British Police Championships for the first time. Winning their way through to the Final which was played at Leeds, their

The RUC team which played Bangor at Greencastle in March 1962. In the Back row is Inspector-General W Howard (fourth from left), and (three places to the right), Adrian Ringland, father of Trevor Ringland the Irish Rugby International. The officiating umpires were the very youthful Billy Jordan, extreme right, and Des Simon, extreme left.

opponents were the London Metropolitan Police, whom they beat 3-1.

Since then the RUC First XI have competed in the competition every year, winning it on 11 occasions against opposition from 26 other police forces. Over the recent years the Club have been represented on the British Police representative team against the Army, Royal Navy and Royal Air Force, by Tommy Hughes, David Meeke, Ricky Cox, Norman McManus, Gary Nelson, Ian Forbes, Norman Mulholland, Terry Mulholland and David Purdy.

Ricky Cox has captained the Ulster Junior side on several occasions. Billy Anderson and David Dunwoody have participated in the Club at both player and administrator level and have represented the RUC at the Ulster Branch.

The unique circumstances surrounding the RUC Hockey Club mean that unlike other Clubs there are no youth teams and therefore no 'nursery' of young talent, necessitating all players joining at Senior level. This in no way diminishes the commitment each week of the players nor their enthusiasm for the game. This, of course, is what the game is all about.

RAPHOE

Hockey has been played in Raphoe since the early 1900s, with a few 'breaks' in between. At the start, Raphoe played in the North West League, travelling to places like Omagh, Strabane, Derry and Convoy.

Although there are very few records for the early years, Raphoe were reasonably successful in that period, with the team winning the North West Senior League and the Charity Cup, in the mid-Twenties.

The Club continued successfully in the North West League (which was affiliated to the Ulster Branch) and the Season of 1945-46 proved to be one of its most successful, winning the North West Senior Cup, North West Senior League and the McAlinden Charity Cup. Their League record for the Season was - played 23; won 20; drew 2; lost 1; goals for 79; goals against 24.

Unfortunately this successful Season was just before the Club had its first major set-back. In the late Forties Raphoe failed to field a team for several Seasons, until in 1951 people like Jack Willoughby and Dr Wray and others re-formed Raphoe Hockey Club.

That team continued once again to be successful in the North West League and even in their first match back, they drew with RNAS (the Navy team) - a significant achievement. This team continued to play until the late Sixties, when the Club again ran into difficulty. The demise of the North West League forced Raphoe to stop, as the travel commitments were too much.

Raphoe formed for the third time in 1972 when the Club's present Chairman - Uel Blair, Billy McConnell, Cairns Witherow and Jeffrey Vance got together to start the Club and to take on the travel commitments. They made a good start, and in their first Season Raphoe won Section Two of the Intermediate League, which became a single League the next year.

In 1974-75 Raphoe fielded two teams, for the first time. The First XI continued to do well, and in the 1975-76 Season they narrowly missed out on promotion to the Senior League, losing 3-2 to Portadown in the play-off. At their Annual Dinner Dance that year, the former Irish Hockey Union President, Mr Walter Dowdall described Raphoe as "a Club that arose out of nothing to what is generally regarded as the most forward looking, efficiently run and progressive Club in the 32 Counties."

In 1976 Raphoe fielded three teams and won promotion to the Senior League Section II, and later continued its success, fielding four mens teams.

The 1978-79 Season was very successful, with Raphoe winning promotion to Senior I and reaching the last eight of the Irish Senior Cup, only to be beaten 5-0 by Dublin YMCA. However, Senior I proved too tough, and they were relegated in their first Season.

Hockey continued to flourish in the town with the opening of a new £30,000 all-weather pitch at the school. Raphoe consolidated over the next few Seasons, and in 1985-86 were promoted again to Senior I. Again, however, it proved too tough and they were relegated in their first Season. Sadly, hockey in the Club declined somewhat over the next few years, and in 1991-92 the Club was only fielding two men's teams.

Raphoe Hockey Club, 1945-46, Winners of the North West Senior League and Cup, and the McAlinden Charity Cup. Out of 23 games the team won 20, drew 2 and lost 1.

Once again Raphoe showed that they were not a team to lie down easily, and fortunes started to rise. The 1993-94 Season proved as successful as any, with Raphoe being promoted to Senior I for the third time, and reaching the last eight of the Irish Senior Cup, only losing 1-0 after extra time to eventual finalists Banbridge. Their final League table position that year was - played 22; won 17; drew 5; lost 0; goals for 47; goals against 9. The 1994-95 Season proved third time lucky for Raphoe, as they stayed in Senior I, and are now about to enter their third Season there. This success proved fruitful for the Club as they now field five mens teams and two Ladies teams.

Under the circumstances Raphoe is a remarkable Club. Situated in the Irish Republic, but playing their hockey in Northern Ireland, they face round-trips of 180 miles on a Saturday, sometimes taking a bus with several teams on board. Travel can cost the Club in the region of £4-5,000 per year.

The Club has produced some fine hockey players, with several Irish Junior representatives, namely Don Caldwell, Richard Eaton, Billy Pearson, and Vincent Devenney, as well as a number of full-Ulster Caps throughout the years. Bearing in mind that the Club only draws players from the Royal and Prior School, the fact that Raphoe have continued to flourish is a credit to all concerned.

SOUTH ANTRIM

At the conclusion of a meeting held in conjunction with the Lisburn Gymnastic and Physical Culture Club on 3 September 1912, a further meeting was held with a view to inaugurate South Antrim Hockey Club. Cecil Coulter was elected as Captain and he gave the members an idea of the probable cost of 'togs' - Stick 7/6d; Boots 4/6d; Jersey 3/10d; Pants 1/6d; Stockings 1/6d ... Total 18 Shillings!

The first general meeting was held on 12 September 1912, when a Club constitution was agreed. The Club colours chosen were Coronation Blue with dark red sash, later changed to red and black horizontal stripes and finally to the present colours of red and black squares. The initial subscription was Senior 7/6d and Juniors 3/6d. A field was rented at Belsize Road, Lisburn at a cost of £2 per half year.

The Club, along with North of Ireland, were admitted to the Ulster Branch at their AGM on 30 September 1912. Gaining new members was obviously not a problem - despite the fact that there were already two other Clubs in Lisburn, a Second XI was formed in November of that year. The First XI were placed in the Minor League and at the end of the first Season had played sixteen games, winning four, losing nine and drawing three.

Although it is not documented in the Minutes, the Club appears to have developed a strong connection with the linen mill at Hilden, and the First President was JM Barbour. Indeed the Barbour family had a long connection with the Club until well after the Second World War. It is interesting to note, bearing in mind that this was the Home Rule period, that the First Patron of the Club was Captain James Craig, MP, later to become Lord Craigavon and the First Prime Minister of Northern Ireland. A Vice-President was CC Craig who later fought at the Somme in 1916 and became MP for South Antrim.

During the First World War only friendly games were played, and it is recorded that thirty-six members served in HM Forces during the War, a remarkable record for a small Club. In 1919 the First XI moved to Junior League hockey and in 1921 joined the Senior League. The home grounds changed frequently until 1921, when they moved to a site at Forthill owned by Friends School. The first major success was the winning of the Kirk and McMeekin Cups in 1921-22.

It appears that sizeable crowds attended both South Antrim and Lisnagarvey games and home fixtures were arranged so as not to clash. Players were keen to travel, and trips were made on Boxing Day 1923 and 1924 to Dublin to play Monkstown. (The cost of overnight stay at Jury's Hotel was 7 Shillings!)

The South Antrim First XI, 1920-21, who won the Northern Junior League.

In February 1925, the Club pavilion was destroyed by fire - the full claim of £100 was paid by the Insurance Company and a new pavilion was opened in October that year by Sir Robert Baird.

South Antrim continued in the Senior League until March 1940 when the Club ceased to function due to the Second World War. The Club recommenced playing in September 1945 and remained in the Senior League until around 1960. However, they were finding it more and more difficult to attract quality players and with the advent of promotion and relegation, the First XI were (by 1970-71) playing in Intermediate League II. Indeed they had barely enough players to field two teams, and only for the loyalty of a small band of enthusiasts the Club may well have ceased to exist.

The South Antrim team who played a President's XI to mark the Club's 75th Anniversary, in 1987. The strengthened South Antrim side included Jimmy Kirkwood, Kenny Morris, and John Clarke.

The year 1972 saw a welcome upturn in the Club's fortunes when the Beechlawn Club from Dunmurry decided to merge with South Antrim. This expanded the playing membership of the Club considerably and enabled a Third XI to be formed. The Junior teams in the Club enjoyed considerable success during the 1970's, and in 1979 the First XI finally made a welcome return to Senior League II hockey.

Since then most of the Club's recruitment has been from Wallace High School although this has diminished over the past few years when the school decided to give priority to rugby rather than hockey. However, relationships with the school remain excellent, and it is imperative for the future of the Club that this link is maintained.

Unfortunately the First XI were relegated to the Intermediate League in the 1993-94 Season, but the next year won the Intermediate Cup and narrowly missed promotion both in 1994-95 and 1995-96.

South Antrim now field four teams; First XI Intermediate League; Second XI Junior League II; Third XI Junior League V; and Fourth XI Junior League VI. Home fixtures have for a number of years been played at Lisburn Leisure Centre, although the First XI are currently playing their games at University of Ulster, Jordanstown.

The Club is fortunate to have a strong committee ably led by Chairman Adrian Hunter and is financially in a sound position - thanks to the dedication of Treasurer Eric Cunningham who joined from Beechlawn in 1972.

Obviously South Antrim wishes to return to Senior League hockey as soon as possible but the long-term aim is to continue providing facilities which will encourage more and more young people in the Lisburn area to play hockey.

WANDERERS

Wanderers Hockey Club was founded in 1985 and played its first competitive match in the Intermediate League in the 1985-86 Season. The Club was based at Larkfield Secondary School on the Black's Road in Dunmurry. The original membership was 13 playing members and in that first Season one team was fielded.

The Club was soon able to field two teams, and in the 1986-87 Season a Second XI was entered in Junior League 5. The Club continued to expand and by the late 1980s a Third XI was formed. For a number of reasons including the need to use artificial surfaces, Wanderers have lived up to their name by rarely playing at the same venue for consecutive Seasons. The Club has played home matches at various locations including Larkfield, Boucher Road, Laurelhill, Valley Leisure Centre, Ormeau, Friends School Lisburn and Jordanstown. This illustrates the difficulties faced by small young Clubs that have limited resources and members.

Now in its eleventh year, the Club has two teams currently in the Intermediate League and Junior League 6 respectively. High points for the Club have been the First XI winning the Intermediate League in 1988-89, 3 Intermediate Cup Final appearances, an Irish Junior Cup Semi-final appearance in 1993-94 and an Irish Senior Cup 3rd round appearance in 1989-90, and for the Second XI a Strabane Cup win in 1989-90. Over the years the Club has provided a number of players for the Ulster Junior squad, including, William Redpath, Gordon Huston, Geoff Blakely, Stanley Dixon, Howard Quin, and Andrew Sullivan.

Wanderers Hockey Club, Winners of the Intermediate Cup in the Season 1988-89.

STATISTICS

Matches Played By Ireland in Ulster Since 1897

Date	Venue	Team	Score
10 March 1900	Balmoral	England	L 1-2
8 March 1902	Balmoral	Scotland	L 0-2
5 March 1904	Ormeau	Scotland	W 8-1
3 March 1906	Cliftonville FC	Scotland	W 7-1
7 March 1908	Stranmillis	Scotland	W 6-0
14 February 1920	Ormeau	Wales	W 9-1
3 March 1923	Banbridge	Scotland	L 0-2
27 March 1926	Ravenhill	England	L 1-2
24 March 1928	Ravenhill	England	W 3-2
27 February 1932	Dunmore	Wales	W 3-1
24 March 1934	Dunmore	England	L 1-2
16 March 1935	Dunmore	Scotland	L 2-3
20 March 1937	Dunmore	Scotland	W 5-0
19 March 1938	Dunmore	England	W 3-0
1 April 1950	Celtic Park	Scotland	W 2-1
10 March 1951	Ravenhill	Wales	W 3-1
29 March 1952	Bladon Drive	Scotland	D 3-3
14 March 1953	Cliftonville	Wales	W 4-0
7 April 1956	Cliftonville	Scotland	W 1-0
18 April 1959	Celtic Park	England	L 1-0
15 April 1961	Celtic Park	England	L 3-4
20 April 1963	Celtic Park	England	L 1-2
25 March 1966	Bladon Drive	Scotland	D 1-1
22 April 1967	Bladon Drive	England	D 0-0
5 April 1969	Bladon Drive	Holland	L 0-1
17 April 1971	Bladon Drive	England	L 0-2
3 September 1977	Blaris	Yugoslavia	W 4-0
27 September 1980	Antrim	Scotland	L 0-2
29 September 1980	Blaris	Scotland	W 5-0
30 April 1983	Banbridge	Italy	W 3-1
1 May 1983	Blaris	Italy	W 2-0
17 June 1988	Blaris	Switzerland	W 7-0
18 June 1988	Blaris	Wales	W 2-1
19 June 1988	Blaris	Belgium	W 2-1
2 September 1988	Blaris	Germany	L 1-2
3 September 1988	Blaris	Germany	L 1-2
16 June 1989	Blaris	Spain	L 3-4
17 June 1989	Blaris	France	L 0-1
18 June 1989	Blaris	USA	W 5-1
8 June 1990	Blaris	France	W 2-0
9 June 1990	Blaris	Russia	W 4-3
10 June 1990	Blaris	Australia	L 0-2
31 May 1991	Blaris	Switzerland	L 1-2
1 June 1991	Blaris	Egypt	W 3-1
2 June 1991	Blaris	Canada	D 1-1
7 September 1991	Antrim	Pakistan	L 1-5

Matches Played By Ireland in Ulster Since 1897 (cont'd)

Date	Venue	Team	Score
8 September 1991	Blaris	Pakistan	L 0-2
23 June 1995	Blaris	Scotland	W 1-0
24 June 1995	Blaris	U.S.A.	W 2-1
25 June 1995	Blaris	Spain	L 2-3
14 September 1996	Blaris	Wales	D 2-2
15 September 1996	Blaris	Scotland	W 1-0

Under-21 European Qualifying Tournament

Date	Venue	Team	Score
26 August 1991	Olympia	Sweden	W 6-0
27 August 1991	Olympia	Wales	L 0-1
29 August 1991	Olympia	Switzerland	D 1-1
30 August 1991	Olympia	France	L 1-2
1 September 1991	Olympia	England	D 1-1

Irish International Players from Ulster
Caps Awarded as at 31 August 1996

ALLISTER, AA	Banbridge	1951-61	24
ALLISTER, CB	Banbridge	1979-87	59
ANDERSON, P	Belfast YMCA	1975-79	11
ANDREWS, O	Galway/North Down	1898-99	4
ARMYTAGE-MOORE, H	Antrim	1899-1900	3
ATKINS, J	Queen's	1988	1
BAILEY, RA	Queen's/Belfast YMCA/ North Stafford	1955-61	17
BAILEY, RTS	Lisnagarvey	1926	1
BANNISTER, GW	Lisnagarvey	1922	1
BOWDEN, John	Lisnagarvey	1938-50	19
BOWDEN, Joseph	Lisnagarvey	1934	1
BOWDEN, Michael	Lisnagarvey	1969	2
BROWN, K	Queen's	1966-71	5
BROWNE, WA	Queen's/Mid Surrey	1928-32	8
BULLOCH, S	Malone	1903-09	3
BURNS, H	Mossley	1978-79	15
BURNS, M	Cookstown/Holywood 87	1979-90	107
CARROL, J (GK)	Belfast YMCA/Banbridge	1937-48	15
CARSON, AG (GK)	Antrim/Belfast YMCA	1970-83	90
CARSON, JC	Queen's	1920-22	6
CARSON, RH (GK)	Banbridge	1974	2
CLARKE, D	Lisnagarvey	1990-96	73
CLARKE, GN	North Antrim	1932-36	3
CLARKE, JG	Belfast YMCA/Lisnagarvey	1972-79	56
COATES, E (GK)	Holywood	1932-35	12
COBURN, J	Banbridge	1921-23	6
COBURN, N	Banbridge	1921-28	13
COOKE, N	Instonians	1990-95	43
COOKE, P	Instonians	1984-91	91
CORKEN, J	Lisnagarvey	1951-55	10
COULTER, W	North Down	1907-08	4
COURTNEY, SC	Ulster	1926	1
CRAWFORD, NG	Belfast YMCA	1974-81	39
CULL, Dalzell G	Oxford University	1964	2
CULL, HC	Banbridge	1921	1
DICK, WM	Cliftonville	1924-36	32
DILLON, EM (GK)	Queen's/Holywood/ Lisnagarvey	1913-27	17
DOWD, A	Lisnagarvey	1990-96	65
DUDDY, K (GK)	North Down	1907	1
DUNLOP, EGN	Sheffield Uni/Lisnagarvey	1974-78	32
ENTHWHISTLE, JG	Antrim	1904	1

GEDDIS, R	Lisnagarvey	1991-96	27
GILROY, B	Mossley	1952-53	6
GORDON, D	Mossley	1986	1
GOTTO, CC	Malone	1903-08	11
GREEN, F	Belfast YMCA	1984	1
GREEN, WS	Royal Air Force	1948-55	22
GREENFIELD, H (GK)	Lisnagarvey	1928-31	9
GREGG, TA	Queen's/Belfast YMCA	1970-80	103
HAMILTON, G	Cookstown	1987	1
HARVEY, JH	Banbridge	1922-31	14
HAYES, R (GK)	Banbridge	1912-14	7
HOLLWAY, P	Queen's/Instonians	1990-95	60
HOLMES, EPC (GK)	Cliftonville	1901-08	19
HOSFORD, G	Loughborough Colleges	1965	1
HULL, FG	Lisnagarvey	1908-10	2
IMRIE, W	Malone	1905	1
IRWIN, M	Instonians	1996	2
JACKSON, C	Annadale	1996	1
JOHNSON, S	Lisnagarvey	1952-57	20
JOHNSTONE, JB	Malone	1909	3
KENNEDY, RL	Banbridge	1908-11	8
KERR, RF	North Down	1899	1
KIRK-SMITH, I	London Uni/Collegians/Dublin Uni	1974-75	6
KIRKWOOD, J	Queen's/Belfast YMCA/Lisnagarvey	1981-95	130
KIRKWOOD, T	Lisnagarvey	1933	1
LAMOUR, D (GK)	Cookstown	1980-90	10
LEEBURN, HW	East Antrim	1933	3
LUTTON, E	Newry Olympic	1993-96	11
McANULTY, D	Banbridge	1991-96	60
McBRATNEY, S (GK)	Cliftonville	1898-1900	3
McCABE, WA	Banbridge	1947-49	5
McCALL, E	Banbridge	1900	1
McCARTNEY, JC	Queen's	1956	2
McCAUSLAND, JC (GK)	Queen's	1901-05	3
McCONNELL, WDR	Belfast YMCA/Holywood 87	1979-91	135
McCORMACK, W	Downpatrick	1912	1
MacDONALD, J	North Down	1928-36	25
MacDONAGH, WP	Dublin Uni/East Antrim/Cliftonville	1923-34	29
McELDERRY, T	Antrim	1900	1
McELROY, TG	Banbridge	1951-62	39
McERVEL, EJ	Malone	1907	1
McGLADDERY, N	Banbridge	1977-85	50

McGREGOR, DD	Lisnagarvey	1922-28	19
McKEE, J	Belfast YMCA/		
	Holywood 87	1980-91	108
McMANUS, D	Hounslow	1970-71	6
McMANUS, JR	Queen's	1956	1
McMILLAN, ARW	Belfast YMCA	1958-71	40
McKNIGHT, RF	Banbridge	1920	1
McVEA, B	Cliftonville	1951-52	6
McVICKER, S	Queen's	1914	1
MADELEY, R	Banbridge/Cannock/		
	Three Rock Rovers	1990-93	39
MALCOLMSON, P	Banbridge	1986	2
MALCOLMSON, SR	Queen's/Banbridge	1921-30	14
MARTIN, F	Clftonville/Hounslow	1974-78	24
MARTIN, SA	Belfast YMCA/		
	Holywood 87	1980-91	105
MERCER, WS	Queen's/Lisnagarvey	1962-68	15
MINAHAN, DA	The Army	1949-51	11
MORRIS, I	Belfast YMCA/Lisnagarvey	1983-90	39
MORRIS, K	Belfast YMCA/		
	Holywood 87	1983-90	66
MORTON, J	Banbridge	1923	1
MORTON, WB	Banbridge	1905	1
O'HARA, GW	Cliftonville/Southgate/		
	Anglo Irish/Three Rock		
	Rovers	1947-57	27
PATTERSON, R	Cliftonville	1969	3
POOTS, RB	Newry Olympic	1957	4
PRIESTLEY, GE	Lisnagarvey	1968	1
PURCE, G	Queen's	1913	1
QUINN, Raymond	Lisnagarvey	1967	2
QUINN, Reginald J	Queen's/Lisnagarvey	1966-72	23
QUINN, WN	Queen's/Lisnagarvey	1972-78	62
RAPHAEL, I	Friends'/Queen's/		
	Lisnagarvey	1969-78	70
RAPHAEL, RB	Lisnagarvey	1947	1
REA, S	Antrim	1902	1
RENTOUL, AT	Queen's	1909-12	3
RENTOUL, JL	Queen's	1909-11	3
RENTOUL, RWR	Queen's	1911	1
RENTOUL, WW	Queen's	1920-22	4
RICHARDSON, P	Lisnagarvey	1990-93	18
ROBINSON, FL	Malone/Staines	1908-14	13
ROSE, AD	Cliftonville	1957-69	14
RUSSELL, N	Lisnagarvey	1923	1
SHANKS, J	Portrush	1955-63	8
SHAW, JD	Lisnagarvey	1963-72	32

SHAW, RB	Lisnagarvey	1963	1
SHERRARD, J	Derry	1923	2
SHIELDS, DS	Instonians	1976-77	7
SHOOTER, K	Queen's	1960	3
SIMS, HC	Banbridge	1911-14	8
SINNAMON, WM	Banbridge	1975-83	61
SLOAN, M	Cookstown	1982-95	149
(108 as Captain)			
SMITH, J	East Antrim	1919	3
SMYTH, EF	Banbridge	1911-12	4
STERRITT, G	Queen's/Cliftonville	1990-96	36
STEVENSON, J	Lisnagarvey	1994-96	20
STURGEON, J	Lisnagarvey	1960	1
TAYLOR, R	Lisnagarvey	1990-96	71
THOMPSON, TG	Cliftonville	1947-48	3
TOLERTON, AJ	Friends/Lisnagarvey	1970-76	42
WILKIN, P (GK)	Lisnagarvey	1964	1
WILSON, RB	Queen's/Belfast YMCA	1956-60	16
WILLIS, R	Mossley/Pembroke Wanderers	1986	3
WOOD, HE	Malone	1910	2
YOUNG, FDB	Cliftonville	1971-74	18

Presidents of the Ulster Branch of the Irish Hockey Union

1897-98	Marquis of Duffern & Ava
1898-99	Marquis of Duffern & Ava
1899-1900	Herbert W Andrews (North Down)
1900-01	George Hurst (Antrim)
1901-02	JHS Davidson (Bangor)
1902-03	EM Clayton (Banbridge)
1903-04	Hugh Mulholland (Lisburn)
1904-05	William T Graham (North Down)
1905-06	William T Graham (North Down)
1906-07	Rev Prof Dick (Cliftonville)
1907-08	RW Glass LLB (Banbridge)
1908-09	Alex M Adams (Cliftonville)
1909-10	Alex M Adams (Cliftonville)
1910-11	H Percy Andrews (North Down)
1911-12	William Heney (Antrim)
1912-13	William Heney (Antrim)
1913-14	William Heney (Antrim)
1914-18	Great War
1919-20	William Heney (Antrim)
1920-21	Andrew G Burney (East Antrim)
1921-22	Samuel A Bulloch (Malone)
1922-23	Robert C Bannister (Lisnagarvey)
1923-24	Raymond A Burke DL (North Down)
1924-25	Robert H Coulter (Antrim)
1925-26	Thomas N Anderson (Banbridge)
1926-27	Andrew Rose (Cliftonville)
1927-28	Alfred Lowe (Cliftonville)
1928-29	James Alexander (East Antrim)
1929-30	James Stevenson (South Antrim)
1930-31	A Charles Montgomery (Cliftonville)
1931-32	John V Addy (Knock)
1932-33	S Francis C MacDonald (East Antrim)
1933-34	Thomas Stanage (Banbridge)
1934-35	George W Bannister (Lisnagarvey)
1935-36	John LO Andrews (North Down)
1936-37	James Coburn (Banbridge)
1937-38	James H Church (Portrush)
1938-39	Nathaniel M Clarke (Antrim)
1939-40	Andrew Fowweather (YMCA)
1940-41	{ Richard K Megran (Banbridge) was
1941-42	the Acting President at the Meetings
1942-43	which were held between 1940-43 }
1943-44	Richard K Megran (Banbridge)
1944-45	W Harold Greenfield (Lisnagarvey)
1945-46	D Norman Coburn (Banbridge)
1946-47	J Rowland Guiler (Wanderers)
1947-48	James S Templeton (Cliftonville)
1948-49	Albert E Hunter (South Antrim)
1949-50	Dr John CS Ritchie (Downpatrick)
1950-51	Robert S Craig (Newry Oly)
1951-52	William A Shooter (Banbridge)
1952-53	Edward D Burton (Wanderers)
1953-54	Rev Charles N Sansom (YMCA)
1954-55	James Wilton (Cliftonville)
1955-56	J Kenneth C Armour (Portrush)
1956-57	Andrew F Hayes (East Antrim)
1957-58	William P Jordan (Cliftonville)
1958-59	Cecil C Pearson (YMCA)
1959-60	Gerard Edwards (Civil Service)
1960-61	Herbert E Henshall (Mossley)
1961-62	Harold Burrows (Bangor)
1962-63	Cecil M Wilkinson (Downpatrick)
1963-64	Owen W Peacock (YMCA)
1964-65	William A Cross (Banbridge)
1965-66	H Desmond Simon (Cliftonville)
1966-67	Alexander Taylor (Dunmurry)
1967-68	James McClurg (Downpatrick)
1968-69	G Percival Taylor (North West)
1969-70	R George Blower (YMCA)
1970-71	James Barry (Holywood)
1971-72	Angus M Jamieson (North West)
1972-73	Walter RT Dowdall (Bangor)
1973-74	W Robert J Fawcett (Antrim)
1974-75	Austin Johnston (North Down)
1975-76	F Alexander Glasby (Cliftonville)
1976-77	George A McIntosh (ICL)
1977-78	Stewart Strange (Cloughfern)
1978-79	W Robert Howard (Lisnagarvey)
1979-80	A Dixon Rose (Cliftonville)
1980-81	Francis Baird (Antrim)
1981-82	Robert Campbell (Civil Service)
1982-83	William A Williamson (East Antrim)
1983-84	John V Smyth (Bangor)
1984-85	S Derek Watt (Mossley)
1985-86	Francis H Hollway (YMCA)
1986-87	John E Kennedy (Lisnagarvey)
1987-88	Brian P Hanna (Instonians)
1988-89	Ronald McNamee (Annadale)
1989-90	William Gillespie (Portadown)
1990-91	WR Carson Clarke (Holywood 87)
1991-92	J Gordon McIlroy (Instonians)
1992-93	Nigel McCullough (Newry Oly)
1993-94	R George Houston (Antrim)
1994-95	Samuel G Jones (Portadown)
1995-96	Francis DB Young (Cliftonville)
1996-97	Michael W Graham (Annadale)

Officers of the Ulster Branch of the Irish Hockey Union

HONORARY SECRETARY

1897-1902	John Moore
1902-11	Samuel A Bulloch
1911-12	Raymond A Burke
1912-14	JH Louden
1914-18	Great War
1919-20	WT Coates
1920-23	James H Church
1923-25	DD Persse
1925-29	James H Church
1929-32	S Francis C MacDonald
1932-34	George W Bannister
1934-43	Andrew Rose
1943-45	Thomas H MacDonald
1945-50	James Wilton
1950-54	James H Church
1954-70	Owen W Peacock
1970-88	H Desmond Simon
1988-93	Michael F Parsons
1993-	WR Carson Clarke

HONORARY TREASURER

1897-1920	W Thomas Graham
1920-50	Robert H Coulter
1950-56	James Wilton
1956-57	Ronald W Jess
1957-67	WH (Peter) Mayes
1967-72	Alexander Taylor
1972-74	Alan Gilmore
1974-81	Francis H Hollway
1981-95	Michael W Graham
1995-	G Roy Colvin

BRANCH SECRETARY

1929-43	Thomas H MacDonald
1947-77	Cecil C Pearson

(No Branch Secretary was appointed after 1977)

FIXTURES SECRETARY

1964-89	R George Blower
1989-93	Peter S Wood
1993-	John V Smyth

Ulster Officials of the Irish Hockey Union

PRESIDENTS

1905-20	WT Graham		1978-79	RG Blower
1924-25	RA Burke		1980-81	FA Glasby
1927-28	AG Burney		1985-87	AD Rose
1931-32	A Rose		1989-91	WR Howard
1934-35	RH Coulter		1993-95	BP Hanna
1939-47	AC Montgomery			
1950-51	RK Megran			
1954-55	WA Shooter			
1958-59	Dr JCS Ritchie			
1965-66	AF Hayes			
1970-71	WP Jordan			
1974-75	HD Simon			
1976-77	WRT Dowdall			

HONORARY TREASURER

1986-	FH Hollway

Irish Senior Cup
(Instituted 1894)

1894	Dundrum	1942	Dublin University	1990	Lisnagarvey
1895	Dublin University	1943	Dublin University	1991	Lisnagarvey
1896	Dundrum	1944	Dublin YMCA	1992	Lisnagarvey
1897	Dublin University	1945	Lisnagarvey	1993	Lisnagarvey
1898	Three Rock Rovers	1946	Lisnagarvey	1994	Lisnagarvey
1899	Dublin University	1947	Dublin University	1995	Instonians
1900	Palmerston	1948	Banbridge	1996	Avoca
1901	Dublin University	1949	Dublin YMCA		
1902	Dublin University	1950	Dublin YMCA		
1903	Palmerston	1951	Lisnagarvey		
1904	Palmerston	1952	Lisnagarvey		
1905	Palmerston	1953	Three Rock Rovers		
1906	Dublin University	1954	Dublin YMCA		
1907	Banbridge	1955	Lansdowne		
1908	Three Rock Rovers	1956	Banbridge		
1909	Dundrum	1957	Dublin YMCA		
1910	Monkstown	1958	Lisnagarvey		
1911	Royal Hibernians	1959	Three Rock Rovers		
1912	Queen's	1960	Lisnagarvey		
1913	Royal Hibernians	1961	Belfast YMCA		
1914	Monkstown	1962	Three Rock Rovers		
1915	No Competition		Lisnagarvey		
1916	No Competition	1963	Three Rock Rovers		
1917	No Competition	1964	Three Rock Rovers		
1918	No Competition	1965	Dublin YMCA		
1919	No Competition	1966	Lisnagarvey		
1920	Royal Hibernians	1967	Cork Ch of Ireland		
1921	Royal Hibernians	1968	Cork Ch of Ireland		
1922	Limerick PYMA	1969	Cork Ch of Ireland		
1923	Banbridge	1970	Lisnagarvey		
1924	Banbridge	1971	Lisnagarvey		
1925	Lisnagarvey	1972	Queen's		
1926	Banbridge	1973	Pembroke Wanderers		
1927	Lisnagarvey	1974	Three Rock Rovers		
1828	Limerick PYMA	1975	Cliftonville		
1929	Railway Union	1976	Cliftonville		
1930	Railway Union	1977	Belfast YMCA		
1931	Railway Union	1978	Dublin YMCA		
1932	Cliftonville	1979	Dublin YMCA		
1933	Pembroke Wanderers	1980	Belfast YMCA		
1934	Dublin University	1981	Queen's		
1935	Dublin University	1982	Banbridge		
1936	Dublin University	1983	Belfast YMCA		
1937	Pembroke Wanderers	1984	Banbridge		
1938	Railway Union	1985	Belfast YMCA		
1939	Three Rock Rovers	1986	Banbridge		
1940	Dublin YMCA	1987	Cookstown		
1941	} Lisnagarvey Limerick PYMA	1988	Lisnagarvey		
		1989	Lisnagarvey		

Irish Junior Cup
(Instituted 1895)

Year	Winner	Year	Winner	Year	Winner
1895	Beechfield	1929	Banbridge II	1963	Lisnagarvey II
1896	Sandymount	1930	Naas	1964	Cliftonville II
1897	Avoca School	1931	Cork Old Grammarians II	1965	Avoca II
1898	Three Rock Rovers II	1932	Portrush	1966	Mossley II
1899	Dublin University II	1933	Portrane Asylum	1967	Lisnagarvey IIB
1900	Corinthians II	1934	Portrane Asylum	1968	Cork Ch of Ireland II
1901	Dublin University II	1935	Newry Olympic	1969	Monkstown II
1902	Dublin University II	1936	Newry Olympic	1970	Lisnagarvey II
1903	Dublin University II	1937	Parkview	1971	Lorraine
1904	Kingstown G S	1938	Pembroke Wanderers II	1972	Lisnagarvey II
1905	Naas	1939	Maryborough	1973	Lisnagarvey II
1906	Monkstown II	1940	Maryborough	1974	Lisnagarvey II
1907	Dublin University II	1941	Maryborough	1975	Railway Union II
1908	Monkstown II	1942	Pembroke Wanderers II	1976	Antrim II
1909	Monkstown II	1943	Portrush	1977	Lisnagarvey II
1910	Three Rock Rovers II	1944	Mossley	1978	Instonians II
1911	Dublin University II	1945	Down	1979	Three Rock Rovers II
1912	Three Rock Rovers II	1946	Portrush	1980	Instonians II
1913	Dublin University II	1947	Antrim II	1981	Belfast YMCA II
1914	Ballinasloe Asylum	1948	Antrim II	1982	Newry Olympic
1915	No Contest	1949	Banbridge II	1983	Cookstown II
1916	No Contest	1950	Glenanne	1984	Cork Ch of Ireland II
1917	No Contest	1951	Monkstown	1985	Cookstown II
1918	No Contest	1952	RUC	1986	Mossley II
1919	No Contest	1953	Banbridge II	1987	Lisnagarvey II
1920	Three Rock Rovers II	1954	Dublin YMCA II	1988	Aer Lingus
1921	Dublin University II	1955	Lisnagarvey II	1989	Banbridge II
1922	Waterford	1956	Lisnagarvey II	1990	Lisnagarvey II
1923	College of Science	1957	Railway Union II	1991	Holywood 87 II
1924	Pembroke Wanderers	1958	Lisnagarvey II	1992	Holywood 87 II
1925	Railway Union II	1959	Lisnagarvey II	1993	Cork Ch or Ireland
1926	Pembroke Wanderers	1960	Lisnagarvey II	1994	Banbridge II
1927	Killyleagh, Co Down	1961	Pembroke Wanderers II	1995	Glenanne II
1928	Ards	1962	Lisnagarvey II	1996	Pembroke Wanderers II

Inter Provincial Tournament
Leinster Regiment Cup-Wimmers
(Instituted 1923)

1923	Ulster	1948	Leinster	1973	Ulster
1924	Ulster	1949	Ulster	1974	Ulster
1925	Leinster	1950	Ulster	1975	Leinster
1926	Ulster	1951	Leinster	1976	Leinster
1927	Ulster	1952	Leinster	1977	Ulster
1928	Ulster	1953	Leinster	1978	Ulster
1929	Ulster	1954	Leinster	1979	Leinster
1930	Leinster Ulster	1955	Ulster	1980	Leinster
1931	Leinster	1956	Leinster	1981	Munster
1932	Ulster	1957	Leinster	1982	Ulster
1933	Leinster	1958	Leinster	1983	Ulster
1934	Leinster	1959	Ulster	1984	Ulster
1935	Leinster	1960	Ulster	1985	Ulster
1936	Ulster	1961	Leinster	1986	Ulster
1937	Leinster	1962	Leinster	1987	Leinster
1938	Leinster	1963	Leinster	1988	Ulster
1939	Leinster	1964	Ulster	1989	Ulster
1940	No Competition	1965	Munster	1990	Ulster
1941	No Competition	1966	Ulster	1991	Ulster
1942	No Competition	1967	Leinster	1992	Ulster
1943	No Competition	1968	Ulster	1993	Ulster
1944	Ulster	1969	Leinster	1994	Ulster
1945	Leinster	1970	No Competition	1995	Leinster
1946	Leinster	1971	Leinster	1996	Ulster
1947	No Competition	1972	Ulster		

Winners of the Championship prior to 1923

1897	Leinster	1905	Leinster	1912	Ulster
	Munster		Ulster	1913	Leinster
1898	Leinster		Connaught		Connaught
1899	Ulster	1906	Leinster	1914	Connaught
1900	Leinster	1907	Leinster	1915-19	Great War
1901	Leinster	1908	Leinster	1920	Leinster
1902	Leinster	1909	Leinster	1921	Leinster
1903	Leinster	1910	Leinster	1922	Ulster
1904	Leinster	1911	Ulster		

Irish Times - Monday, 25 January 1897

Inter-Provincial Hockey Match
Played on Saturday, 23 January 1897
in Cork City

LEINSTER v MUNSTER

The First Inter-provincial hockey match between Munster and Leinster was played on Saturday afternoon on the Cork Ground at Blackrock, the result being a draw, each side scoring three goals. Notwithstanding the adverse atmospheric conditions, an extremely large crowd travelled to Blackrock to witness the match. The turf was in good condition, but the snow which fell in the morning tendered it a trifle slippery. The match itself was most interesting; it was fast and several brilliant passages were witnessed on both sides.

Leinster:
Goal;
    TC Perrott;
Full Backs;
    ED Rutherford (Three Rock Rovers), and B Ramsey (Donnybrook);
Halves;
    Blake (Donnybrook), TM Walsh (Palmerstown), and Perrott (Donnybrook);
Forwards;
    F Dobbin (Trinity), WSC Crawley (Trinity), Loch (Donnybrook); HE Rutherford (Three Rock Rovers), and Bowles.

Munster:
Goal;
    FJ Lee (Cork);
Full Backs;
    FJ Murphy (Glenbrook), and RJ Booth (Queen's College);
Halves;
    J Daly (Cork), F McCarthy (Queen's College), and J 'Francis' (Glenbrook);
Forwards;
    A Beale (Cork), F Dale (Cork), F Lyons (Cork), R Corry (Cork), and V Taylor (Glenbrook).

Referee: Mr Devlin

Leinster played with the wind in the first half, but the home side were the first to attack and Taylor scored for Munster. In the second period, play was more even and exciting and Taylor and Dale both registered goals for the Southerners. Subsequently the visitors improved considerably, and before the end drew level; Walsh, Dobbin and one of the forwards scoring.

LEINSTER - 3 Goals   **MUNSTER** - 3 Goals

(NOTE: - The references to 'Queen's College' on the Munster team applied to Queen's College Cork, which together with 'Queen's Belfast' and 'Queen's Galway' formed the three Queen's Colleges in Ireland, established by Queen Victoria in 1845.)

Kirk Cup[1]

1897-98	North Staffs	1933-34	Lisnagarvey	1964-65	Portrush
1898-99	Antrim	1934-35	Banbridge	1965-66	Antrim
1899-1900	North Down	1935-36	North Down	1966-67	Parkview
1900-01	Antrim	1936-37	North Down	1967-68	Cliftonville
1901-02	North Down	1937-38	Banbridge	1968-69	Cliftonville
1902-03	Strabane	1938-39	Lisnagarvey	1969-70	Portrush
1903-04	Cliftonville	1939-40	No Competition	1970-71	Lisnagarvey
1904-05	Antrim	1940-41	No Competition	1971-72	Antrim
1905-06	Banbridge	1941-42	Lisnagarvey		Instonians
1906-07	Antrim	1942-43	Lisnagarvey	1972-73	Lisnagarvey
1907-08	Malone	1943-44	North Down	1973-74	Lisnagarvey
	North Down	1944-45	Lisnagarvey	1974-75	Instonians
1908-09	Banbridge	1945-46	Lisnagarvey	1975-76	Instonians
1909-10	Banbridge	1946-47	Portrush	1976-77	YMCA
1910-11	Banbridge	1947-48	Lisnagarvey	1977-78	Lisnagarvey
1911-12	Cliftonville	1948-49	Portrush	1978-79	YMCA
1912-13	Banbridge	1949-50	Banbridge	1979-80	Lisnagarvey
1913-14	Banbridge	1950-51	Banbridge	1980-81	Instonians
1914-18	No Competition	1951-52	Withheld	1981-82	Lisnagarvey
1919-20	Banbridge	1952-53	Lisnagarvey	1982-83	Banbridge
1920-21	North Down	1953-54	Lisnagarvey	1983-84	Mossley
1921-22	South Antrim	1954-55	Withheld	1984-85	YMCA
1922-23	Lisnagarvey	1955-56	Parkview	1985-86	Banbridge
1923-24	Lisnagarvey		Lisnagarvey	1986-87	Banbridge
1924-25	Lisnagarvey	1904-05	Antrim	1987-88	Banbridge
1925-26	Banbridge	1956-57	Banbridge	1988-89	Cookstown
1926-27	Banbridge	1957-58	YMCA	1989-90	Lisnagarvey
1927-28	Antrim	1958-59	YMCA	1990-91	Holywood 87
1928-29	North Down	1959-60	YMCA	1991-92	Holywood 87
1929-30	Cliftonville	1960-61	Lisnagarvey	1992-93	Holywood 87
1930-31	Cliftonville	1961-62	Lisnagarvey	1993-94	Instonians
1931-32	South Antrim	1962-63	No Competition	1994-95	Lisnagarvey
1932-33	East Antrim	1963-64	Lisnagarvey	1995-96	Lisnagarvey

[1] The Cup was presented to the Branch in 1897, by the late Mr John Kirk JP (Vice-President of Antrim Hockey Club) and known originally as the 'Ulster Senior Challenge Cup' and now as the 'Kirk Cup', and is open to all Senior League teams and such other teams as shall be approved by the Council.

Anderson Cup[1]

1919-20	Banbridge	1945-46	Lisnagarvey	1971-72	Instonians
1920-21	Banbridge	1946-47	Lisnargarvey	1972-73	Banbridge
1921-22	Antrim	1947-48	Antrim	1973-74	Banbridge
1922-23	Lisnagarvey	1948-49	Antrim	1974-75	Banbridge
1923-24	Banbridge	1949-50	Portrush	1975-76	Lisnagarvey
1924-25	Lisnagarvey	1950-51	Antrim	1976-77	Annadale
1925-26	Antrim	1951-52	Lisnargarvey	1977-78	Instonians
1926-27	Banbridge	1952-53	Antrim	1978-79	YMCA
1927-28	Banbridge	1953-54	Lisnagarvey	1979-80	Lisnagarvey
1928-29	Antrim	1954-55	Lisnagarvey	1980-81	Lisnagarvey
1929-30	Cliftonville	1955-56	Lisnagarvey	1981-82	Banbridge
1930-31	Banbridge	1956-57	Queen's	1982-83	Cookstown
1931-32	Cliftonville	1957-58	Lisnagarvey	1983-84	Banbridge
1932-33	Banbridge	1958-59	Parkview	1984-85	YMCA
1933-34	Lisnagarvey	1959-60	Lisnagarvey	1985-86	Banbridge
1934-35	Lisnagarvey	1960-61	Lisnagarvey	1986-87	Lisnagarvey
1935-36	Queen's	1961-62	Cliftonville	1987-88	Holywood 87
1936-37	Cliftonville	1962-63	Portrush	1988-89	Mossley
1937-38	Lisnagarvey	1963-64	Lisnagarvey	1989-90	Holywood 87
1938-39	Antrim	1964-65	Portrush	1990-91	Banbridge
1939-40	No Competition	1965-66	Cliftonville	1991-92	Banbridge
1940-41	No Competition	1966-67	Mossley	1992-93	Cookstown
1941-42	Queen's	1967-68	YMCA	1993-94	Lisnagarvey
1942-43	Lisnagarvey	1968-69	FSOB	1994-95	Instonians
1943-44	Banbridge	1969-70	Banbridge	1995-96	Lisnagargey
1944-45	Banbridge	1970-71	Instonians		

[1] The Cup was presented to the Branch in 1919 by the late Mr TN Anderson (Banbridge Hockey Club) in memory of his brother, Captain JG Anderson MC RAMC of the 1st/6th Black Watch Battalion who was killed on active service in France during the First World War, and known as the 'Anderson Cup', and is open to all Senior League teams and such other teams as shall be approved by the Council.

Keightley Cup[1]

1899-1900	North Down	1935-36	North Down	1966-67	Cliftonville
1900-01	Antrim	1936-37	North Down	1967-68	Cliftonville
1901-02	Banbridge	1937-38	Lisnagarvey	1968-69	Cliftonville
1902-03	Antrim	1938-39	Lisnagarvey	1969-70	Lisnagarvey
1903-04	Banbridge	1939-40	No Competition	1970-71	Cliftonville
1904-05	Antrim	1940-41	No Competition	1971-72	Lisnagarvey
1905-06	Malone	1941-42	No Competition	1972-73	Cliftonville
1906-07	Cliftonville	1942-43	Lisnagarvey	1973-74	Cliftonville
1907-08	Antrim	1943-44	Lisnagarvey	1974-75	Instonians
1908-09	Banbridge	1944-45	Lisnagarvey	1975-76	Cliftonville
1909-10	Banbridge	1945-46	Banbridge	1976-77	Lisnagarvey
1910-11	Banbridge	1946-47	Banbridge	1977-78	Lisnagarvey
1911-12	Queen's	1947-48	Banbridge	1978-79	YMCA
1912-13	Banbridge	1948-49	Antrim	1979-80	YMCA
1913-14	Banbridge	1949-50	Lisnagarvey	1980-81	Lisnagarvey
1914-18	No Competition	1950-51	Lisnagarvey	1981-82	YMCA
1919-20	Banbridge	1951-52	Lisnagarvey	1982-83	Cookstown
1920-21	Antrim	1952-53	Lisnagarvey	1983-84	YMCA
1921-22	Banbridge	1953-54	Lisnagarvey	1984-85	YMCA
1922-23	Lisnagarvey	1954-55	Lisnagarvey	1985-86	Banbridge
1923-24	East Antrim	1955-56	YMCA	1986-87	Banbridge
1924-25	Lisnagarvey	1956-57	Banbridge	1987-88	Banbridge
1925-26	Banbridge	1957-58	Banbridge	1988-89	Banbridge
1926-27	Antrim		Portrush	1989-90	Lisnagarvey
1927-28	Antrim	1958-59	Lisnagarvey	1990-91	Lisnagarvey
1928-29	Cliftonville	1959-60	Lisnagarvey	1991-92	Lisnagarvey
1929-30	Antrim	1960-61	Lisnagarvey	1992-93	Holywood 87
1930-31	Cliftonville	1961-62	Banbridge	1993-94	Lisnagarvey
1931-32	North Down	1962-63	Lisnagarvey	1994-95	Lisnagarvey
1932-33	North Down	1963-64	YMCA	1995-96	Instonians
1933-34	Lisnagarvey	1964-65	Lisnagarvey		
1934-35	North Down	1965-66	Lisnagarvey		

[1] The Cup was presented to the Branch in 1899, by the late Sir Samuel Keightley LLD (President of Lisburn Hockey Club) and known as 'The Keightley Cup' is held for one year by the team winning the Senior League. As the Senior League had not been organised for the Season 1899-1900, this Cup was played for, and won by North Down, in a Knock-out Competition. The Senior League was re-formed the next Season and the Winners have been awarded this Cup ever since.

Corken Cup[1]

1957-58	Lisnagarvey	1970-71	Lisnagarvey	1983-84	Banbridge
1958-59	Lisnagarvey	1971-72	Queen's	1984-85	Belfast YMCA
1959-60	Lisnagarvey	1972-73	Lisnagarvey	1985-86	Banbridge
1960-61	YMCA	1973-74	Lisnagarvey	1986-87	Cookstown
1961-62	Lisnagarvey	1974-75	Cliftonville	1987-88	Lisnagarvey
1962-63	Banbridge	1975-76	Cliftonville	1988-89	Lisnagarvey
1963-64	Portrush	1976-77	Belfast YMCA	1989-90	Lisnagarvey
1964-65	Portrush	1977-78	Lisnagarvey	1990-91	Lisnagarvey
1965-66	Lisnagarvey	1978-79	Belfast YMCA	1991-92	Lisnagarvey
1966-67	Cliftonville	1979-80	Belfast YMCA	1992-93	Lisnagarvey
1967-68	FSOB	1980-81	Queen's	1993-94	Lisnagarvey
1968-69	Queen's	1981-82	Banbridge	1994-95	Instonians
1969-70	Lisnagarvey	1982-83	Belfast YMCA		

McCabe Cup[2]

1968-69	Lisnagarvey 2nds	1978-79	Lisnagarvey 2nds	1988-89	Banbridge 2nds
1969-70	Lisnagarvey 2nds	1979-80	Instonians 2nds	1989-90	Lisnagarvey 2nds
1970-71	Lisnagarvey 2nds	1980-81	Belfast YMCA 2nds	1990-91	Holywood 87 2nds
1971-72	Lisnagarvey 2nds	1981-82	Newry	1991-92	Holywood 87 2nds
1972-73	Lisnagarvey 2nds	1982-83	Cookstown 2nds	1992-93	Lisnagarvey 2nds
1973-74	Lisnagarvey 2nds	1983-84	Belfast YMCA 2nds	1993-94	Banbridge 2nds
1974-75	Lisnagarvey 2nds	1984-85	Cookstown 2nds	1994-95	Banbridge 2nds
1975-76	Antrim 2nds	1985-86	Mossley 2nds	1995-96	Banbridge 2nds
1976-77	Lisnagarvey 2nds	1986-87	Lisnagarvey 2nds		
1977-78	Instonians 2nds	1987-88	Lisnagarvey 2nds		

[1] The Cup was presented to the Branch in 1957 by Mrs Mary Corken in memory of her husband, the late Jimmy Corken (Lisnagarvey Hockey Club) and known as 'The Corken Cup. It is awarded to the Ulster team which reaches the furthest stage of the Irish Senior Cup Competition.

[2] The Cup was presented to the Branch in 1968 by Banbridge Hockey Club in memory of the late P S McCabe, and known as 'The McCabe Cup' and is awarded to the Ulster team which reaches the furthest stage of the Irish Junior Cup Competition.

Hospital Cup[1]

1933-34	Banbridge A	1954-55	No Competition	1975-76	NICS 3rds
1934-35	North Staffs Reg	1955-56	No Competition	1976-77	Raphoe 3rds
1935-36	Parkview	1956-57	King's Scholars	1977-78	Lisnagarvey 6ths
1936-37	Civil Service	1957-58	No Competition	1978-79	Raphoe 4ths
1937-38	East Lancs Reg	1958-59	No Competition	1979-80	Cloughfern 2nds
1938-39	Banbridge 3rds	1959-60	Montalto	1980-81	Cookstown 4ths
1939-40	No Competition	1960-61	Bangor	1981-82	RUC 3rds
1940-41	No Competition	1961-62	Cliftonville 2nds	1982-83	Ballynahinch 2nds
1941-42	RUC	1962-63	No Competition	1983-84	Newry 4ths
1942-43	Down	1963-64	No Competition	1984-85	Saintfield 2nds
1943-44	Mossley 2nds	1964-65	No Competition	1985-86	Kilkeel 2nds
1944-45	Antrim Olympic 2nds	1965-66	No Competition	1986-87	North Down 5ths
1945-46	Mossley	1966-67	No Competition	1987-88	Cookstown 5ths
1946-47	Antrim 2nds	1967-68	No Competition	1988-89	Lisnagarvey 7ths
1947-48	Lisnagarvey 2nds	1968-69	No Competition	1989-90	Ballynahinch 2nds
1948-49	Banbridge 3rds	1969-70	Annadale 3rds	1990-91	Kilkeel 3rds
1949-50	Antrim 2nds	1970-71	Annadale 4ths	1991-92	Raphoe 3rds
1950-51	Cliftonville 2nds	1971-72	FSOB 4ths	1992-93	Collegians 4ths
1951-52	Banbridge 3rds	1972-73	Bangor 4ths	1993-94	Newry Olympic 5ths
1952-53	Cookstown	1973-74	YMCA 4ths	1994-95	Annadale 5ths
1953-54	No Competition	1974-75	Portadown 3rds	1995-96	Cookstown 5ths

[1] The Cup was presented to the Branch in 1933 by the late Dr MJ Nolan (Down County Mental Hospital Hockey Club) and known as 'The County Hospital Cup' was played as a Knock-out, mid-week Competition from 1933-35. From 1935-69 'The County Hospital Cup' was played for as a Knock-out Cup Competition open to all teams not over Intermediate status. Played off in two Sections - Intermediate and Junior/Minor, the Section Winners meeting in the Final. From 1969 'The County Hospital Cup' has been awarded to the team winning Junior League Section 6.

Ireland's Saturday Night Cup[1]

1934-35	Down	1955-56	Parkview	1976-77	Bangor
1935-36	Bangor	1956-57	Parkview	1977-78	NICS
1936-37	Parkview	1957-58	Portrush	1978-79	Raphoe
1937-38	Portrush	1958-59	Mossley	1979-80	Queen's
1938-39	Portrush	1959-60	Cliftonville	1980-81	Portadown
1939-40	No Competition	1960-61	Parkview	1981-82	Bangor
1940-41	No Competition	1961-62	Bangor	1982-83	Annadale
1941-42	No Competition	1962-63	Portrush	1983-84	RUC
1942-43	No Competition	1963-64	Parkview	1984-85	Annadale
1943-44	Mossley	1964-65	Mossley	1985-86	Raphoe
1944-45	Mossley	1965-66	Instonians	1986-87	RUC
1945-46	Mossley	1966-67	RUC	1987-88	Collegians
1946-47	Cancelled - Weather	1967-68	Mossley	1988-89	Queen's
1947-48	Portrush	1968-69	FSOB	1989-90	Newry Olympic
1948-49	No Competition	1969-70	Parkview	1990-91	Bangor
1949-50	Parkview	1970-71	Parkview	1991-92	Cliftonville
1950-51	Mossley	1971-72	Collegians	1992-93	Bangor
1951-52	Parkview	1972-73	Banbridge	1993-94	Raphoe
1952-53	Parkview	1973-74	YMCA	1994-95	Bangor
1953-54	Down	1974-75	Cookstown	1995-96	Cliftonville
1954-55	Parkview	1975-76	Annadale		

[1] The Cup was presented to the Branch in 1934, by the proprietors of the 'Ireland's Saturday Night' and known as 'The Ireland's Saturday Night Cup'. From 1934-39, 1947-48 and 1951-53 the Cup was awarded to the Winners of the Qualifying League. From 1943-46 the Cup was awarded to the Winners of Intermediate League Section A. From 1949-51 and 1953-58 the Cup was awarded to the Winners of Senior League Section B. From 1958-69 the Cup was awarded to the Winners of Qualifying League Section A. From 1969 'The Ireland's Saturday Night Cup has been awarded to the Winners of Senior League Section II.

Cliftonville Cup[1]

1958-59	RUC	1971-72	Stranmillis	1984-85	Down
1959-60	Montalto	1972-73	Newry	1985-86	Collegians
1960-61	Bangor	1973-74	East Antrim	1986-87	Kilkeel
1961-62	Old Bleach	1974-75	NICS	1987-88	NICS
1962-63	Instonians	1975-76	Portadown	1988-89	Wanderers
1963-64	Portadown	1976-77	Raphoe	1989-90	North Down
1964-65	Lissara	1977-78	Collegians	1990-91	Ballynahinch
1965-66	FSOB	1978-79	South Antrim	1991-92	Portadown
1966-67	East Antrim	1979-80	North Down	1992-93	Portrush
1967-68	Cookstown	1980-81	Corinthians	1993-94	Parkview
1968-69	North Down	1981-82	Newry	1994-95	RUC
1969-70	Collegians	1982-83	East Antrim	1995-96	North Down
1970-71	Annadale	1983-84	Collegians		

[1] The Cup was presented to the Branch in 1958, by Cliftonville Hockey Club in memory of Past Presidents, Officials and Players of the Cliftonville Club who gave service to the Ulster Branch and known as 'The Cliftonville Cup'. From 1958-69 the Cup was awarded to the Winners of Qualifying League Section B. From 1969-73 the Cup was awarded to the Winners of Inter- mediate League Section 1. From 1973 'The Cliftonville Cup' has been awarded to the Winners of the Intermediate League.

Braddell Shield[1]

1898-99	Ulster H C	1933-34	Bangor	1966-67	Mossley 3rds
1899-1900	Antrim 2nds	1934-35	Newry Olympic	1967-68	Newry Olympic 2nds
1900-01	Antrim 2nds	1935-36	Mossley	1968-69	Annadale
1901-02	Monaghan	1936-37	South Antrim 3rds	1969-70	Cloughfern 2nds
1902-03	Sydenham	1937-38	RUC	1970-71	Annadale 2nds
1903-04	Holywood	1938-39	RUC	1971-72	Annadale 3rds
1904-05	Downpatrick	1939-40	No Competition	1972-73	Bangor 3rds
1905-06	North Down 2nds	1940-41	No Competition	1973-74	NICS 2nds
1906-07	Lisnagarvey	1941-42	No Competition	1974-75	South Antrim 2nds
1907-08	Clones	1942-43	No Competition	1975-76	Michelin 2nds
1908-09	North Down 2nds	1943-44	Ormeau 2nds	1976-77	Raphoe 2nds
	Randalstown	1944-45	North Down 3rds	1977-78	FSOB 4ths
1909-10	Larne	1945-46	Cliftonville 3rds	1978-79	Parkview 2nds
1910-11	Ballymoney	1946-47	Saintfield	1979-80	Raphoe 2nds
1911-12	East Antrim	1947-48	Parkview 2nds	1980-81	Mossley 3rds
1912-13	Lisnagarvey 2nds	1948-49	Lisnagarvey 3rds	1981-82	Bangor 4ths
1913-14	Holywood	1949-50	Saintfield 2nds	1982-83	Newry Olympic 3rds
1914-18	No Competition	1950-51	Old Bleach	1983-84	RUC 3rds
1919-20	Holywood	1951-52	Mossley 3rds	1984-85	Banbridge 3rds
1920-21	Lisnagarvey 2nds	1952-53	Banbridge 3rds	1985-86	Bangor 3rds
1921-22	Portrush	1953-54	Ballymena	1986-87	Cookstown 4ths
1922-23	Cliftonville 2nds	1954-55	YMCA 3rds	1987-88	Kilkeel 2nds
1923-24	Antrim 2nds	1955-56	Montalto 2nds	1988-89	Instonians 4ths
1924-25	Down	1956-57	Montalto 2nds	1989-90	Down 2nds
1925-26	Wanderers	1957-58	Lisnagarvey 3rds	1990-91	Mossley 3rds
1926-27	City of Derry 2nds	1958-59	RUC 2nds	1991-92	Ballynahinch 2nds
1927-28	Albert Foundry	1959-60	Lissara	1992-93	Cookstown 4ths
1928-29	Albert Foundry	1960-61	Antrim 3rds	1993-94	Annadale 4ths
1929-30	Richhill	1961-62	YMCA 3rds	1994-95	Newry Olympic 4ths
1930-31	Albert Foundry	1962-63	No Competition	1995-96	Raphoe 3rds
1931-32	Albert Foundry	1963-64	Lisnagarvey 3rds		
1932-33	Down County	1964-65	YMCA 3rds		
	Hospital	1965-66	Short & Harland		

[1] The Shield was presented to the Branch in 1899, by the late Mr C Playfair of Messrs Joseph Braddell & Sons and known as the 'Braddell Shield'. From 1899 until 1969 the 'Braddell Shield' was played for in a Knock-out Competition among Junior teams. From 1969 the 'Braddell Shield' has been awarded to the team winning Junior League, Section 5.

McClements Cup[1]

1991-92   Parkview 2nds
1992-93   Cookstown 2nds
1993-94   Kilkeel 2nds
1994-95   RUC 2nds
1995-96   Lisnagarvey 2nds

Strabane Cup[2]

1983-84   Mossley 5ths
1984-85   Portrush 3rds
1985-86   Cookstown 5ths
1986-87   Banbridge 5ths
1987-88   Parkview 3rds
1988-89   Portrush 3rds
1989-90   Wanderers 2nds
1990-91   Lisnagarvey 5ths
1991-92   Antrim 4ths
1992-93   Antrim 4ths
1993-94   Cookstown 5ths
1994-95   Antrim 4ths
1995-96   Antrim 4ths

[1] The Cup was presented to the Branch in 1991, by Mrs Mamie McClements in memory of her husband Mr David McClements (Lisnagarvey Hockey Club) and known as 'The McClements Cup'. It is open to those teams in the Intermediate League and Junior League Sections 1 and 2 who do not enter the Irish Junior Cup or who lose their first match in that Competition.

[2] The Cup was presented to the Branch in 1983, by Strabane Hockey Club (from funds remaining after their dissolution) and known as 'The Strabane Cup'. It is awarded to the Winners of a Knock-out Competition between teams in Junior League Sections 7 and 8.

Mulholland Shield[1]

1903-04	Banford	1938-39	HMS Caroline	1969-70	Annadale
1904-05	Lisnagarvey	1939-40	No Competition	1970-71	ICL
1905-06	North Down 2nds	1940-41	No Competition	1971-72	Kilkeel
1906-07	Malone 2nds	1941-42	No Competition	1972-73	Instonians 3rds
1907-08	Antrim 2nds	1942-43	No Competition	1973-74	Portadown 2nds
1908-09	Larne	1943-44	No Competition		Bangor 2nds
1909-10	Banbridge 2nds	1944-45	No Competition	1974-75	Antrim 4ths
1910-11	Lisnagarvey	1945-46	Crossgar	1975-76	Michelin 2nds
1911-12	North Down 2nds	1946-47	Cancelled - Weather	1976-77	FSOB 3rds
1912-13	Banbridge 2nds	1947-48	No Competition	1977-78	North Down 3rds
1913-14	Antrim 2nds	1948-49	No Competition	1978-79	FSOB 3rds
1914-18	No Competition	1949-50	Banbridge Y C	1979-80	East Antrim 2nds
1919-20	Antrim 2nds	1950-51	Kings Scholars	1980-81	Newry Olympic 2nds
1920-21	South Antrim 2nds	1951-52	Old Bleach 2nds	1981-82	RUC 2nds
1921-22	Holywood 3rds	1952-53	Ballymena 2nds	1982-83	Cliftonville 2nds
1922-23	Ards 3rds	1953-54	Ballymena 2nds	1983-84	NICS 2nds
1923-24	Down 2nds	1954-55	Saintfield 3rds	1984-85	Mossley 3rds
1924-25	Banbridge Tech Sch	1955-56	Cliftonville 4ths	1985-86	Banbridge 3rds
1925-26	Banbridge Tech Sch	1956-57	Cliftonville 4ths	1986-87	Instonians 3rds
1926-27	Cregagh	1957-58	Saintfield 3rds	1987-88	RUC 3rds
1927-28	Richhill	1958-59	Lisnagarvey 4ths	1988-89	Bangor 3rds
1928-29	Ballynahinch	1959-60	Parkview 3rds	1989-90	FSOB 2nds
1929-30	Riddles	1960-61	Lisnagarvey 4ths	1990-91	Bangor 3rds
1930-31	Down CMH	1961-62	Antrim 4ths	1991-92	Bangor 3rds
1931-32	Ballynahinch	1962-63	Cliftonville 4ths	1992-93	Banbridge 3rds
1932-33	Banbridge Tech	1963-64	Banbridge 4ths	1993-94	Annadale 4ths
1933-34	Trinity Coll Mission	1964-65	*No Record*	1994-95	Annadale 3rds
1934-35	Dunmurry 2nds	1965-66	Instonians 4ths	1995-96	Instonians 3rds
1935-36	Whitehouse	1966-67	Crossgar 2nds		
1936-37	Crossgar	1967-68	Instonians 4ths		
1937-38	Crossgar	1968-69	Instonians 4ths		

[1] The Shield was presented to the Branch in 1903, by the late Mr Hugh Mulholland (Lisburn Hockey Club) and known as 'The Mulholland Shield'. From 1903-69 the Shield was awarded to the team winning the Minor League. From 1969-72 the Shield was played for in a Knock-out Competition for teams in Intermediate League Section 2 and Junior League Sections 3 and 4. From 1972 'The Mulholland Shield' has been played for in a Knock-out Competition for teams in Junior League Sections 3 and 4.

McMeekin Cup[1]

1920-21	South Antrim 2nds	1946-47	Banbridge Boys Club	1972-73	South Antrim 2nds
1921-22	South Antrim 3rds	1947-48	No Competition	1973-74	RUC 2nds
1922-23	East Antrim 3rds	1948-49	No Competition	1974-75	Collegians 3rds
1923-24	Anglo American Oil	1949-50	Banbridge Y C	1975-76	South Antrim 4ths
1924-25	South Antrim 3rds	1950-51	Kings Scholars	1976-77	YMCA 4ths
1925-26	South Antrim 3rds	1951-52	Ballynahinch 2nds	1977-78	Lisnagarvey 6ths
1926-27	Cregagh	1952-53	Ballymena 2nds	1978-79	Portrush 3rds
1927-28	Ballycastle	1953-54	Ballymena 2nds	1979-80	Raphoe 4ths
1928-29	Willowfield 2nds	1954-55	Saintfield 3rds	1980-81	Mossley 4ths
1929-30	King's Scholars	1955-56	Cliftonville 4ths	1981-82	FSOB 4ths
1930-31	Glentaisie	1956-57	Cliftonville 4ths	1982-83	Cliftonville 3rds
1931-32	South Down	1957-58	Lisnagarvey 4ths	1983-84	FSOB 4ths
1932-33	Trinity Coll Mission	1958-59	Lisnagarvey 4ths	1984-85	Saintfield 2nds
1933-34	Albert Foundry	1959-60	Antrim 4ths	1985-86	Cookstown 4ths
1934-35	Whitehall	1960-61	Lisnagarvey 4ths	1986-87	Kilkeel 2nds
1935-36	Whitehouse	1961-62	YMCA 4ths	1987-88	Instonians 4ths
1936-37	Ards	1962-63	Mossley 4ths	1988-89	Cliftonville 3rds
1937-38	Mossley 2nds	1963-64	Cliftonville 4ths	1989-90	Newry 4ths
1938-39	Hydepark 2nds	1964-65	*No Record*	1990-91	Kilkeel 3rds
1939-40	No Competition	1965-66	Queen's 4ths	1991-92	Mossley 4ths
1940-41	No Competition	1966-67	Parkview 3rds	1992-93	Mossley 4ths
1941-42	No Competition	1967-68	Instonians 4ths	1993-94	Newry 5ths
1942-43	No Competition	1968-69	Cookstown 4ths	1994-95	Kilkeel 3rds
1943-44	No Competition	1969-70	Instonians 4ths	1995-96	Cookstown 5ths
1944-45	No Competition	1970-71	Lisnagarvey 4ths		
1945-46	Short & Harlands	1971-72	FSOB 4ths		

[1] The Cup was presented to the Branch in 1920 by the late Mr Hugh McMeekin (President of East Antrim Hockey Club) and known as 'The McMeekin Cup'. From 1920-69 the Cup was played for in a Knock-out Competition for teams in the Minor League. From 1969 'The McMeekin Cup' has been played for in a Knock-out Competition for teams in Junior League Sections 5 and 6.

Linden Cup[1]

1922-23	Ards	1948-49	Mossley 2nds	1972-73	Raphoe
1923-24	Holywood 2nds	1949-50	Antrim 2nds	1973-74	Civil Service
1924-25	Antrim 2nds	1950-51	Mossley 2nds	1974-75	Michelin
1925-26	Antrim 2nds	1951-52	Banbridge 2nds	1975-76	No Competition
1926-27	Down	1952-53	Saintfield	1976-77	No Competition
1927-28	Cliftonville 2nds	1953-54	Banbridge 2nds	1977-78	Collegians
1928-29	Ards	1954-55	YMCA 2nds	1978-79	No Competition
1929-30	South Antrim 2nds		Saintfield	1979-80	No Competition
1930-31	Portrush		Montalto	1980-81	Down
1931-32	Down	1955-56	Lisnagarvey 2nds	1981-82	Newry
1932-33	Down	1956-57	Lisnagarvey 2nds	1982-83	Down
1933-34	CPA	1957-58	Lisnagarvey 2nds	1983-84	Down
1934-35	Bangor	1958-59	North Down 2nds	1984-85	Down
1935-36	Banbridge 2nds	1959-60	RUC 2nds	1985-86	Collegians
1936-37	Banbridge 2nds	1960-61	Lisnagarvey 2nds	1986-87	NICS
1937-38	Banbridge 2nds	1961-62	Lisnagarvey 2nds	1987-88	NICS
1938-39	Banbridge 2nds	1962-63	Lisnagarvey 2nds	1988-89	Portrush
1939-40	No Competition	1963-64	Lisnagarvey 2nds	1989-90	North Down
1940-41	No Competition	1964-65	Lisnagarvey 2A	1990-91	Portadown
1941-42	No Competition	1965-66	Lisnagarvey 2B	1991-92	Portadown
1942-43	Mossley	1966-67	Lisnagarvey 2A	1992-93	Larne
1943-44	Banbridge 2nds	1967-68	Lisnagarvey 2A	1993-94	Larne
1944-45	Banbridge 2nds	1968-69	Lisnagarvey 2A	1994-95	South Antrim
1945-46	Banbridge 2nds	1969-70	Annadale	1995-96	North Down
1946-47	Cancelled - Weather	1970-71	Ballynahinch		
1947-48	Antrim 2nds	1971-72	Michelin		

[1] The Cup was presented to the Branch in 1922, by the late Mr SA Bulloch (Outgoing Branch President) and known as 'The Linden Cup' was held for one year by the team winning the Intermediate League from 1922-43 and from 1947-58. The Section Winners played off for the Cup. From 1943-46, the Intermediate League Section B Winners were awarded the Cup. From 1958-69, the Intermediate League Section A Winners were awarded the Cup. From 1969-73, the Intermediate League Section 2 Winners were awarded the Cup. From 1973 'The Linden Cup' has been played for, in various forms, as a Knock-out Cup Competition for Intermediate Clubs.

Davidson Cup[1]

1901-02	Ballymena	1935-36	Saintfield	1966-67	Antrim 3 'B'
1902-03	Sydenham	1936-37	Dunadry	1967-68	Mossley 3 'A'
1903-04	Holywood	1937-38	Albert Foundry 2nds	1968-69	Annadale
1904-05	Downpatrick	1938-39	Banbridge	1969-70	Parkview 2nds
1905-06	East Antrim	1939-40	No Competition	1970-71	Portrush 2nds
1906-07	Lisnagarvey	1940-41	No Competition	1971-72	YMCA 2nds
1907-08	Silverstream	1941-42	No Competition	1972-73	Annadale 2nds
1908-09	Downpatrick 2nds	1942-43	242 Training Reg	1973-74	Lisnagarvey 3rds
1909-10	North Down 2nds	1943-44	Mossley 2nds	1974-75	Instonians 3rds
1910-11	Sydenham	1944-45	Mossley 2nds	1975-76	North Down 2nds
1911-12	East Antrim	1945-46	Mossley 2nds	1976-77	FSOB 2nds
1912-13	Antrim	1946-47	Cancelled - Weather	1977-78	Portrush 2nds
1913-14	Downpatrick	1947-48	Parkview 2nds	1978-79	YMCA 2nds
1914-18	No Competition	1948-49	Saintfield 2nds	1979-80	Raphoe 2nds
1919-20	Holywood	1949-50	Saintfield 2nds	1980-81	Mossley 2nds
1920-21	South Antrim	1950-51	Banbridge Y C	1981-82	Banbridge 2nds
1921-22	Lisnagarvey 2nds	1951-52	Banbridge 3rds	1982-83	Raphoe 2nds
1922-23	Parkview	1952-53	Lissara	1983-84	RUC 2nds
1923-24	Antrim 2nds	1953-54	Cliftonville 3rds	1984-85	Newry 2nds
1924-25	Parkview	1954-55	Saintfield 2nds	1985-86	Raphoe 2nds
1925-26	Wanderers	1955-56	Saintfield 2nds	1986-87	Banbridge 2nds
1926-27	Albert Foundry	1956-57	Montalto 2nds	1987-88	Bangor 2nds
1927-28	Doagh	1957-58	YMCA 3rds	1988-89	Newry 2nds
1928-29	Cliftonville 3rds	1958-59	Lisnagarvey 3rds	1989-90	Bangor 2nds
1929-30	Wanderers	1959-60	Lisnagarvey 3rds	1990-91	Instonians 3rds
1930-31	Cregagh	1960-61	Lissara	1991-92	Annadale 2nds
1931-32	Waringstown	1961-62	Cloughfern	1992-93	Bangor 2nds
1932-33	Down County	1962-63	Courtaulds	1993-94	Kilkeel 2nds
	Hospital	1963-64	YMCA 3rds	1994-95	RUC 2nds
1933-34	Bangor	1964-65	Ballynahinch	1995-96	Instonians 2nds
1934-35	Parkview	1965-66	Portadown 3rds		

[1] This Cup was presented to the Branch, in 1901, by the late JHS Davidson (Bangor Hockey Club) and known as the 'Davidson Cup'. From 1901-69 the 'Davidson Cup' was presented to the overall Winner of the Junior League. The Section Winners played off for the Cup. From 1969 the 'Davidson Cup' has been awarded to the team winning Junior League Section 2.

Bannister Cup[1]

1922-23	Portrush	1947-48	Parkview	1971-72	Lisnagarvey 2nds
1923-24	Belmont	1948-49	Mossley 2nds	1972-73	Lisnagarvey 2nds
1924-25	Portrush	1949-50	RUC	1973-74	Lisnagarvey 2nds
1925-26	Belmont	1950-51	Lisnagarvey 2nds	1974-75	Lisnagarvey 2nds
1926-27	Down	1951-52	Antrim 2nds	1975-76	Lisnagarvey 2nds
1927-28	Ards	1952-53	Cliftonville 2nds	1976-77	Lisnagarvey 2nds
1928-29	Ards	1953-54	Lisnagarvey 2nds	1977-78	Lisnagarvey 2nds
1929-30	Down	1954-55	YMCA 2nds	1978-79	Lisnagarvey 2nds
1930-31	North Down 2nds	1955-56	Lisnagarvey 2nds	1979-80	Lisnagarvey 2nds
1931-32	CPA	1956-57	Lisnagarvey 2nds	1980-81	Instonians 2nds
1932-33	Down	1957-58	Lisnagarvey 2nds	1981-82	Lisnagarvey 2nds
1933-34	Wanderers	1958-59	Lisnagarvey 2nds	1982-83	Cookstown 2nds
1934-35	North Staffs Reg	1959-60	Lisnagarvey 2nds	1983-84	Cookstown 2nds
1935-36	South Antrim 2nds	1960-61	Old Bleach	1984-85	Cookstown 2nds
1936-37	Parkview	1961-62	Antrim 2nds	1985-86	YMCA 2nds
1937-38	Banbridge 2nds	1962-63	Banbridge 2nds	1986-87	Lisnagarvey 2nds
1938-39	CPA	1963-64	Lisnagarvey 2nds	1987-88	Lisnagarvey 2nds
1939-40	No Competition	1964-65	Lisnagarvey 2nds	1988-89	Lisnagarvey 2nds
1940-41	No Competition	1965-66	Lisnagarvey 2nds	1989-90	Lisnagarvey 3rds
1941-42	Mossley & Shorts	1966-67	Lisnagarvey 2nds	1990-91	Lisnagarvey 2nds
1942-43	Albert Foundry	1967-68	Crossgar	1991-92	Banbridge 2nds
1943-44	Lisnagarvey 2nds	1968-69	Banbridge 2nds	1992-93	Banbridge 2nds
1944-45	Portrush		Lisnagarvey 2nds	1993-94	Holywood 2nds
1945-46	Mossley	1969-70	Mossley 2nds	1994-95	Banbridge 2nds
1946-47	Cliftonville 2nds	1970-71	Lisnagarvey 2nds	1995-96	Banbridge 2nds

[1] The Cup was presented to the Branch in 1922, by the late RC Bannister (President of Lisnagarvey Hockey Club) and was known originally as 'The Intermediate Charity Cup' and now known as 'The Bannister Cup'. It was played for by Intermediate League teams in a Knock-out Competition from 1922-58. From 1958-69 the Cup was open to Qualifying League B and Intermediate League teams. From 1969 'The Bannister Cup' has been awarded to the team winning Junior League Section 1.

Ludlow Cup[1]

1977-78	Antrim	1984-85	North Down 5ths	1991-92	Holywood 87 5ths
1878-79	Portrush 4ths	1985-86	Portrush 3rds	1992-93	Newry Olympic 5ths
1979-80	RUC 3rds	1986-87	South Antrim 5ths	1993-94	Ballynahinch 3rds
1980-81	Bangor 5ths	1987-88	Lisnagarvey 7ths	1994-95	Raphoe 4ths
1981-82	Parkview 3rds	1988-89	Portrush 3rds	1995-96	Armagh 2nds
1982-83	Annadale 5ths	1989-90	Wanderers 2nds		
1983-84	Banbridge 4ths	1990-91	Kilkeel 4ths		

North West Festival[2]

1978-79	Queen's 4ths	1984-85	Omagh 2nds	1990-91	Lisnagarvey 8ths
1979-80	No Competition	1985-86	Newry 5ths	1991-92	Portadown 3rds
1980-81	Corinthians 2nds	1986-87	Lisnagarvey 7ths	1992-93	Collegians 5ths
1981-82	No Competition	1987-88	Parkview 4ths	1993-94	Cookstown 5ths
1982-83	Newry 4ths	1988-89	Wanderers 2nds	1994-95	NICS 6ths
1983-84	No Competition	1989-90	Kilkeel 4ths	1995-96	Armagh 3rds

Junior League Cup[3]

1986-87	Collegians 5ths	1990-91	Omagh 2nds	1994-95	No Competition
1987-88	Crossgar 2nds	1991-92	Bangor 7ths	1995-96	No Competition
1988-89	Raphoe 3rds	1992-93	Mossley 5ths		
1989-90	Holywood 87 5ths	1993-94	Newry 6ths		

[1] The Cup was presented to the Branch in 1977, by Antrim Hockey Club in memory of William Ludlow and known as 'The Ludlow Cup' was awarded in the first year, to the Winner of a Colts League. From 1978 'The Ludlow Cup' has been awarded to the Winner of Junior League Section 7.

[2] The Cup was presented to the Branch in 1978, from the old North West District and known as 'The Festival Cup'. It has been awarded to the Winners of Junior League Section 8

[3] The Cup was presented to the Branch in 1986, and known as the Junior League Cup and it has been awarded to the Winners of Junior League Section 9.

Priory Cup[1]

1925-26	Shaftesbury School	1950-51	Old Bleach 2nds	1974-75	Portadown 2nds
1926-27	Durham Light Inft	1951-52	Old Bleach 2nds	1975-76	Antrim 4ths
1927-28	Queen's	1952-53	YMCA 4ths	1976-77	Bangor 3rds
1928-29	Banbridge Tech	1953-54	Ballymena 2nds	1977-78	Raphoe 2nds
1929-30	Banbridge Tech	1954-55	Lisnagarvey 4ths	1978-79	South Antrim 2nds
1930-31	Lisburn Tech	1955-56	Cliftonville 4ths	1979-80	East Antrim 2nds
1931-32	Lisburn Tech	1956-57	Cliftonville 4ths	1980-81	Bangor 3rds
1932-33	South Down	1957-58	Cliftonville 4ths	1981-82	RUC 2nds
1933-34	Trinity Coll Mission	1958-59	Lisnagarvey 4ths	1982-83	Cliftonville 2nds
1934-35	Trinity Coll Mission	1959-60	Lisnagarvey 4ths	1983-84	Newry 3rds
1935-36	Mossley 2nds	1960-61	Lisnagarvey 4ths	1984-85	YMCA 3rds
1936-37	Hydepark 2nds	1961-62	Antrim 4ths	1985-86	Portrush 2nds
1937-38	St Donards 2nds	1962-63	Mossley 4ths	1986-87	Banbridge 3rds
1938-39	St Donards 2nds	1963-64	Cliftonville Colts	1987-88	Instonians 3rds
1939-40	No Competition	1964-65	Antrim 4ths	1988-89	Lisnagarvey 4ths
1940-41	No Competition	1965-66	Queen's 4ths	1989-90	Parkview 2nds
1941-42	No Competition	1966-67	Parkview 3rds	1990-91	Antrim 2nds
1942-43	No Competition	1967-68	Cliftonville 4ths	1991-92	Newry 3rds
1943-44	No Competition	1968-69	Instonians 4ths	1992-93	Raphoe 2nds
1944-45	No Competition	1969-70	Mossley 3rds	1993-94	Ballynahinch 2nds
1945-46	Crossgar	1970-71	Antrim 3rds	1994-95	Annadale 3rds
1946-47	Parkview 2nds	1971-72	Annadale 2nds	1995-96	Antrim 2nds
1948-49	No Competition	1972-73	Instonians 3rds		
1949-50	Banbridge Y C	1973-74	Banbridge 3rds		

[1] The Cup was presented to the Branch in 1925, by the late RA Burke DL, and known as 'The Priory Cup'. It was played for in a 'Wednesday League Competition' from 1925-28. From 1928-32 it was played as a Technical Schools Knock-out Cup Competition and as a Minor League Knock-out Cup Competition from 1932-69. From 1969 'The Priory Cup' has been awarded to the Winners of Junior League Section 3.

Athletic Stores Cup[1]

1931-32	Waringstown	1953-54	Lissara	1975-76	Kilkeel 2nds
1932-33	Bangor	1954-55	Saintfield 2nds	1976-77	Newry Olympic 3rds
1933-34	Banbridge Tech Sch	1955-56	Saintfield 2nds	1977-78	Raphoe 3rds
1934-35	Parkview	1956-57	Derry YMCA	1978-79	Collegians 3rds
1935-36	Saintfield	1957-58	Lisnagarvey 3rds	1979-80	Raphoe 4ths
1936-37	Cullybackey	1958-59	Lisnagarvey 3rds	1980-81	Bangor 4ths
1937-38	Mossley	1959-60	Lissara	1981-82	Newry 3rds
1938-39	Antrim 2nds	1960-61	Parkview 3rds	1982-83	RUC 3rds
1939-40	No Competition	1961-62	YMCA 3rds	1983-84	Cliftonville 3rds
1940-41	No Competition	1962-63	YMCA 3rds	1984-85	FSOB 4ths
1941-42	Dunmurry	1963-64	Cliftonville 3rds	1985-86	Cookstown 4ths
1942-43	Ormeau 2nds	1964-65	Mossley 3rds	1986-87	Kilkeel 2nds
1943-44	Mossley 2nds	1965-66	Gallaghers	1987-88	Banbridge 4ths
1944-45	RAF Bishopscourt	1966-67	Antrim 3B	1988-89	Cookstown 5ths
1945-46	Mossley 2nds	1967-68	Collegians	1989-90	Newry Olympic 4ths
1946-47	Saintfield	1968-69	Annadale	1990-91	Ballynahinch 2nds
1947-48	North Down 3rds	1969-70	Annadale 2nds	1991-92	Parkview 3rds
1948-49	Antrim 3rds	1970-71	Annadale 2nds	1992-93	Bangor 4ths
1949-50	Saintfield	1971-72	Lisnagarvey 4ths	1993-94	Larne 2nds
1950-51	Banbridge Y C	1972-73	Down 2nds	1994-95	Raphoe 3rds
1951-52	Montalto	1973-74	Bangor 4ths	1995-96	Instonians 4ths
1952-53	Banbridge 3rds	1974-75	Raphoe 2nds		

[1] The Cup was presented to the Branch in 1931, by the late Mr V Bleakley of the Athletic Stores, Belfast and known as 'The Athletic Stores Cup'. It was played, in the first year as a Knock-out Cup Competition for Junior and Minor League teams. From 1932-69 it was the Knock-out Cup Competition for Junior League teams. From 1969 'The Athletic Stores Cup' has been awarded to the Winners of Junior League Section 5.

SCHOOLS CUP WINNERS

Burney Cup[1]
(First XI)

1919-20	RBAI	1947-48	Newry H S	1972-73	Cookstown H S
1920-21	BRA	1948-49	Friends S	1973-74	Cookstown H S
1921-22	BRA	1949-50	Newry H S	1974-75	Friends S
1922-23	Banbridge T S	1950-51	Bushmills G S	1975-76	Friends S
1923-24	Banbridge T S	1951-52	Friends S	1976-77	Friends S
1924-25	Ballycastle H S	1952-53	Friends S	1977-78	Friends S
1925-26	Ballycastle H S	1953-54	Friends S	1978-79	Newry H S
1926-27	Shaftesbury House	1954-55	Cookstown H S	1979-80	Cookstown H S
1927-28	Ballycastle H S	1955-56	Banbridge A	1980-81	Newry H S
1928-29	Banbridge A	1956-57	Campbell C	1981-82	Banbridge A
1929-30	Ballycastle H S	1957-58	Friends S	1982-83	Bangor G S
1930-31	Ballyclare I S	1958-59	Friends S	1983-84	Newry H S
1931-32	Banbridge A	1959-60	Friends S	1984-85	Cookstown H S
1932-33	Ballycastle H S	1960-61	RBAI	1985-86	Campbell C
1933-34	Ballycastle H S	1961-62	Ballycastle H S	1986-87	RBAI
1934-35	Ballyclare H S	1962-63	RBAI	1987-88	RBAI
1935-36	Newry H S		Friends S	1988-89	Wallace H S
1936-37	Ballycastle H S	1963-64	Ballycastle H S	1989-90	Cookstown H
1937-38	Ballycastle H S	1964-65	MCB	1990-91	Cookstown H S
1938-39	Banbridge A	1965-66	Friends S	1991-92	RBAI
1939-40	Friends S	1966-67	RBAI	1992-93	Sullivan U S
1940-41	Banbridge A	1967-68	RBAI	1993-94	RBAI
1941-42	No Competition		Friends S	1994-95	RBAI
1942-43	No Competition	1968-69	Cookstown H S	1995-96	Cookstown H S
1943-44	Friends S	1969-70	RBAI		
1944-45	Banbridge	1970-71	RBAI		
1945-46	Friends S		Friends S		
1946-47	Friends S	1971-72	Cookstown H S		

[1] The Cup was presented to the Branch in 1920, by the late Mr AG Burney (President of East Antrim Hockey Club and known as the 'Ulster Schools Cup' or 'The Burney Cup' which is to be organised as decided by the Schools Committee (Current Rule). Open to teams of boys 19 years of age or under on 1 April immediately preceding the draw thereof.

SCHOOLS CUP WINNERS (cont'd)

Richardson Cup
(U-15)

1946-47	Omagh A	1965-66	Cookstown H S	1982-83	Banbridge A
1947-48	Bushmills G S	1966-67	Friends S	1983-84	RBAI
1948-49	Banbridge A		Royal & Prior S	1984-85	Royal & Prior S
1949-50	Friends S	1967-68	Cookstown H S	1985-86	Cookstown H S
1950-51	Newry H S	1968-69	Cookstown H S	1986-87	Bangor G S
1951-52	Banbridge A	1969-70	Cookstown H S	1987-88	RBAI
1952-53	Cookstown H S		Newry H S	1988-89	Portadown C
1953-54	Banbridge A	1970-71	Cookstown H S	1989-90	Bangor G S
1954-55	Friends S	1971-72	Kilkeel H S		Sullivan U S
1955-56	Wallace H S	1972-73	Newry H S	1990-91	Banbridge A
1956-57	Wallace H S	1973-74	Friends S	1991-92	RBAI
1957-58	Bushmills G S	1974-75	Newry H S	1992-93	RBAI
1958-59	Friends S	1975-76	Cookstown H S	1993-94	Friends S
1959-60	RBAI	1976-77	Friends S	1994-95	Cookstown H S
1960-61	Wallace H S	1977-78	Newry H S	1995-96	RBAI
	Ashfield S		Royal & Prior S		
1961-62	Wallace H S	1978-79	Bangor H S		
1962-63	Ashfield S	1979-80	Newry H S		
1963-64	Friends S	1980-81	Newry H S		
1964-65	Cookstown H S		Wallace H S		
	Wallace H S	1981-82	Newry H S		

McCullough Cup[1]

1964-65	Ballycastle H S	1975-76	Cookstown H S	1986-87	RBAI
1965-66	MCB		Bangor G S	1987-88	RBAI
1966-67	Newry H S	1976-77	Friends S	1988-89	Wallace H S
1967-68	Annadale G S	1977-78	Friends S	1989-90	RBAI
1968-69	RBAI	1978-79	Cookstown H S	1990-91	Bangor G S
1969-70	RBAI	1979-80	Friends S	1991-92	RBAI
1970-71	RBAI	1980-81	Friends S	1992-93	RBAI
	Kilkeel H S	1981-82	Wallace H S	1993-94	Banbridge A
1971-72	RBAI	1982-83	Bangor G S	1994-95	RBAI
1972-73	Cookstown H S	1983-84	Wallace H S	1995-96	Wellington C
1973-74	Cookstown H S	1984-85	Cookstown H S		
1974-75	RBAI	1985-86	Banbridge A		

[1] The Cup was presented to the Branch in 1961, by the parents of the late Ian McCullough, a pupil of Newry Grammar School and known as 'The McCullough Cup'. To be organised as decided by the Schools Committee (Current Rule). Open to teams of boys 19 years of age and under on 30 June immediately preceding the draw thereof. This Competition shall be open to Schools playing hockey in the Christmas term.

SCHOOLS CUP WINNERS (cont'd)

Dowdall Cup
(Second XI)

1974-75	Bangor G S	1981-82	Newry H S	1988-89	Cookstown H S
	Friends S	1982-83	Wallace H S	1989-90	RBAI
1975-76	Newry H S	1983-84	Campbell C	1990-91	Wallace H S
1976-77	Newtownbreda H S	1984-85	MCB	1991-92	Friends S
1977-78	Royal & Prior S		Wallace H S	1992-93	Banbridge A
1978-79	Newtownbreda H S	1985-86	Wallace H S	1993-94	Banbridge A
1979-80	Campbell C	1986-87	Campbell C	1994-95	RBAI
1980-81	Bangor G S	1987-88	Wallace H S	1995-96	RBAI

Ferris Cup
(U-14)

1974-75	Ballycastle H S	1981-82	Newry H S	1989-90	Banbridge A
1975-76	Ballycastle H S	1982-83	Newry H S	1990-91	Newry H S
1976-77	Newry H S	1983-84	Wallace H S		Sullivan U S
1977-78	Bangor G S	1984-85	Cookstown H S	1991-92	MCB
1978-79	Bangor G S	1985-86	Bangor G S	1992-93	RBAI
	Newry H S	1986-87	Cookstown H S	1993-94	Cookstown H S
1979-80	Royal & Prior S	1987-88	Newry H S	1994-95	Bangor G S
1980-81	Newry H S	1988-89	RBAI	1995-96	Regent H S

Prior Shield[1]
(U-14)

1980-81	Campbell C	1987-88	Sullivan U S	1993-94	Grosvenor H S
1981-82	Royal & Prior S	1988-89	Portadown C	1994-95	Grosvenor H S
1982-83	Royal & Prior S	1989-90	Portadown C		RBAI 2nds
1983-84	Ballycastle H S	1990-91	RBAI 2nds	1995-96	Regent H S
1984-85	Ballycastle H S	1991-92	Wellington C		
1985-86	Wallace H S 2nds		Bangor G S 2nds		
1986-87	MCB 2nds	1992-93	BRA		

[1] Open to Second XIs and First XIs of Schools not in the McCullough Cup.

SCHOOLS CUP WINNERS (cont'd)

Bannister Bowl[1]
(U-13)

1980-81	Newry H S	1988-89	Cookstown H S	1993-94	RBAI
1981-82	Friends S		Banbridge A		Bangor G S
1982-83	RBAI	1989-90	Friends S	1994-95	Newry H S
1983-84	Ballycastle H S		Banbridge A		Regent H S
1984-85	Newry H S	1990-91	MCB	1995-96	RBAI
1985-86	Bangor G S	1991-92	RBAI		
	Friends S	1992-93	RBAI		
1986-87	Banbridge A		Bangor G S		
1987-88	RBAI				

[1] The Cup was presented to the Branch in 1981, by Mrs Bannister, and known as 'The Bannister Bowl' and is open to teams of boys 13 years of age and under on 30 June immediately preceding the Season in which the Competition is played.

Schools' Hockey

Cup	Season First Held	Open to
Taylor Cup	1962-63	Secondary Schools
Burney Cup	1919-20	First XI
Richardson Cup	1946-47	U-15
McCullough Cup	1961-62	First XI[1]
Ferris Cup	1974-75	U-14
Dowdall Cup	1974-75	Second XI
Prior Shield	1980-81	First XI & Second XI[2]
Bannister Bowl	1980-81	U-13
Indoor Cup	1982-83	Invitation to 8 Schools
Irish Schools Championship	1982-83	Open to 8 Ulster, 4 Leinster and 4 Munster Schools

Inter-pros	Individual Matches
	Ulster v Leinster v Munster v South East
	1976-77 Introduced weekend tournament
	1983-84 Introduced U-16 and U-18 weekend event

Internationals	
	v Scotland 1955: v England 1958: v Wales 1960
	Quad Tournament 1964 for U-19
	Addition of U-16 by Ireland in 1984
	U-19 changed to U-18

[1] Played as a League Cup in the Christmas Term with Semi-Final and Final
[2] League Cup open to First XI not in the McCullough Cup and Second XI

ULSTER BRANCH INDOOR HOCKEY ASSOCIATION
TROPHY WINNERS 1978-92

James Howard Memorial Cup[1]

1978-79	Target Men	1983-84	Team Volkswagen	1988-89	Holywood Kaliber
1979-80	Target Men	1984-85	Team Volkswagen	1989-90	Holywood Kaliber
1980-81	Team Volvo	1985-86	Team Volkswagen	1990-91	Holywood Kaliber
1981-82	Team Volkswagen	1986-87	Team Kaliber	1991-92	Instonians
1982-83	Team Volkswagen	1987-88	Team Kaiber		

James McClurg Memorial Cup[2]

1979-80	Banbridge	1983-84	FSOB	1987-88	Annadale
1980-81	Antrim	1984-85	East Antrim	1988-89	Queen's
1981-82	Bangor	1985-86	Civil Service		
1982-83	Banbridge	1986-87	Newry Olympic		

Carson Clarke Knock-Out Cup[3]

1981-82	Team Volkswagen	1985-86	Team Volkswagen	1989-90	Lisnagarvey
1982-83	Team Volkswagen	1986-87	Team Kaliber	1990-91	Holywood Kaliber
1983-84	Garvey Nationwide	1987-88	Team Kaliber	1991-92	Holywood 87
1984-85	Team Volkswagen	1988-89	Holywood Kaliber		

Angus Hamilton Schools Cup[4]

1982-83	Bangor GS	1986-87	RBAI	1990-91	RBAI
1983-84	Annadale GS	1987-88	FSOB	1991-92	Methodist College
1984-85	Newry HS	1988-89	Methodist College	1992-93	FSOB
1985-86	RBAI	1989-90	RBAI		

[1] The Cup was presented to the Branch in 1978, by Mr WR Howard in memory of his father, and known as the 'James Howard Memorial Cup', shall be held for one year by the team winning the Indoor League, Division 1.
[2] The Cup was presented to the Branch in 1979, by Mr J McClurg, and known as the 'James McClurg Cup' and shall be held for one year by the team winning the Indoor League, Division 2.
[3] The Cup was presented to the Branch in 1981, by Mr WRC Clarke and known as the 'Carson Clarke Perpetual Cup' and shall be held for one year by the team winning the Indoor Knock-out Competition.
[4] The Cup was presented to the Branch in 1982, by Mr AK Hamilton and known as the 'Angus Hamilton Cup' shall be held for one year by the team winning the Schools Indoor Tournament.

ULSTER BRANCH INDOOR HOCKEY ASSOCIATION
TROPHY WINNERS 1978-92

7Up Cup[1]

1987-88	Instonians	1990-91	Instonians
1988-89	Friends Provident	1991-92	Instonians
1989-90	Friends Provident		

Andrew Rose Memorial Cup
Under-21 Inter-Provincial

1984-85	Ulster	1987-88	Ulster
1985-86	Ulster	1988-89	Ulster
1986-87	Ulster		

Paul O'Reilly Cup
Senior Inter-Provincial

1979-80	Ulster	1983-84	Ulster	1987-88	Ulster
1980-81	Ulster	1984-85	Leinster	1988-89	Leinster
1981-82	Ulster	1985-86	Leinster		
1982-83	Leinster	1986-87	Ulster		

Switzer Trophy
National Club Championships

1979-80	Monkstown	1984-85	Team Volkswagen	1989-90	Avoca
1980-81	Team Volvo	1985-86	Team Volkswagen	1990-91	Holywood Kaliber
1981-82	Team Volkswagen	1986-87	Avoca	1991-92	Holywood 87
1982-83	Team Volkswagen	1987-88	Avoca		
1983-84	Team Volkswagen	1988-89	Holywood Kaliber		

Officers of the Indoor Association

Chairman		Honorary Secretary	
1978-89	WR Howard	1978-89	WRC Clarke
1989-92	RG Blower	1989-93	E Coulter
1992-93	W Dowdall		

[1] The Cup was presented to the Branch, in 1988, by 7Up Bottlers and known as the '7Up Cup' and shall be held for one year by the team winning the Under-20 League.